GROWING
OLDER
TOGETHER

GROWING OLDER TOGETHER

A COUPLE'S GUIDE TO UNDERSTANDING AND COPING
WITH THE CHALLENGES OF LATER LIFE

BARBARA SILVERSTONE
HELEN KANDEL HYMAN

PANTHEON BOOKS

NEW YORK

Library of Congress Cataloging-in-Publication Data
Silverstone, Barbara, 1931–
    Growing older together : a couple's guide to understanding and coping with the challenges of later life / Barbara Silverstone and Helen Kandel Hyman.
        p.   cm.
    Includes bibliographical references and index.
    ISBN 0-679-72155-X
    1. Aged—Life skills guides. 2. Married people—Life skills guides. 3. Aging. 4. Life change events in old age. I. Hyman, Helen. II. Title.
HQ1061.S489 1992
646.7′9—dc20   92-54118

Book Design by Maura Fadden Rosenthal

Manufactured in the United States of America
First American Edition

To our husbands,
Stan and Herb

CONTENTS

P R E F A C E

We have raised more questions in this book than we can answer because little attention has been given until recently to the subject of older couples. While there is now a rich accumulation of knowledge about the aging process and about the elderly, there is little in the way of clinical and research findings focusing directly on partners growing old together. Our knowledge of aging and the family tends to center on intergenerational relationships. Our knowledge about marriage and intimate partnerships tends to center on younger couples.

We therefore are like explorers embarked on uncharted waters. The ideas and material we include stem from our clinical and personal experience, knowledge of gerontology and its literature, interviews with professional experts, and conversations with and observations of older couples.

There are increasing numbers of older couples in our society—married, unmarried, heterosexual and homosexual—grappling together with the many challenges of late life. Without offering solutions, we have tried to describe the dilemmas presented by old age and the rapidly changing world around us. Our goals are to stimulate research and new approaches, not to prescribe cures, to bring out in the open rarely discussed but common problems older partners face, and to help them deal with the pain and enjoy the pleasures of extended years together.

The book does not pretend to speak to all older couples, but touches on issues central to the majority. It does not deal with the specific economic problems afflicting couples on or below the poverty line, nor have we looked at the variety of attitudes toward marriage or specific traditional patterns followed by different cultural, ethnic, and religious groups in our society. While we have attempted to keep the book general enough to be applicable to a readership of diverse ethnic, gender, and racial identity, we recognize that we deal largely with middle-class, middle-income couples. Nevertheless, we hope we have identified some universal issues and that some parts of this book, if not all, will have broad appeal.

B.S.

H.K.H.

April 1992

ACKNOWLEDGMENTS

Our appreciation goes out first to the many couples who were willing to speak openly to us about the pleasures and pains they were encountering as they were growing older together. Their experiences helped us to shape the chapters that follow. We are also grateful to our original editor, Susan Rabiner, who first recognized the need for this book and then asked us to write it. Once again we must thank Charlotte Kirschner, MSW, who, after making essential research contributions to all three editions of *You and Your Aging Parent,* continued all through the development of this book to be an invaluable source of information and criticism. We are grateful to Marion Rodriguez for her cheerful willingness to type numerous revisions of each chapter, and to Dr. Amy Horowitz and Arlene Gordon for helpful consultation. Finally, we must both thank Dr. Stanley Silverstone, who has worn three hats: those of consultant, critic, and, whenever we needed one, cheerleader.

GROWING
OLDER
TOGETHER

PROLOGUE

"Then the prince lifted the princess onto his prancing steed and together they rode off to his splendid castle," read the storyteller, closing the book.

"And what happened then?" asked the child.

"Then they got married," replied the storyteller.

"I know, but what happened then?" repeated the child.

"Then they lived happily ever after," explained the storyteller gently.

"I know that, too," snapped the child impatiently. "But what happened *after* that?"

What did indeed happen? Fairy tales end at weddings. What did happen after the flourish of trumpets and the tootling of fifes and the rolling of drums announced to the world that the prince and princess were man and wife? What was their marriage like? Did they really live "happily ever after"? How long did "ever after" last? Forever? Or only until the prince began to chase after Snow White's handmaidens in the palace gardens? Until he resumed his favorite manly sport—making war? Until he grew tired of endless domestic nights of feasting and revelry? Did he then long instead to joust with his knights and drink a couple of horns of mead down in the tavern beyond the castle moat?

And Cinderella? Did she outgrow her glass slippers? Did she soon need to loosen the silken girdles of her ball gowns? Did she start dallying playfully with cute palace pages while her prince was forever off playing his war games? Did she one day steal the key to her chastity belt and enjoy delicious romps with handsome equerries who were always there for her when the prince was not?

And as the years passed, were there children? Was the prince an absent father, the princess an overprotective mother? Did she berate him for his indulgent permissiveness, and did he admonish her for her relentless discipline? Or perhaps vice versa? Were the royal coffers one day stripped of treasure? Did the golden sovereigns melt away? Was the palace forced to economize on luxury? Did he blame her for extravagance, and did she blame him for penny-pinching?

And as the years passed, did the prince undergo a mid-life crisis and the princess a hysterectomy? Did she decide to color her golden hair and he to take up jogging along the palace walls? Did the prince begin to realize he would never be a world-conqueror and did she admit to herself that her beauty was fading? Did they renegotiate their marriage vows and agree to play by less strict rules—he with his games, she with hers?

And as the years passed, was he concerned about his cholesterol and she about her osteoporosis? Did his armor rust and its joints creak? Did her skin wrinkle and her breasts sag? Did she decide to let her hair go white? Did he quit jogging? Did she worry about losing her memory and he about losing his erection?

And as the years passed, did they find themselves living separate lives in separate suites along separate corridors of the palace? Did either or both of them ever admit they had lost each other somewhere along the way?

OR

Did he know that after years of noisy palace pageantry full of knights and ladies and children and dogs and cats and horses and servants, he really wanted no one but her? And she? Did she want no one but him? And did they spend their days walking hand in hand in the palace gardens waiting for sunset?

"Look, honey, the glass slipper still fits."

1

INTRODUCTION

Frances: I can't fight him—never could. So I go along with him. I let him sell the house and now he's buying that camper he's always dreamed about. He's worked hard all his life, so I guess he oughta have his dream. But it's his dream, not mine. I'm too old to be a gypsy. You know what I want? To stay right here close to our kids and near a good hospital. Who knows when we'll need one?

Tony: Finally! No more punching time clocks! No more gutters to clean, leaves to rake! No more house! I can't wait to get going. We'll be free—nothing holding us down. We can go where we want, do what we want! Can't she understand how great it'll be? Not her! Not Mrs. Sourpuss. We'll come back for a wedding, or a new grandchild, or just to visit. Isn't that enough for her? We're still young, still healthy. Doesn't she want some adventure before it's too late?

. . .

. . .

Tina: It's 3 A.M. I'm wide awake and in a panic. My heart's pounding and I'm drenched with sweat. Something is terrifying me! I reach out for David's hand and move closer to his warm body lying next to mine. I feel comforted and safe, but only for a minute, because next come those terrible questions: "What if he's not here one night?" "What'll happen to me if he dies?" "Why won't he take care of himself?" "Didn't that heart attack scare him enough?" "I saw him snitch that cream puff last night." "How dare he risk his life?" "How dare he do this to me?" And then the anger starts.

. . .

Shirley: We get up in the morning. We eat breakfast. We go for a walk. We go through the day together, but we're not together. We haven't been together for years. Sometimes I feel he took off forty years ago but just left his body behind. We eat together, but we don't talk. We sleep together, but we don't touch. We never fight. We're beyond fighting. How did we let ourselves waste our lives this way?

Dave: She says it's because she loves me—that's why she's on my case all the time. It's driving me crazy! "Don't eat that!" and "You've been smoking—I can smell the tobacco!" and "Did you forget your pill again?" "Turn off the TV. It's past your bedtime." Nag! Nag! Nag! It's not me she loves—it's being the boss. That's what she's always wanted. Now, just because of that little scare with my heart, she thinks she's got a right to run the whole show. We're not kids anymore. We don't have much time left. Why does she have to wreck it?

. . .

Paul: Why do they say being alone is so terrible? Don't they know that being lonely even when you're with someone is worse? Why didn't I get out years ago? I guess I stayed for the children. Was it too late when they left? Could I have started a new life then? What stopped me? Why did she stay? She doesn't like me either. Forget about love! Was there ever any? I can't say we're killing each other—we don't die. We just keep on going. With nothing. . . .

rances and Tony . . . Tina and Dave . . . Shirley and Paul. Six people all over sixty-five with more life behind them than ahead. They are three couples among the millions, married or partnered, growing old together as we approach the year 2000. Such couples reflect a twentieth-century phenomenon: the aging of society. Even in the recent past only one out of ten people could expect to live to be sixty-five. Today 80 percent of Americans live past that age. The most dramatic increase of all is the extended longevity of people over eighty-five—the fastest-growing segment of the population. There are nearly 30 million men and women over sixty-five in the United States today—more than 12 percent of the population. We have more seniors than teenagers. We are no longer a nation of kids. By the year 2020 when the Baby Boom generation reaches Social Security time, the elderly population is expected to rise to 51 million—17 percent of the total. A Senior Boom lies ahead.

Because more people are living longer, their marriages have a chance to live longer, too. Marriages, therefore, for better or worse, may last until couples are over eighty, ninety, or even a hundred.

As a young groom standing at the altar today looks at his about-to-be bride, he may realize suddenly that he could live another forty, fifty, sixty or more years with this same woman. The bride, in her turn, may realize the same thing about her about-to-be husband. Each one could be excused for having a fleeting moment of panic at the words "till death do us part."

At the turn of the century wives often became widows and husbands widowers when they were still young, often barely into middle age. This is now rarely the case. According to anthropologist Margaret Mead, we have a very antiquated view of marriage. In the old days, when a couple said "till death do us part," death was likely to part them pretty quickly. That's why marriages seemed to last forever. Everyone was dead!

The age-old institution of marriage, although constantly threatened with extinction, still manages to hold its ground and shows no sign of retiring. Marital figures reveal that one out of every five marriages of the 1980s will celebrate a golden wedding. Even today it is no longer unusual for couples who married in the 1940s, when life expectancy was much lower, to pass the golden milestone and head for platinum. In the late 1960s, at the height of the youth culture, the Beatles wondered in song if someone would need them and feed them at sixty-four. Sixty-four then, less than twenty-five years ago, seemed like the end of the line. If the Beatles were singing today, they might choose a more appropriate decade for the title of their song: "When I'm Eighty-four" or "When I'm Ninety-four." Both fit the rhyme and rhythm patterns just as well and are much more timely. These days sixty-four—and even older—seems to be the appropriate time for jogging, tennis, and frequently for remarrying.

The dramatic rise in life expectancy, with both men and women, sometimes couples, surviving into their eighties, nineties, and even beyond a hundred, has brought blessings with it. Good relationships between couples and with their younger relatives are being extended, offering more years of shared experiences. Many older couples are able to retire, relax, and enjoy life after years of work pressures and family responsibilities. Some continue happily in careers that have always been gratifying. Others, eager for a change of pace or scenery, have the opportunity to explore new experiences: hobbies, second careers, political pursuits, volunteer activities.

But the benefits of extended living should not blind us to the pains. The heavy down side to aging—particularly for the over-seventy-five population—must be acknowledged. Aging brings with it a much higher risk that something—or everything—will go wrong. Whereas improved scientific knowledge and medical care have allowed millions of people to survive into the later decades, there is no guarantee that their survival will be healthy, happy, or rewarding. There are greater hazards in these years—physical, emotional, economic. The losses multiply: friends and relatives disappear, physical beauty and strength vanish; status and self-respect may dwindle, too, when paid work is finished. For most of us the most painful of all is the loss of independence.

Extended years also mean that relationships will be prolonged that may never have been fulfilling—witness Paul and Shirley. As life continues, stressful relationships with grown children and other relatives can keep on smoldering or flaring up. Sons or daughters may be disappointing in their choices of careers, mates, or lifestyles. They may refuse to grow up, and drain aging parents emotionally and financially. Siblings may have open breaks over money or inheritances. Antagonistic in-law relationships, suppressed over the years, may erupt into open hostilities.

More than half of the approximately 26 million men and women over sixty-five are married or have a permanent partner. These pairs include husbands and wives, long-term companions, and gay men and women. Their relationships vary in length. Some couples have lasted forty, fifty, even sixty or more years together, others remarried at some point in mid-life, and still others are newlyweds or newly partnered—with one or both over sixty-five. These latter couples, formerly widowed or divorced, may have rediscovered romance in their sixties, seventies, or eighties. Hearts and flowers and moonlight and roses are not the exclusive property of the young. Neither is sexual pleasure.

There is something heartwarming and reassuring about portraits of golden-agers—their silver heads posed closely together, their wrinkled hands tenderly intertwined. To younger couples still grappling with the strains and pressures of their own marriages, and continually being warned that their union has only a 50 percent chance of survival, these aging couples suggest a lifetime of unconflicted relationships, of peace, harmony, and contentment. For a minority of couples these pictures may even be true. For the majority, however, marriage is a fluid, not a static, relationship.

"I wonder if we'll ever make it through our *next* anniversary!" one middle-aged wife wails. "How did they make it through fifty?" The answer to that question is probably "With difficulty!" or with perseverance, hard work, or sometimes with habit and resignation.

A fortyish divorcee visiting her aunt in a nursing home was always moved by an old couple she passed each time, sitting close together in the solarium. The woman was usually disoriented and in tears. The man always held her tenderly, stroking her hand and murmuring comforting words. The visitor, on learning that the two were in their nineties and had been married seventy years, one day could not resist asking the old man what it was like to be married all those years. He smiled, thought for a moment, and then said with a twinkle, "You gotta take a lot of shit."

Like the tide, a marriage or a partnership is ever-changing. It will go through a series of transitions, constantly readjusting and readapting according to the demands of each new stage of life. Most partnerships have ups and downs—alternating highs and lows. Few relationships can sustain uninterrupted bliss, although some couples will make this claim. An unfortunate minority stay together despite years of uninterrupted conflict.

Two people, furthermore, rarely see eye-to-eye when it comes to a life crisis: infidelity, or a financial disaster, or illness, or a career disappointment, a son's divorce, a daughter's widowhood. They may have their own troubled relationship to deal with as well as the crisis before they can move ahead to a new period of harmony. Whether or not their conflicts in the past were successfully resolved may have a profound effect on their relationships in late life.

At their golden wedding anniversary, couples whose marriages have been through so many transitions and emotions may greet the dawn of their new day with a sense of satisfaction, not only for having survived, but for years well spent and for challenges accepted. Reaching any advanced age together may be a fine accomplishment in itself, but these couples are not usually granted peace as their reward. They cannot now sit back and relax and enjoy the satisfaction of a job well done. Nor can elderly newlyweds expect smooth sailing. Just when their energies may be flagging and their resiliency lower, their relationship must ready itself to deal with a new challenge—old age itself. Think of the frightening possibilities lying in wait: failing physical health, diminishing mental capacities, catastrophic illness, chronic disability, sexual dysfunction, boredom, reduced income, meaninglessness, uselessness, and the worst specter of all—total dependency.

These negative possibilities are likely to have a profound effect on aging couples. They may begin to wonder about their own relationship to each other. Can they face being together through these final years? Can they face *not* being together—being alone? Which scenario is the scariest? To think about the negative possibilities is to open up a Pandora's box of terrors. Perhaps this is why there is such an attempt these days to deny them or to ignore them. "Think Positive" seems to be the slogan of choice when it comes to aging. Talk about "the golden years," "prime time," "the best years of our lives," and the like.

The aging segment of the population includes millions of consumers, yet popular magazines and TV commercials devote little space or time to promoting products that cater to the "downbeat" aspects of aging. Hearing aids, hernia belts, prosthetic devices, wheelchairs, and other appliances that could improve the quality of life for disabled older people are rarely featured. A rare exception is the cheery, colorful TV commercials extolling the joys of adult diapers. Delta Air Lines, while offering senior discount coupons to aging flyers, feels forced to add the words "for the young in heart" to sugar-coat the bitter pill of the word "senior."

Gerontological research studies of older people report many positive findings. In general, to the surprise of their younger counterparts, the majority of the elderly are active, independent, and living satisfying lives. But just because a large percentage are doing well, the smaller percentage doing poorly should not be overlooked. It has been said that statistics are "people without tears." In any honest discussion of old age people-*with*-tears must be included. Furthermore, many older couples doing well today may run into trouble tomorrow, and we can never forget that death is a certainty, waiting to claim each one of us. So it's never safe—or fair—or humane—to turn our backs on the "downbeat" aspects of aging.

What if you are among the many millions of couples who are having trouble getting along? What good will it do you to read books or watch TV shows about "wonderful" or "remarkable" or "admirable" older people who are getting along splendidly? You probably want to learn, instead, if there is anything you can do about your problems, whether there are any solutions out there and if so how to find them. How do other couples like you handle their situations? Have they discovered techniques you've never tried? Above all, you probably want to know you are not alone!

Marriage as an institution is constantly being studied, probed, put under the microscope in all its various stages by professionals—sociologists, psychiatrists, psychologists, social workers, etc.—but this intense scrutiny seems to dissolve when the day for retirement and Social Security dawns. The professionals may have continued to think that there weren't enough couples over sixty-five to warrant study. Or perhaps they thought there weren't enough problems at these ages to make serious investigation worthwhile. But the numbers of these marriages creep up every year. The problems older couples face are just as varied—and just as interesting—as those of younger ones.

So it's time to turn the spotlight on the wide variety of couples who are lumped together in that meaningless category "sixty-five-and-over." Within it is such variety—those approaching late life and those actually experiencing it. They span two or three generations—those in late middle age, the young-old in their late sixties and seventies, and the old-old, eighty-five and over. The chapters ahead are for them and also for widowed or divorced older men and women who are considering— or hoping for—a new marriage or a new partnership.

Readers should understand that because the majority of couples consist of husband and wife, and for the sake of simplicity, the word "marriage" is used most frequently throughout the chapters. However, by extension, the words "marriage" as well as "husband" and "wife" should be seen as including the many couples who are growing old together outside of traditional formal arrangements: long-standing heterosexual companions and homosexual partnerships, male and female.

These couples, who number in the millions, are survivors that reflect the aging of our society. This book is a tribute to them and to their strength in adversity. Just as their numbers are unprecedented, so are their experiences. They have few role models to study. They are explorers mapping out new territory.

In the coming chapters we will attempt to offer a road map and a compass through this dangerous terrain. We will not indulge in euphemisms. Our main focus will be on the serious problems many have to face—the pain and loss they suffer and how a couple's relationship becomes cemented or eroded when adversity strikes.

The transition from middle age to old age is inevitably accompanied by a strong emotional upheaval—the late-life crisis. Aging can change the way couples feel about themselves and the way each partner feels about, and relates to, the other. How couples resolve the late-life crisis will determine whether their old age is satisfying, merely bearable, or truly miserable.

Another determining factor must be included: each partner's view of the same relationship. Although friends, relatives, and the outside world tend to consider every couple as a unit—the Browns, the Riccios, the

Hoffmans; or Jack and Mary, Tom and Bill, Flo and Marge—these pairs are, in fact, two separate individuals with their own personal feelings, reactions, needs. Each one marches to a different drummer. The sociologist Jessie Bernard claims that in every marriage there are *two* marriages—*his* marriage and *her* marriage—and that these two rarely coincide.

There may even be a third marriage, one the couple jointly presents to the outside world and sometimes even to each other. Three couples—Frances and Tony, Tina and Dave, Shirley and Paul—opened this book. Each side had a very different story to tell about the same relationship. This theme—the "double identity" of every partnership—runs through all the chapters.

No book could pretend to cover all the situations facing couples in late life. You may not find your own examined. Instead, we hope to sensitize you to think through your own personal problems more realistically, or perhaps understand them more clearly. Understanding may not solve things, but it's a step along the way; after all, if you don't understand what's going on, how can you hope to solve your problems, or at least learn how to live with them? The complexity of the marital relationship will be examined, the transitions, the positive or negative feelings—passions included—which have been discarded by the wayside or toted along right through into late life.

The paradoxes of old age will be weighed: the mysteries, terrors, and painful dilemmas on one side balanced by the challenges and opportunities on the other. What is the emotional impact of these paradoxes on the couple? On each person in the partnership? To a great extent, aging is a uniquely personal experience that cannot be totally shared with someone else no matter how close the bond. We are born alone and we die alone. The individual experience cannot be overlooked, nor will the crises that must be shared by the couple when things go wrong. Relationships, for better or worse—with each other, with children, grandchildren, relatives, and friends—will be explored as well as the influence these have on older couples.

Other weighty questions are raised: What does retirement represent? How does it affect each partner? What is the likely effect of diminishing finances? What happens when one partner is disabled—temporarily or chronically—and the other is not? The burdens of the caregiver and the feelings of the care-receiver will be examined as well as the strain on their marriage. What kind of outside help is available? Who can afford it?

Perhaps the most painful questions faced by couples relate to nursing-home placement. When is this necessary? What steps must be taken? The growth of hospice care will be described as well as the importance, in the final years, of renegotiating contracts. These late-life revisions are significant not only for the partners themselves but for their children and other relatives.

Finally, how do couples contemplate the inevitable—death? As individuals? As partners? Do they agree on the use of life supports, living wills, medical power of attorney, funeral plans, cremation? The inescapable breakup of every relationship—and the prospect of life alone for the survivor—must be faced by every couple, even those fortunate few who sail splendidly through late life.

Special resources will be included in the appendixes—a guide to counseling agencies, selected nursing homes, and home-care agencies. A reference list includes a bibliography as well as discussions of a variety of situations that older couples may encounter.

Men and women in couples, if they are fortunate, do not have to "go it alone" through the threatening and uncharted territory of old age. There may not be strong love between the two—their relationship may be thorny rather than smooth. They may not even like each other much or enjoy the time they are forced, by the infirmities of aging, to spend together. But there is usually some bond of caring. This bond allows each partner to feel secure in the thought, "I have someone there for me." Nowhere else in the life cycle do the words "in sickness and in health, for better or for worse" have deeper meaning.

Each person has a partner sharing the pleasures and alleviating the pain of aging—a hand to hold through these late years right up to the final moment when it has to be a solo flight. The following story, told and retold for hundreds of years, underscores the value of partnership in times of adversity.

A weary traveler found himself lost in the midst of a dark, dangerous forest. No matter which way he turned, he could find no way out. Finally, he came upon another weary traveler.

"Good sir!" he cried out in desperation. "Please, I beg you, show me how to escape from this terrifying place!"

"Alas!" sighed the second traveler. "I am just as lost as you are."

"What can we do?" wailed the first.

"I cannot answer with certainty," said the second. "But here—take my hand. Perhaps together we will find the path neither of us could find alone."

So holding hands the two braved the terrors lurking in the dark forest and soon reached the edge of it—together.

2

Did he regret he had never fulfilled his early promise? Or finally admit he never had much promise to fulfill?

And she? Was she no longer a star? Did younger princesses outshine her? Did the young gallants pass her by in the corridors without a backward glance? Did they no longer fight each other for her favors?

FACING UP TO
GROWING OLD

Every year Freda and Hank Alcott dreamed of going back to Bermuda where they had honeymooned, but every year their vacation money had to go for some other family emergency. Finally, they got back to Bermuda for a second honeymoon—twenty-nine years after the first. In their late fifties they felt like a couple of kids—swimming, snorkeling, sailing, dancing, making love.

On their last day Freda, dressed and ready to leave, waited while Hank took one last swim. She shaded her eyes watching his athletic figure splashing out of the surf. But as he came nearer, she noticed something else, too. The hair on his chest was almost white and the flesh on his arms was sagging. For the first time he looked vulnerable, almost frail. She felt tender, protective, but then a flash of panic swept over her. "Oh, my God!" she almost cried out loud. "He's getting *old!*"

Her heart pounded and she found it hard to breathe. All sorts of crazy thoughts raced through her mind—"What's going to happen? What if he gets sick? What if he dies? What will I do? And *me!* I'm getting old, too!"

"Such a sad face," Hank said affectionately as he came closer. "What's wrong?"

Freda looked at him blankly for a moment and then shook her head, smiling. "I guess I just hate to leave. And—I've been thinking—maybe I'll junk that blue bathing suit. I'm really getting too old for a two-piece."

*F*reda and Hank knew they'd be old eventually. They'd talked about it—even joked about it. But it always seemed something far, far away in the distant future. Suddenly, the future seemed closer. At that moment in Bermuda, Freda received the first flash of her approaching *late-life crisis*. She did not know it, of course, and if someone had told her, she would have reacted with shock. "Don't tell me about another crisis! Wasn't that mid-life one enough?"

THAT FAMILIAR MID-LIFE CRISIS

Of all life's transitions mid-life has been awarded top billing in recent years and not only by professionals. Anyone who reads popular magazines or watches talk shows cannot avoid hearing about the mid-life crisis, which comes at no specific age—usually somewhere in the forties—and refers to those confusing, disturbing, conflicting emotions that are suffered whenever the message "You are no longer young!" is picked up.

These emotions may be merely disconcerting, coming and going at different times. Or they may be unrelenting, almost overwhelming as described by John Cheever in his journal:

In middle age there is a mystery, there is mystification. The most I can make out of this hour is a kind of loneliness. Even the beauty of the visible world seems to crumble, yes, even love. I feel there has been some miscarriage, some wrong turning, but I do not know when it took place and I have no hope of finding it.

The mid-life crisis often involves giving up a particular dream, one with no specific goal such as the scientist's—winning the Nobel Prize—or the Hollywood starlet's—winning an Oscar. The dream may be merely a vague yearning to "be someone," "go somewhere," to be noticed, to excel in something, to be applauded. With the mid-life crisis comes the reality: the dream will probably not come true. There's no pot of gold at the end of the rainbow.

Along with accepting reality comes a tendency to look back, to pinpoint past mistakes, Cheever's "wrong turnings." A man may agonize over a long list of "I should'ves": "I should've gone to college." "I should've taken that other job." "I should've married that other girl." A woman may obsess about the man she did not marry, the career she gave up for her children, or the children she gave up for her career. This is the time to find someone to blame: wife, husband, children, teachers, parents, bosses. Some people see it also as a time for change before it's too late and rush to try a new line of work, a new place to live, a new wife, husband, lover, companion.

Others may pass through the transition with little drama, willing to accept the message "You're no longer young" as an inescapable fact of life. Even so, there's no denying that almost everyone has moments of sadness, regret, nostalgia for the passing years.

On a beautiful spring morning forty-one-year-old Gary Fitch went for his regular five-mile run, came home with enough time for some rushed but pleasurable sex with his wife, and then ate his usual healthy breakfast. He was gratified to notice the appreciative glances his wife gave his body as they both dressed for work. His high spirits were further buoyed by additional appreciative glances turned his way by several attractive women at the bus stop. As everyone crowded onto the bus, Gary and one of the young women headed for the same seat. Although a step in front, he gallantly waved her ahead. "Oh, no!" she insisted. "You take it, sir!" Gary sat down heavily and stared glumly into space. He had a frustrating day at the office and when he got home picked a nasty fight with his wife.

That simple little three-letter word "sir" sent a powerful message to Gary, telling him that even though he was active, vigorous, healthy, and sexy, he wasn't young anymore. Imagine how much more devastating the message will be if a day comes when an attractive young woman rises up and *gives* him her seat on the bus! The new message "I'm getting old!" is the theme of the late-life crisis.

THAT UNFAMILIAR LATE-LIFE CRISIS

Although the mid-life crisis is widely acknowledged, few people foresee that there may be an equally strong emotional upheaval accompanying the transition from middle age to old age. As increasing numbers of couples survive into the later decades, the evidence is mounting that their feelings—individual or shared—about growing old and being old have a powerful impact on their relationships and how they weather their final years together. Some of these feelings are barely conscious ones or, if they surface, are quickly stifled. It takes a pretty strong ego to face the future honestly.

Don't be fooled by the couples who insist they are able to visualize growing old. "What do you mean we're not facing it?" one husband reacted defensively. "Didn't we visit all those retirement homes until we found the right one for us? Haven't we worked out a sensible pension plan? Don't we ask ourselves questions all the time?" Such a forward-thinking couple gets an A for effort, but there still may be questions neither one dares ask.

It's not easy for any of us to ask ourselves: "What do I feel about aging?" "What do I fear most about it?" "What's the most positive scenario? The most negative?" "Who do I want to be stranded with in old age?" "Will my partner be there for me?" "Will someone—any-one—be there for me?" "Will I be alone?"

There may be troubled times ahead. Couples may discover that surviving their mid-life crisis and learning to live happily without active parenthood, youthful beauty, and passionate lovemaking is no guarantee of a peaceful transition into late life. This transition may be traumatic. Even though the search for the fountain of youth has been going on since the beginning of time, middle age—crises and all—is a highly regarded time. Why else would it be called "the prime of life"? Old age seems to offer few rewards. This is understandable since this stage of life conjures up all those negative possibilities—poverty, loneliness, illness, disability, sexlessness, withdrawal, uselessness, as well as loss of status, self-esteem, and respect.

These negative descriptions may apply to some old people but far from the majority. They are not universal. As more and more better-educated and health-conscious middle-agers move into late life, it is likely that the negative views of old age will change to more positive ones. That time has not yet come; our children may reap the benefits even if we do not.

But facts are facts. Even the most optimistic among us have to admit that disaster and loss lurk just around the corner, and the older we get, the closer we come to the one certainty the future holds—death. Everyone laughs at the statement attributed to Yogi Berra, "The future ain't what it used to be!" But for those in late life that statement holds a chilling reality. The future, once stretching out endlessly ahead, now has definite limits.

THE PARADOXES OF AGING

It's no wonder that it's hard to get a clear picture of old age, because in addition to all the negative myths this stage of life embraces so many paradoxes. It is a time feared by some, welcomed by others. For some it means giving up cherished patterns. For others it means opportunities they never had before. It represents boredom; it is stimulation. Like Freda Alcott, we may begin to pick up messages about late life when we are only in our fifties. But when we see all the octogenarians and centenarians in our society, we also get the opposite message—one that tells us we may live another thirty or forty years. Presidents can be in office into their late seventies; Supreme Court justices, into their eighties.

Old age is certainly a time of change, often radical change, for the worse and for the better, too. Much is out of our control, but much depends on our own personalities, how we see ourselves, our partners, and the years that remain to us.

HOW OLD IS OLD?

Late life defies definition. The usual chronological measures of aging are crumbling as healthy, active people live in large numbers into their seventies and eighties, some of them resembling their middle-aged counterparts—or even their middle-aged children.

A man or woman may "turn" sixty or seventy-five, but neither turns "old" on that day. Perhaps one of the problems is the word itself, which brings along with it that terrifying list of negative ideas. If a man of eighty is alert, vigorous, creative, and athletic, everyone says, "Isn't Sam wonderful! He sure doesn't act old." This naturally implies that if he acted old he would present the opposite picture. When someone commented in amazement to Gloria Steinem that she didn't look forty, she replied, "This is what forty looks like." And so it is with "old." "Old" has so many faces. It comes in all shapes and sizes, strengths and weaknesses, personalities and behavior patterns. The danger is that all too often the variety is forgotten and only negative possibilities remembered. This is probably why so many people are almost phobic about their own aging.

Compare the terms "elder statesman," frequently used in the past, and "village elder," still used in some primitive societies today, with the term "senior citizen" used broadside in the United States to describe everyone over sixty-five. "Elder statesman" and "village elder" suggest dignity, wisdom, respect, and personal value. "Senior citizen" carries no such positive connotations. It is merely a meaningless tag to put on nearly 30 million men and women who have only one thing in common—they are all over sixty-five. More and more people, including a recent president, defy the traditional view of "OLD."

Try testing your own Age IQ with the following portraits:

> Frances and Phil Lester are waiting impatiently for the twins' arrival. Everything is ready. Frances has prepared all the food the boys love. Phil has hauled bikes, fishing gear, and kites out of the shed. The two of them had been looking forward to this visit all summer. Even though Frances's arthritis has been slowing her

down quite a lot and Phil had given everyone a scare with that heart attack last winter, they weren't worried about keeping two active ten-year-old boys amused.

How old are the Lesters? 55–65? 65–75? 75–85?

. . .

Jane and Ted Cooley are also waiting for a visit, but not so eagerly. They lived so quietly most of the time. How were they going to cope with Betsey and her three active children? And Betsey wanted to stay a week this time. *A whole week!* But how could they say no to their only daughter? Jane sighs—just thinking about the week ahead makes her tired. Many days she's nearly crippled with arthritis. How will she manage the meals for all those hungry appetites? And how would Ted react to all the noise and confusion? His pacemaker has made his heart condition less worrisome, but he does need a quiet routine. Would the excitement be too much for him?

How old are the Cooleys? 55–65? 65–75? 75–85?

It would seem that the Cooleys are older because they fit the popular image of old people better than the Lesters do. In fact, Frances Lester is seventy-nine and Phil is eighty-two. They are eagerly awaiting the arrival of their great-grandchildren. Jane Cooley is sixty-five and Ted is sixty-eight. They are dreading the arrival of their grandchildren. Neither the Lesters nor the Cooleys can be called typical older people. They are merely two of the millions of American older couples over sixty-five.

TELEGRAPHING THE MESSAGE

Although late life probably starts somewhere in the late sixties or seventies, the intimations of the late-life crisis usually start earlier, as they did for Freda Alcott. Experts now note that somewhere in their fifties individuals begin to pick up the message "You're not as young as you used to be" or "You're getting old!" Ironically, the messages may be telegraphed to men and women just when they are peak-career. Tom

Brokaw, the NBC anchorman, described his own message in the *New York Times* "About Men" column: "At 50, you begin to examine the pass book of your life with a new urgency. Suddenly all those casual promissory notes of years gone by are overdue. Oh, migod, I still haven't learned French. Or chess. Or whatever."

The messages become louder and more insistent as the years go by:

> Larry on his fiftieth birthday was shocked when a friend congratulated him, saying, "From now on no one will say you died young."
>
> . . .
>
> Fifty-eight-year-old Jane felt "over the hill" when she realized taxi drivers and salespeople were calling her "young lady"!
>
> . . .
>
> Fifty-nine-year-old Peter was dismayed to discover that he was older than everyone else in his office—including his boss!

The aging of children and grandchildren also delivers a powerful message about late life to couples, some of whom find the arrival of a first grandchild more of a blow than a blessing. When the Parsons were in their sixties and celebrated their son's fortieth birthday, they were more disconcerted than he was. If he was middle-aged, then they were really getting old, weren't they? The fact that their granddaughter was ready for college reiterated the same message.

Retirement, whenever it occurs, and even if it is voluntary, telegraphs a message. One man opted for retirement instead of going with his firm when it relocated. No one made him retire. It was his decision. Yet the first time he heard himself referred to as a "retiree" he felt much older than he had felt the week before when he sat behind his desk. The death of a contemporary probably sends the strongest message of all.

SOME CAN IGNORE THE MESSAGES

Couples who have delayed parenthood until their forties may be too involved with children and teenagers to pick up other messages. Those whose parents are still alive can honestly believe their own old age is far away in the distant future. "How can I be old? I still have Mother!"

SOME CAN DENY THE MESSAGES

Denial can work wonders. Makeup, hair dyes, and cosmetic surgery can preserve a youthful appearance. Regular exercise programs and healthy diets can preserve youthful bodies. "I can still get into my prom dress!" "I'm running the marathon tomorrow!" "I do three sets of singles—no sweat. I can take on any of those youngsters in my office."

BUT THE MESSAGES KEEP COMING

Old notions about the precise dividing line between life stages are fading along with a few—but not nearly enough—negative stereotypes about aging. Individual variations are endless. Young adulthood over-laps with middle age, middle age with old age. But—there is no going backward. We can't stop, either. We have to keep moving ahead. Time, for every one of us, marches on! It doesn't matter whether we pick up the messages, postpone hearing them, or deny them vehe-mently, the biological clock keeps on ticking away—nothing stops it.

While it's true that life expectancy has risen dramatically in recent years, with more people living longer, the life span—the length of time the human body can survive—has hardly risen since biblical times. A man dying at 114 still makes headlines. A woman may feel like a girl, look like a girl, act like a girl, but that biological clock always knows her true age, and one day, inevitably, it will have to stop.

THE PERSONAL FACTOR

The leading roles in this book are played by couples. The main focus is on the way they live out their lives together as they grow older. But how the partners deal with their own personal aging is a very individual process. Each one is likely to see late life in a different light. This, in turn, affects the relationship. One may see the future as black, the other as rosy. One may dread the dangers ahead while the other—considering the alternative—may be glad to be alive. Fortunate couples may be able to communicate their feelings, compensate for each other's weaknesses, share each other's strengths. But even so, we age alone according to our own personal timetables and our own individual emotions.

IT'S AN EVER-CHANGING WORLD

Late life certainly has its down side—there's no denying it. Even without major upheavals—catastrophic or disabling illness, financial disaster—change is everywhere, not only in the world outside but inside each man and woman. Changes in the outside world, political and global, can cause confusion enough. It's hard for anyone to keep up with geography—the endless renaming of countries, the reshaping of borders, the collapse of political systems, the overthrow of leaders. Change also comes with the deterioration of neighborhoods or their gentrification. An elderly couple, even though they have lived in the same place for decades, may feel bewildered when they walk out on formerly familiar streets and find no familiar landmarks. Impersonal giant supermarkets and malls replace the old shops and their friendly shopkeepers. Valued long-term relationships with trusted professional advisers may be terminated by death, disability, or retirement. These are often replaced by doctors, lawyers, dentists, and even local policemen who look like children to their aging patients, clients, and neighbors.

Change can also involve technological "advances" that do not seem "user-friendly" to inexperienced older people. Although at ease with the automobile, the telephone, the airplane, and television—inventions which would have astounded most of their own parents—today's elderly now have to grapple with the computer, the CD, the cellular telephone, the VCR, and the microwave. "Take that damn thing back to the store! I want my old toaster again!" bellowed the cantankerous eighty-year-old when his children presented him with a microwave oven. He would never admit that he secretly consulted his ten-year-old grandson when he had problems with his TV or his VCR—gifts which he had accepted with equally bad grace.

Changes in living patterns may be expected but, even so, not easy to accept. Changes in language cause confusion, misunderstanding, or outright shock! Perhaps the most upsetting of all changes are those that take place inside us—in our bodies, our organs, our minds, our psyches. When one or more of these essential functions slows down or becomes seriously disabled, coping with the simple demands of daily life becomes sadly complicated.

All the bodily functions that were almost taken for granted in the past or at least seemed to operate smoothly most of the time now may demand constant attention. "Nothing works anymore!" growls an irritable retiree to his wife as he lines up his daily medications on the breakfast table. "I'm sick of catering to my digestion, my arteries, my bowels."

Across the table from him she is probably lining up her own daily requirements. Both are acutely aware of their diminished pleasures. One or both of them may give more than a passing thought to the likelihood of increased dependency in the future, the loss of control of their lives, their own mortality and closeness to death.

THE LOSSES MULTIPLY

The most profound, painful, but inevitable change for late-lifers is the loss of close relatives and friends. Despite increased life expectancy, some people live longer than others—some die too young. The price we all have to pay for getting older is outliving the people we love. Some losses are more deeply felt than others. Extended mourning is natural following the death of a parent, a husband, a wife, a lover, a close friend, or—worst of all—a child.

The loss of more remote relatives and acquaintances may be less painful but serve as ongoing reminders of our own closeness to death. One seventy-year-old announced almost with pride, "There are more dead people in my address book than living ones," as she crossed out another name after reading that morning's obituary page. Another contemporary also reads the obits, but more selectively. She is only interested in learning about people whose age at death is at least ten years greater than her own.

Other losses may be less obvious but still have significant meaning: for those of us whose main identity is derived from our work, retirement may mean loss of status and power. Retirement may also mean loss of financial resources and buying power as inflation takes its annual toll of a fixed income. Loss of beauty and decreased sexuality are blows to both men and women.

THE GRAB BAG OF EMOTIONAL REACTIONS

Anxiety, preceding and accompanying change and loss, is understandable. Even if we are in high spirits and great shape ourselves, we can't avoid noticing the problems besetting people around us. Younger people lucky enough to have been untouched by trouble often convince themselves that bad things happen to "the other guy" and not to them. As we grow older, we lose that comforting illusion and know that anything can happen to anyone at any time! What's wrong with a little anxiety about that?

Sadness and *depression* can also be anticipatory reactions to what lies ahead—preparing for the worst. These emotions are normally suffered when tragedy does happen—the loss of someone loved or something valued. This is normal, too. It's also normal to mourn the loss of pleasures and favorite pastimes when disabling illness or financial reverses occur. If mourning is too intense or prolonged, however, professional intervention may be needed.

But mourning, within bounds, is an important process everyone needs to work through before adjusting to a significant loss. Some people in late life seem sad, depressed, or anxious most of the time. This may be because they have an unrelenting series of external or internal losses to deal with. It is also one of the reasons why the rate of suicide for the population over sixty-five is so high.

THE SILVER LINING

What a dismal scenario has just been presented for late life. It would not be surprising if most older people were emotional wrecks and the suicide rate even higher. But here is another paradox: the opposite seems to be true. The morale of the great majority of older people is remarkably high. According to pollster Lou Harris, older people are fairly content with their lives and even seem optimistic about their limited futures. These findings would seem to belong in Ripley's "Believe It or Not." The reason for the Harris findings must lie in the fact that for all the changes for the worse facing people late in life there are also possibilities for change for the better. In the Chinese language the word "crisis" is formed by two separate characters—one stands for "danger" and the other for "opportunity." So it is with the late-life crisis. There's danger ahead—but also opportunity.

Given the litany of negative changes, what possible change for the better can there be? For some people, not having to struggle for a living is compensation enough, provided they have a reasonable income. Others find relief from parental responsibilities or from competition. Still other late-lifers thrive on perpetual vacations—a luxury some, but far from all, can afford. The chance for adventure is a blessing many discover and—finally, at long last—the chance to make some old dreams into realities before it's too late. For those who recoil at the mere idea of a life of leisure, the raising of the retirement age enables older people to stay on the job longer or—if forced to retire—find second and even third careers. Because life now for the majority goes on for many years after retirement, those deeply attached to children and grandchildren have more time to enjoy their companionship.

A caveat is needed here: positive changes in late life, as gerontologists report, are closely tied to economic security and adequate resources. A significant number of older people live at or close to the poverty line. Poverty for old and young alike curtails opportunities—for pleasure and for good health. (See Chapter 6.)

One of the most significant changes for the better is that society is slowly beginning to revise its attitude toward old age and therefore toward old people. No one can deny that stereotypes still exist and that ageism is still prevalent in many places. When Lewis Carroll wrote these lines over a hundred years ago—

> *"You are old, Father William," the young man said,*
> *"And your hair has become very white;*
> *And yet you incessantly stand on your head—*
> *Do you think, at your age, it is right?"*

—the dividing lines between what was acceptable behavior for young and old were much stricter. Today if an eighty-year-old can stand on his head, sail solo across the ocean, climb mountains, or take a lover, society is more likely to cheer than sneer. Not only have attitudes toward senior behavior become looser but so has the general acceptance of what old people are capable of doing. Now, as the ranks of the healthy elderly mushroom into the millions, they are beginning to be seen as an important resource to be tapped.

THE FOUR R'S OF AGING

Times are changing. It can no longer be assumed that the pessimistic view of aging is the common view. To be sure, there are many painful emotions to deal with, but it is now believed that human beings adapt to these and to the aging process in many different ways, and not all of them are negative. Some are downright remarkable!

These adaptations can be divided into four main categories that can legitimately be called the four R's of old age. No individual can be neatly pigeonholed in any one of these permanently or be expected to stay in any one forever. Each man or woman may seesaw among the R's depending on how life progresses and what unanticipated blows or blessings occur.

RESIGNATION

Resigned people, although still alive, have given up on life. In the words of the song made famous by singer-comedian Gracie Fields in World War II, "She's dead but she won't lie down!" Such people see old age as shrouded in the familiar negative myths. They may not be bitter but merely passive, accepting what fate has dished out to them.

Psychoanalyst Erik Erikson writes about integrity versus despair in old age. The resigners choose despair. Their body language—as well as their words—is likely to send out the message "Who cares?" or "What's the difference?" or "What's the use?" Resigners are their own worst enemies because they not only do nothing to help themselves but often alienate family and friends—and their partners—by rejecting everyone's advice or help. Resignation may also mask depression or be a defense against future loss and change: "Nothing more can touch me now."

RESISTANCE AND RAGE

This is the flip side of the coin of resignation. Angry resisters also see their old age in negative terms, but react with fury at the insults and assaults life has leveled at them. Resisters are not always angry. They may resist through denial. If they admit time's passing at all, they are more likely to say "I'm no spring chicken" rather than "I'm getting old."

Some resisters will fight to the death, refusing to give in to any realistic disability. "Speak up! Stop mumbling!" a hearing-impaired resister keeps on shouting in fury to his exasperated wife, refusing to admit his deafness and get a hearing aid.

Resisters do their best to deny negative emotions, rejecting the aging process and even defying death. Both women and men in this group are likely to try out each new cosmetic—wrinkle creams, hair colors, baldness cures, eye makeup—as soon as it comes out on the market, as well as face-lifts, tummy tucks, or breast reductions. They experiment with each new diet, fitness program, and exercise machines if they can afford them.

These steps may indeed slow down the aging process and result in improved health, but they cannot stop the clock. The resisters who rage may prefer this emotion to the sadness and depression of their resigned contemporaries. Their fury may be turned on the Fates that have visited miseries on them, on their doctors who don't cure them, on friends and relatives who fail them, and even on their bodies, which have betrayed them. They obey the order of the poet Dylan Thomas: "Rage, rage against the dying of the light." Better rage than pain, although those whose fury is unrelenting risk suffering other losses—the sympathy and support and patience of everyone around them.

RELAXATION

This seems a favorite adaptation for many. Why fight aging or be miserable about it? It's better to enjoy what life there is and get as much out of it as possible. "Live for Today!" is their motto. Relaxed late-lifers are likely to revel in the release from tension and from the stresses and strivings of their earlier years. "What a joy this is!" a relaxed octogenarian may gloat. "I don't have to do anything I don't want to do anymore. Finally, I can do what I want to do."

The aging French gallant played by Maurice Chevalier in the Lerner and Loewe musical *Gigi* sang convincingly that he was glad not to be young anymore. And many relaxers share his opinion, although they have to accept another reality included in the song: that "forevermore is shorter than before," a more poetic version of Yogi Berra's "The future ain't what it used to be."

RENEWAL

Anyone who adapts this way goes beyond the pleasures of relaxation and discovers in late life a wide range of creative opportunities. The American poet Longfellow claimed:

> *Age is opportunity no less*
> *Than youth itself, though in another dress,*
> *And as evening twilight fades away*
> *The sky is filled with stars invisible by day.*

Untapped talents may surface for the first time. Grandma Moses is a prime example of renewal. She did not start painting until she was seventy-six. Late-lifers may return to old passions ignored for years or discover new ones—music, painting, writing, handicrafts, religion, travel. They may renew themselves through their children and grandchildren. For some the act of renewal is more compelling than ever because time ahead is growing shorter.

CHOOSING THE RIGHT R

Personality plays a great part in the adaptation-of-choice made by each individual. But it is not the only determiner. No one can guarantee that those with lifelong outgoing, optimistic attitudes will be the ones who opt for relaxation or renewal. Negative experiences in life may send everything into reverse. Other factors, many out of anyone's control, also determine adaptation—biological, cultural, familial, financial, and emotional.

There are those who believe in such sayings as "Once a complainer, always a complainer" or "Once a martyr, always a martyr." This view implies that the adaptation a person makes in late life follows a course mapped out in early life. If a man has always been thrown for a loop by hardship, pity him in old age! He's sure to be in despair. By contrast, those who have weathered crisis well in the past may continue this admirable trait. But much evidence disputes this view and suggests that earlier patterns are not etched in stone.

People grow and change over the years; some profit and learn from experience, even from adversity. Surprisingly enough, some find the challenges of old age less stressful than the ones of earlier years. Hidden strengths may surface, ready to be tapped. Such people may surprise everyone who knew them earlier. One more essential ingredient must be added to the formula determining an individual's successful or unsuccessful adaptation: the relationship with a husband, wife, lover, a "significant other."

THE IMPACT ON COUPLES

The late-life crisis will have a profound effect on couples whether they realize what's going on or not. For many it is another transition in a life they have shared for years. Those who pair up late in life will have made their own separate adaptations. These may have to be readapted because of their new relationship. Every decade in life is important, but the decades of the fifties and sixties can be a significant turning point for married couples as they begin to pick up the first messages of their future together.

If they weather this period successfully, their feelings for each other are likely to be enriched and strengthened. Patterns of living established early in their marriage, then revised and renegotiated at later periods, once again need to be reexamined and reinterpreted. The "shared biography" adds resiliency and strength to marriage in later years. The sociologist Matilda Riley has written about her own fifty years of marriage:

> For one thing we share over half a century of experience. Because we are similar in age, we have shared the experiences of aging, biologically, psychologically and socially, from young adulthood to old age. Because we were born at approximately the same time we shared much the same historical experiences. We have also shared our own personal family experiences. We shared the bearing and raising of young children during our first quarter century together, during our second quarter we adjusted to our couplehood, to our added roles of parents-in-law and grandparents. The third quarter of our married life by the laws of probability should convert us additionally into grandparents-in-law and great-grandparents. In sum, prolonged marriages like ours afford extensive common experiences with aging, with historical change and with changing family relationships.

Even in the closest relationships couples do not usually experience old age in tandem. Being of the same age—as the Rileys are—does not guarantee that both partners will experience the late-life crisis at the same time. Personal timetables are variable. Being of different ages may present further divergence—a husband in his late fifties may be contemplating retirement and favoring a home-centered life while his wife, ten years younger, may be tasting independence in the outside world for the first time.

THE SHARED CRISIS

Late life for couples may be harmonious or, ironically, discordant for the first time. Differing adaptations to old age may drive a wedge into some relationships, setting two people at odds with each other just when they need each other the most. The relaxer may frustrate the renewer. A resister husband forever raging against his infirmities may also rage against his resigned wife. "Stop telling me to make the best of it!" She, in turn, may find it increasingly hard to give him the care and support he needs. She may take every opportunity to get away from him, leaving him more isolated and furious than ever.

Couples who find the messages of late life threatening may feel stronger and better fortified for the future if they can talk about their concerns with someone else, preferably each other. That's easier said than done, since many couples may not understand what's bothering them. They may not know why they keep getting vague feelings of dissatisfaction or of hostility, why they are restless, out of step, out of sorts. These may be the ones who have never been able to "get in touch with their feelings," or to share their feelings with anyone, including themselves. They may never have learned to talk—or to listen—to each other. They may never have had time or, thanks to the distractions and pressures of their early years, they may have forgotten how.

Some gerontologists are convinced that late life for couples can actually be the most satisfying years of marriage and point to a curvilinear pattern in long-lived relationships: this pattern charts a "honeymoon high" which takes a downhill slide in satisfaction and then, unless a divorce occurs, levels off through mid-life. A new "high" can be reached again in the later years. Older couples, therefore, should indeed seem blessed—and many of them are.

Research findings about old age, as in other areas, do not always agree. Other patterns are emerging, suggesting that this enviable second "high" eludes many couples and that a happy ending cannot be guaranteed every marriage that survives into the late-life stage. Marital relationships do not necessarily get better as couples age—they sometimes get worse. Each couple writes its own scenario—some of these work better than others.

SEVERAL SCENARIOS

The diversity among couples, rather than their similarity, is the strong underlying theme of this book. When two people make a home together, and a life together, they have to figure out for themselves how best to deal with the necessary demands and how to make their personalities blend as smoothly as possible. Couples are endlessly inventive not only in their early relationship but through its duration. How they face the transition into late life and how they cope with these years show the same diversity.

It is hard to predict the future, as well. There are couples like the Rileys who seem to have moved through the many years of their marriage successfully. We would surely feel safe, wouldn't we, in predicting that they will meet the challenges of late life equally successfully? But what about those couples who have had a fairly smooth history, have dealt with earlier crises and transitions successfully, and then unpredictably split apart when they reach the final years?

What about those who have had a miserable history, who have given each other little satisfaction and whose pattern of mutual animosity has been nonstop through the years? We might expect the stresses of late life to compound their misery. But we might be wrong. Couples who have had a rocky biography can grow and profit from a lifetime of painful experiences. By late life their problems may have dissipated, the conflicts resolved. They may reap a reward—a welcome period of serenity at long last.

The diversity of marital patterns includes a series of almost endless combinations. The few scenarios that follow cannot represent them all. They merely serve to dramatize how some couples approach late life and then move on through it.

THE INSEPARABLES

> *John Anderson my jo, John,*
> *We clamb the hill thegither;*
> *And mony a canty day, John,*
> *We've had wi' ane anither:*
>
> *Now we maun totter down, John,*
> *But hand in hand we'll go'*
> *And sleep thegither at the foot,*
> *John Anderson my jo.*

The eighteenth-century Scottish poet Robert Burns gave the world this tender portrait of the "inseparables," together forever. Such pairs sustain their love and their commitment to each other to the end—and after. They are venerable Bobbsey twins—white-haired and wrinkled—speaking always of *our* walk, *our* nap, *our* pills. People talk about them with amazement or perhaps irritation. "They think alike, they talk alike, they're even beginning to look alike!" Neither has a complete identity without the other. One such wife does not feel a separate person even when making a phone call. She invariably announces, "Hello! This is Mildred and Dave calling."

Cynics may claim that the inseparables usually include one submissive partner who has been willing to accept the authority of the dominant one, but this is not always the case. Some couples seem to maintain an even balance.

Inseparables may have been married for many years or for only a few. The strength of such a relationship is hard to fathom. There are no simple explanations. The personal maturity of the two people is not necessarily the answer. Being madly in love is no answer either. Too many relationships that start off on fire sputter out when the fire dies down. Mystery writer Agatha Christie, married for years to an archeologist, had her own explanation. "An archeologist is the best husband any woman can have. The older she gets the more interested he is in her."

Flexibility may be the greatest asset these couples have. Perhaps they have always been able to adjust and grow in relationship to each other and to adjust to changes in the world outside. Their motto may be "Ride with the Tide." Rigidity can be a handicap in every aspect of life, marriage included. It might be expected that the inseparables would adapt to late life in the same way, opting for the same *R,* and this is often the case. But some couples adapt in contrasting rather than similar ways: instead of causing conflict, the positive approach of one compensates for the negative outlook of the other. Inseparables are less likely to settle on negative adaptations—rage or resignation—to aging. Since their identities are so entangled, neither side can face life without the other. When one partner dies, the other usually follows soon after.

THE COLLABORATORS

These couples are also closely connected but are less deeply emotionally wrapped up in each other. They may be genuinely fond of each other, but theirs is more of a practical working partnership. Each side can stand alone, but both may have discovered early in their relationship that thinking together brings better results than thinking separately. Collaborators are colleagues, working efficiently together, pooling ideas, figuring out solutions. Whenever trouble comes—for either or both—

they "problem-solve" together, weighing pros and cons, alternative solutions. Undoubtedly, there are disagreements, arguments, even resentments or recriminations along the way, but the end result is likely to be a positive one arrived at jointly.

> Julie and Ted Convers are a good example of collaborators. They had worked together all their married life. They openly discussed and shared decisions about money matters, sexual behavior, as well as where to live, how to furnish their homes, what kind of vacations to take, and whom to invite for dinner. Being human, they could not avoid some painful fights in the process.
>
> When their teenage son ran into trouble, they consulted a family therapist together. Then came the moment when Ted wanted to retire. Julie did not. They tackled this problem with habitual thoughtful discussion, arriving eventually—after some heated arguments—at a solution that worked for both of them. Ted was willing to postpone his retirement for a couple of years and during that time worked out a schedule of volunteer activities. Julie meanwhile took a reduction in salary in order to readjust her schedule, arranging more vacations and time off so she and Ted could be together more often.

The ups and downs of late life are likely to force a couple into becoming collaborators even when they have usually taken unilateral action in earlier years.

THE QUIET DESPAIRERS

Sophia Tolstoy, wife of the great Russian writer, described their relationship in her diaries:

> *If only people knew how . . . even more painful is the realization in the last days of our life together, that there are no mutual feelings between us, and that for the whole of my life I have single-mindedly and unwaveringly loved a man who was utterly selfish and returned all my feelings with a withering and pitiless scorn.*

In Sophia Tolstoy's day escape from an unsatisfying marriage was almost impossible. Death was usually the only escape. If marriages did break up, the event carried with it a dreadful social stigma usually borne by the woman. Today some couples extricate themselves before either side has suffered serious damage; sometimes they escape too quickly before giving the whole thing a try. But many modern women—and men, too—still resemble Sophia. Marriage becomes a trap from which they never manage to escape. They may be willing to remain trapped "for the good of the children" or for the good of the bank account, claiming they cannot afford a divorce. Or they may remain out of fear: "What will I do?" "Where will I go?" "Who will be there for me?"

How sad it is to think of the many couples who have gone through life giving and receiving little support from each other. Although sharing the same house, even the same bedroom, they may live miles apart emotionally. Neither partner may have the slightest idea of what the other is thinking or feeling about growing old or about anything else. We see them in restaurants, on park benches, in vacation spots—with blank expressions, exchanging silences. One nationwide study reported the amazing finding that married couples talk to each other—*really* talk about something meaningful—around seventeen minutes a week. This adds up to perhaps an hour a month. Hardly enough to nourish a relationship.

Despairers may put on a false face when they greet the world, presenting themselves as a happy couple, physically caring and providing for each other and their children, socializing and vacationing together. Their sex life may not be bad; it may even be good. Emotionally, however, they may feel starved, forever hungry for the nourishment missing in their relationship. Perhaps neither one has ever been able to bond with another person. Perhaps they were simply mismatched years before. The reasons for their distance may be buried deep in their separate pasts.

By staying together, silently suffering, they do nothing to change their relationship or to form new ones that might nourish them as they grow older. One or both of the despairers usually adapts to old age with resignation. Richard Bausch described this quiet desperation when he wrote to his wife in his story "Letter to the Lady of the House":

> *Everything we say seems rather aggravatingly mindless and automatic, like something one stranger might say to another . . . we go so long these days without having anything to do with each other. . . .*

THE NOT-SO-QUIET DESPAIRERS

Other couples may suffer out loud and in public. They want the world to know their pain. They may have a history of fighting—bickering, sniping, carping, and even physically abusing each other—and may continue this pattern right into their final years. This may surprise and disturb friends and families who may feel that such behavior is hardly appropriate at this stage of life. But why should this pattern stop just because the antagonists are getting old? Or perhaps the antagonism never surfaced in the past and only emerged when the couples had no buffers, such as work or children, to separate them. Once thrown directly face-to-face with each other they may discover they can't stand each other.

But they won't let go. Fighting may have always been a way of life for them, or it may become one. They may not even be aware of what they sacrifice with their behavior—not only their own peace and serenity but other relationships, too, as children and friends prefer to keep their distance rather than witness or be drawn into marital battles. When other social outlets are then denied them, they are thrown even more closely together and their life together becomes an endless round of conflict. Even so, they probably will not change. This may be the only way they have found to relate to each other. If they didn't fight, how would they communicate?

> Henry and Lauraine Koslof fought their way through the fifty-three years of their marriage. Their conflicts intensified in later life because they spent so much time together. Henry brooded constantly about the financial losses he suffered by retiring, and Alice about her arthritis, which interfered with many activities she used to enjoy. But neither shared their painful feelings with the other. Their only emotional outlet came, as it always had, from fighting. They would be lost without each other.

In Carrie Fisher's novel *Postcards from the Edge,* Suzanne's grandmother talks about her long marriage. "I've stayed with your grandfather now for fifty-odd years. I don't like him, but I picked him. I'm proud of the fact that we've had this long marriage. I can't say it's all happy, it's not always a good life, but we have our life together . . ." When Suzanne replies, ". . . but you and Grandpaw hate each other," Gran answers, "Where did you get *that* idea? We don't hate each other. He just mostly stays in the back of the house and I stay in the front, but we see each other. We have our history together. We are each other's lives, and I don't hate my life."

Later Gran says, "This is what I don't understand about your generation. You just stop getting along? You have to work at getting along. It has to be something you care about, a priority." And Suzanne replies, "Gran, you should put out a relationship video. There's Dr. Ruth for sex, and then, once they've had the sex, *you* could tell people how to stay together."

THE PARALLEL PAIRS

The marital relationship for these couples is more of a business arrangement than a marriage. The "I" predominates, rarely the "we." There may even be a tacit or open acknowledgment of an emotional estrangement—perhaps there is a sexual one, too. A pair traveling together on parallel tracks may remain together for the same reasons as the despairers—social, economic, or family reasons, or simply the fear of being alone. But there's a difference: this twosome may not even bother to play the role of happily married husband and wife, or lovers. It may be common knowledge that they rarely go anywhere together, do anything together. "If I need another single man at a dinner party, I always invite the Baileys," quipped a hostess. "She's sure to refuse and he's sure to come alone."

Eighty years ago, in the preface to his play *Getting Married*, George Bernard Shaw wrote with cynicism:

> *The typical [British] husband sees much less of his wife than he does of his business partner, his fellow clerk, or whoever works beside him day by day. Man and wife do not, as a rule, live together; they only breakfast together, dine together, and sleep in the same room. In most cases the woman knows nothing of the man's working life and he knows nothing of her working life (he calls it her home life). . . . The majority of married couples never get to know one another at all; they only get accustomed to having the same house, the same children, and the same income. . . .*

Shaw always enjoyed making such cynical exaggerations, but parallel
-track couples often play out his scenario. They make no bones about
going their separate ways. One—or both—moves beyond the marriage
to find activities or relationships more nourishing emotionally and
sexually. Sometimes the arrangement is one-sided and then one partner—usually the woman but sometimes the man—is left stranded and
martyred. Martyrs, however, usually find some kind of satisfaction in
their martyrdom. "Parallel pairs" have an advantage over despairers
because by finding substitutes they are more likely to make a satisfying
adaptation to late life. They can enjoy relaxing and renewing opportunities without hindrance from a resentful partner. If there is someone
to share these activities with, so much the better.

A gratifying substitute relationship that satisfies intimate needs may
improve rather than destroy a marriage. It may neutralize long-standing
rancor and frustration, permitting a husband to remain on remarkably
friendly terms with his wife, and vice versa.

The rub is likely to come, however, if illness strikes or when one of
the two is disabled, thus putting an end to extramarital or solo pursuits.
Financial resources diminished by retirement may no longer support
the luxury of parallel lives. Couples then find themselves face-to-face,
together as they may not have been for years. What do they say to each
other then? How do they feel about each other?

Couples may never have taken separate routes but discover the
option only as they grow older. A husband may approach late life in one
way, his wife in the opposite. He wants *in;* she wants *out.* He may see
these later years as "time for *us*"; she, recently released from the home
front, may see this period as "time for *me.*" The conflicting approaches
may cause serious trouble in a marriage for the first time and shock
couples who always considered themselves so well balanced and traveling in tandem. Perhaps only one of them, probably the husband,
thought their balancing act was so successful. Perhaps the other, probably the wife, was only biding time until free to do "my thing."

THE TIE BREAKERS

None of the above scenarios may work. Some older couples just cannot
make it together and have to escape a relationship that has become

unbearable. Separation and divorce, while still infrequent, are on the rise and marriage counselors report a challenge rarely seen in the past—helping a couple make it through their eighties. Troubled relationships should not be surprising. Just as life crises can draw people together, they can also drive them apart or make a bad situation worse. Old age confers no immunity from conflict. Even at seventy, eighty, or ninety, separation or divorce may be the only solution. (See Chapter 3 for divorce.)

Despite all the variations in the timetables of the aging process, there is one certainty: late life is a stage that couples will share more closely than any other period. Through their earlier years partners generally had separate responsibilities—he did his thing, she did hers. When experiences converged, they were shared, but many, including the mid-life transition, were generally solo adventures for each partner. Their passage into late life is more likely to be a duet.

Late life brings with it a release from many of the responsibilities that distracted couples in the past—work, children, in-laws, money—and kept them from sharing their feelings except at specially eventful times. Late life offers them many more less-pressured hours together. These can be gratifyingly filled, or aimlessly wasted. Just think what happens when a man retires at sixty! He and his wife could possibly become twenty-four-hour-a-day companions for the next thirty years.

Even without such an unlikely scenario, there's bound to be greater closeness, good or bad. *Her* marriage and *his* marriage may even become *their* marriage one day.

The individual feelings both partners have about growing old affect their relationship, and vice versa: their relationship affects how they feel about growing old. Two people may be in complete disagreement about their own personal aging, but when each one is able to counteract the other's fears and weaknesses with reassurance and understanding, both become stronger in the process.

This support rarely comes out of the blue. It depends largely on the shared biography of the couple and how it developed over the years: what emotional baggage each one brought to the relationship; who has made promises, who has broken them; which roles each one played; what contribution each expected from the other; who talked, who listened. Support depends on a further factor: the partners' ability and willingness to readjust their relationship, to make it adapt better to late life, to shift priorities, to forget expectations, to forgive old grievances, to revise long-standing patterns.

Even in late life there's still time to renegotiate a marriage contract, whether it's been in force for five years or for fifty.

C H A P T E R

3

Years before, when he tenderly
fitted the glass slipper on her dainty
foot, had he promised her the
moon and the stars?

And she? Had she believed those
promises?

FACING UP
TO YOUR
RELATIONSHIP

Mattie: What a nice party! They've all gone to so much trouble! We're lucky to have such good children—and grandchildren—and great-grandchildren. They all wanted to celebrate our golden wedding anniversary with us. But what's all the fuss about? We haven't done anything miraculous—like inventing penicillin. All we've done is stay together for a lot of years. Plenty of them were good, too. But not all. Some were terrible—I even hate to remember them. But I won't forget them either. And Joe—he's been a good

Joe: Look at her over there—she's got that expression on her face! I'll be damned if I know what she's thinking. I've never known—even after all these years. It drives me crazy. We're supposed to be celebrating all these fifty years we've lived together. I still don't feel I know what goes on in that head of hers. Has she been happy with me? I don't even know that! God—I was crazy about her way back. Was she that way, too—about me? I don't really know—not for sure. I used to wonder if she'd leave me. But I'm not afraid enough husband, I guess—no prince for sure. He's done some pretty nasty stuff in his day, believe me! But we can't live without each other. So I guess they're right—we ought to celebrate!

anymore. We'll make it through to the end together. That's something to celebrate, isn't it?

*E*ven though the guests of honor tell different stories about their long years together, the golden wedding anniversary is truly a milestone to celebrate, whether with a lavish party or a small family get-together. As the champagne corks pop and the band plays on, Mattie and Joe's guests are unlikely to give a thought to the endless ups and downs, some more serious than others, the celebrated couple has lived through. Few marriages are completely immune from strain and pressure. These may be caused by the personal conflicts within the relationship or, just as often, by events outside a couple's control: problems caused by illness, finances, children, careers.

The marriage celebrated at the anniversary party is really not the one that took place fifty years earlier. The partners may be the same, but their current relationship is probably very different, the result of many different transitions. A unifying thread of love, intimacy, caring, responsibility—or sometimes merely habit—has kept all these stages connected.

A LONG SAGA OR A SHORT STORY

Long-married pairs can look back on at least three major transition periods—stages they have weathered together in their marriage—first as a young couple, then as a middle-aged, and finally as an aging couple. The transitions, and the mini-transitions within each one, involved new challenges that placed different demands on their relationship.

Each challenge required a change of attitude, a shifting of priorities, a reassigning of responsibilities. The original vows probably had to be reinterpreted, the original partnership reorganized. Unless some traumatic event occurs, the transition process for many couples—perhaps most—goes on almost unconsciously. Few people are likely to look at their watches and announce, "Okay, time for a new transition!" The change goes on almost without the participants' awareness until one day they wake up and realize that something has changed, that they are seeing their lives, or each other, with different eyes. They may not like what they see, or they may embrace the changes with relief and pleasure.

Change, transition, and readjustment are required in all marriages—not just long-lasting ones. While Mattie and Joe were celebrating fifty years together, other couples their age or older were getting married for the first time, remarried, or recombined. Octogenarians celebrate paper or china anniversaries as well as gold and platinum.

WHAT'S THE FORMULA?

No one formula works across the board in getting through transitions of a relationship and making adjustments, although there are plenty of how-to books filled with suggestions. Some couples get through one transition period with flying colors and adapt with ease to the next one. Others find every new stage traumatic and threatening to their relationship. Or things may not be so black and white—one transition may be much more painful than the next.

A couple may thrive during their early child-rearing years but find the retirement period stressful and unsatisfying. A mid-life crisis may threaten a couple's relationship, but if they muddle through this period intact they may find renewed closeness in retirement.

It is often almost impossible for an outsider—even a close friend or relative—to predict the future of any two people who have made a permanent commitment to each other.

Sam and Gina were considered the "star" couple of their group. Not only were they good-looking and well-heeled, but everything always seemed to break well for them. Each had a reasonably successful career that provided financial security. They raised three attractive children, entertained frequently, and even seemed able to weather successfully whatever difficulties cropped up over the years.

Everyone called them "the golden couple."

Sam and Gina were divorced after thirty-four years of marriage.

. . .

George and Frances had frequent clashes even before they were married. Their families hoped that their stormy relationship would quiet down after the wedding, but the storms continued. They seemed able to disagree on everything—how to raise their children, how to spend money, what kind of vacations to take, what movies to see, and which spices to use in the boeuf bourguignon.

Everyone said this marriage would never last.

George and Frances celebrated their fifty-fifth wedding anniversary last year.

Why? What went wrong? What went right? What worked? What didn't? How could the marriage that looked so "bad" last forever and the golden marriage turn sour? Did a "lasting forever" marriage know only happiness and satisfaction? Probably not. When a marriage goes sour, does it necessarily mean that there was never happiness or satisfaction? Likewise, probably not. Most relationships ride a roller coaster of joy and sorrow. Some couples tire of the ride and get off—others stick it out to the end. What kind of marital Krazy Glue is so strong it can hold some couples together for decades yet so fragile it is in danger of shattering at any time?

It would be a miracle if anyone now, as the twentieth century rushes to a close, could dream up a recipe for a long-lasting, successful marriage. But no such miracle is in sight yet. Marital wizards are still searching for the perfect brew.

The brew may not have been perfect in the past, but it was usually the only one on the market. In other times marriage had an important economic and social function as well as a personal one (and this remains the case in some societies today). Each partner had specific roles to play. What used to be clear-cut is now murky. Some social prophets have been predicting the *end* of marriage before the end of the century. The institution still stands, although it has been rocked by radical changes in recent years, particularly since the end of World War II. The revolution promises to continue into the twenty-first century. The women's movement, which helped women move out of the home and into the workplace, the rising divorce rate, contraception, abortion, have all been contributing factors in transforming the age-old institution.

Still another factor is longevity. In the past, couples in their fifties or sixties were resigned to the state of their marriage. It was too late to escape, since they didn't expect to live much longer. Couples of the same age today may see twenty or thirty years of life ahead of them. Why spend these in misery? Why not throw out the bad marriage and try for a good one instead?

But despite all the gloomy predictions by social Cassandras and despite all the strikes against it, marriage—and other long-term permanent relationships—still stands strong and is the way of life favored by the majority. Even when marriage is ended by death or divorce, many of the newly single—not just the young, but middle-aged and aged as well—keep on searching for the next partner, the next husband, the next wife. It seems that most people prefer to grow old as one half of a couple rather than going it alone through old age.

HIS FEELINGS, HER FEELINGS

No couple enters late life with a clean slate. At the golden anniversary party, couples like Mattie and Joe may feel a sense of great satisfaction, not only for having survived, but for years well spent and challenges met. Others may reach the same milestone trailing a history of acrimony, resentment, and mutual dissatisfaction—emotions likely to affect the way they adapt to late life. One extreme was highlighted by philosopher Will Durant in an interview on his ninetieth birthday:

> *Like my father, I've learned that the love we have in our youth is superficial compared to the love that an old man has for his old wife. "My old gray-haired wife" my father used to call my mother. And I can still remember her saying as she passed the food around at their 50th anniversary, "I thank God for giving me this old man to take care of."*

At the other end of the scale of satisfaction is the description of a marriage given by Tillie Olsen in her story "Tell Me a Riddle."

> *For forty-seven years they had been married. How deep back the stubborn gnarled roots of their quarrel reach, no one could say—but only now, when tending to the needs of others no longer shackled them together, the roots swelled up visible, split the earth between them, and the tearing shook even to the children, long since grown.*

In between these two extremes are couples like Mattie and Joe who have enjoyed good times and weathered bad ones together. It should never be forgotten that it takes two people to make a couple and that each one has a separate set of feelings, which may sometimes mesh and sometimes conflict. A wife may keep her feelings private, burying them deep within herself; her husband may be more open, making her and the world aware of his emotions. Or the two may maintain a successful facade, like Gina and Sam, never letting anyone know there is turmoil going on beneath the surface. Even when bonded together into a couple, partners are likely to experience separate emotions in response to each other's behavior and to external events as well as to their own aging, as described in Chapter 2. The list of emotions is endless: love, hate, passion, bitterness, joy, boredom, worship, toleration, commitment, disregard, tenderness, revulsion, devotion, emptiness, respect, fear, pride, scorn, jealousy, disappointment, trust, mistrust. What a grab bag of emotions! They may be transitory or permanent. They may arise from changing circumstances or from new discoveries one partner makes about the other at any point in a marriage. These feelings are not limited to any specific age. They can be just as powerful for older couples as for younger ones.

A misguided notion about aging is that people's feelings are less intense as they grow older. Just because hearing and eyesight diminish with age, just because thinking and walking become slower, why should it be assumed that the intensity of emotions diminishes, too? It may even be that some feelings intensify in the waning years of life due to a greater appreciation of the time left or to greater regret for past losses.

Some feelings from earlier years may be discarded, others placed in the comfortable perspective that time and experience can bring; some may grow stronger and some may even be experienced for the first time in old age. One obvious example of this is the intense joy and sense of renewal felt by older people at the birth of a grandchild or great-grandchild. Another example is the raging fury some older people experience when a physical disability robs them of their independence.

It is important to recognize that this mixed bag of emotions plays a crucial role in the personal relationships of the old as well as the young. These feelings are part of the normal human experience at every age.

THE LEGACIES—HIS AND HERS

Intense feelings, positive and negative, are not only responses to current situations. They can have deep roots going back generations. The legacy brought to their marriage years ago by a couple now in their eighties—or recently by aging newlyweds—can continue to exert a powerful pull on their relationship. The legacy can be concrete, visible, and ever present, such as a host of in-laws, old friends, and stepchildren. The legacy carries with it customs, beliefs, patterns of living, behavior, superstitions. It also carries the baggage of emotions connected to persons and situations supposedly left behind. This baggage may have the most profound effect on a couple's relationship at any age.

Wedding ceremonies through history have served to unite kingdoms, dynasties, and estates, aggrandizing power, wealth, and influence. On a smaller scale they have united tribes, clans, and families. Today love rather than family considerations is the motivating force behind most marriages. Notice of family involvement is usually limited to wedding invitations and announcements in newspapers. The main focus is on the bride and groom, who sometimes see themselves as two against the world, as if they had sprung full-grown, like Venus, from the waves.

In reality, whether a wedding takes place with royal splendor or in a speedy ceremony at City Hall—whether the happy couple is twenty-five or seventy-five—the families of both sides are in attendance. It doesn't matter whether the bride packs trunks full of trousseau satins and laces or merely stuffs some extra jeans and T-shirts into a knapsack, she still cannot avoid toting along plenty of emotional baggage collected through years of life with her family members. Neither can her groom. Their families are present in spirit if not in flesh.

Unrecognized family strengths and talents going back several generations may provide unexpected resources to the new couple when adversities crop up over the years. Family problems may exert equal influence. If these have not been resolved before the wedding, they may sooner or later cause trouble that, in turn, may be passed down to generations coming after.

Over and over again, TV and newspapers report on instances of child or wife abuse by persons who were once abused children themselves and who carried their legacy of mistreatment into their adult lives. The legacy may well have been inherited by their own parents and their parents' parents. Alcoholic parents often produce alcoholic children, who, in turn, pass on their addictive traits. These are extreme cases that make headlines, but other legacies seemingly more benign are also passed on and can profoundly influence marital relationships in each succeeding generation. Family upheavals—early death, illness, serious financial reverses, separation—can give rise to feelings of abandonment, terror, rejection, insecurity, and inferiority.

One of the most poisonous legacies to be passed on is one of distrust. How people fit in or do not fit into their family structure also plays a part. Those who have felt pushed aside may never believe anyone really values them and may never be able to trust the love and loyalty of a wife, a husband, a lover, or a friend. "You're behaving just like your mother!" an exasperated seventy-year-old husband yells time after time to his suspicious wife. All her life she may have tried to be everything her paranoid mother was not, but her legacy kept scuttling her attempts. On her side, she may have always felt that her source of great pain—her husband's coldness and unsociable disposition—was directly inherited from his father.

These emotions reverberate down through the ages, affecting behavior and relationships between family members and between spouses. A wife who always had a conflicted relationship with her mother may find it difficult to deal with the ups and downs of parenting and grandparenting. Her husband may be able to compensate for her inadequacies, but his own family legacy may get in his way and block him from taking any constructive action. Their children may carry the legacy into their adult lives and bestow it on their children.

Medical doctors sometimes put together genograms—charts of their patient's medical history. Genetic counselors map genograms, too, blueprints showing the genetic inheritance of each parent during a pregnancy. Similarly, family therapists and marriage counselors today often construct genograms for their patients, highlighting current problems and tracing them back to their roots in family history.

Two people may not have any idea of each other's legacies until they are living together in an intimate relationship. The demands of intimacy may activate the legacies and put them into play for the first time. Learning how to deal with, and to live with, someone else's legacy may be a continuing challenge through the length of a relationship. Their legacies may help determine whether a couple work with or against each other in coping with life when they are old.

PROMISES, PROMISES!—HIS MARRIAGE CONTRACT AND HERS

"Watch out for the promises you make when you're a-courting," a father warned his son many years ago. "She may actually expect you to keep them after you're married." And so may the bride today. She may also want her husband to live up to her expectations of him and to keep promises she assumed he had made but never did. He may want the same from her. Since the two never put these expectations into words, neither one may have the slightest idea of what's going on in the other's head. Each one may have romanticized views of the other—or be blinded by love.

Why is it that so often husbands and wives report after years or even months of marriage, "He's changed," or "She's changed"? Probably neither has changed. What's happened is that the two, after tasting real life, finally see each other as the flesh-and-blood human beings they have always been. Loving each other "warts and all," realizing that unreasonable expectations are unreasonable, can create bonds strong enough to sustain couples over the long haul. But this bond eludes some couples, who keep on berating each other for promises broken and expectations unmet.

Centuries ago the ancients invented marriage contracts, chiseled permanently on stone or written on parchment, to ensure that verbal

promises made before the ceremony were kept afterward. These contracts were drafted, revised, and finally signed by bridal couples, usually
with the help and/or interference of their families. The documents laid
out not only financial arrangements, but often duties and obligations
expected from the bride and the groom. Some religious and civil
ceremonies include contracts today. The *ketubah,* the traditional Jewish
marriage contract dating back centuries, is still signed before many
Jewish weddings. Since, according to Jewish law, the right to divorce
rests solely with the husband, the *ketubah* sets forth provisions to protect
the wife should the marriage break up.

Aware of difficulties that might arise in the future and hoping to
forestall at least some of them, a number of couples today compose their
own contracts, allocating financial, social, domestic, and even emotional responsibilities. Such a document may seem like a sensible, realistic approach to modern marriage, but it cannot cover every eventuality.
More important than the points included, and even the fine print, are
the hidden agendas of husband and wife, the unwritten assumptions
and the undefined expectations each has about the other. The expectations may not even be conscious—they may even be contradictory, like
the impossible command "Go away closer!"

Strong emotions are interlaced with the unwritten and unarticulated
expectations each partner brings to the relationship. Some of these can
be met by the other, but some can never be satisfied.

> When Marion fell in love with Jerry, she felt she had found the
> father she never had but always wanted. Jerry was an older man,
> sophisticated, cultured, and eager to take care of her in every way.
> He even offered her financial security. When they got married,
> she was not only in love but, for the first time in her life, she felt
> safe and secure. And she was, for a time. But then she began to
> realize that he had his own insecurities, too, and expected to turn
> to her for comfort and support when he was stressed-out at work,
> and especially if he didn't feel well—which began to happen
> frequently. When he had his heart attack and needed even more
> care, her world seemed to fall apart. He could no longer fulfill her
> expectations, so she felt deserted and betrayed.

The modern marriage contract is unlikely to raise questions like
"How much space do I need?" "Am I willing to share power? To give

up some?" "Will I ever understand his (her) deepest needs?" "Could I satisfy them?" If such questions were raised at all and appropriate clauses inserted, how could they be legally enforced?

The unilateral unvoiced contracts each partner carries into marriage include an endless list of unspoken assumptions about what one expects from the other. Relationships can be rocked when these expectations are not met. An advertisement from a large insurance company declares, "Nothing binds us one to the other like a promise kept. Nothing divides us like a promise broken." Some experts believe that couples who go into marriage with lower rather than higher expectations have the best chance of lasting success.

Newlyweds, old as well as young, are often devastated when they have their first quarrels, but quarreling, they may discover to their surprise, doesn't have to be a sign of a *bad* marriage. It may be a useful form of communication whereby the two can air their shattered expectations, reveal disappointments in each other's behavior, and accept more realistic patterns in their relationship. A warning is necessary here: The right kind of quarreling can open the door to further discussion, leading to greater closeness and understanding. But the wrong kind of quarreling—involving personal attacks, hitting below the belt—can lead to greater distance. For example, hammering away at *you*—"You only think of yourself!" "You're always leaving me alone!" "You promised you'd be there for me"—will only cause resentment or defensiveness. The *I* perspective may be more persuasive: "I feel left out" or "I feel lonely" or "I need you!"

Frustrated or shattered expectations—clauses in the unwritten marriage contract—can spell trouble for couples not only in their early days but through all their years together. They may have an especially jarring effect when couples grow older. Now that time is running out for them and it seems too late to make changes, each one may look back and resent all over again promises seemingly broken by the other. The pendulum may swing in the opposite direction for more fortunate couples. Over the years they may gain in understanding, uncover each other's hidden agenda, and learn how to satisfy each other's needs through the final stage of life.

CHANGING ROLES

Three different influences help to shape a couple's relationship. There are external influences—health, money, jobs; and internal emotional influences—the personalities of the partners, the legacies each brings along, the expectations each one has of the other. The third influence stems from the roles each one assumes in the marriage—breadwinner, homemaker, lover, chauffeur, nurse, confidant, handyman, chef, dietician, etc. These roles do not remain constant over the years and are certain to change. As they are adapted to suit current needs, the relationship inevitably changes, and vice versa: as the relationship changes, roles inevitably change, too. Nowhere are role changes more likely to be seen than in late life.

Despite all the changes that have transformed the institution, there are just as many roles to be assumed in today's marriage as there were in yesterday's. The roles may be modified; they may be shared or interchangeable. They are no longer so rigidly gender-linked.

These role modifications alter but in no way diminish the benefits of being half of a couple. Marriage still has plenty to offer. No other institution can include so much in one package: parenting, financial support, caregiving, companionship, sexual gratification, a confidant, and that special bond with "someone who is always there for me."

No wonder marriage is so popular—witness the high rate of marriage and remarriage. No wonder it often fails—witness the high rate of divorce. No wonder such a strong bond develops between two people when their marriage succeeds. Not all successful marriages embrace every possible benefit—it's not necessary to *have it all*. There are happy childless couples; happy couples without much money; happy couples who find companionship—even confidants—outside of marriage.

The partners in each couple work out the design of their own relationship; there are no hard-and-fast rules to follow anymore. This is probably the reason why the institution still stands firm today— because it permits such great diversity.

HIS ROLE? HER ROLE?

Freeing roles from their gender-linked history may have been liberating, but this freedom also placed a strain on modern marriage. The partners no longer fill traditional roles in lockstep. Formerly, the wife had her domain and the husband his—spheres of influence and prerogatives were clear. Today, with more women in the workplace, husband and wife are often operating in, and sometimes competing for, the same turf.

"Who does what when?" "How much must I do?" "What can I expect from you?" "How often?" These are questions many couples are asking themselves right now. A straw in the wind suggesting that traditional "macho" qualities are no longer the only ones that make a single man a good catch is the frequent inclusion in Personals ads of "good cook" as a desirable asset: "Computer whiz, 35, athletic but romantic, *gourmet cook,* looking to share talents with like-minded partner."

The role revolution may not affect couples who are already in late life. Seventy-five-year-old Jane may want the house to herself. She would find her husband, Bill, an intrusion in her kitchen. Bill, in turn, probably still insists on retaining "power of the tractor." He keeps Jane out of the garage and away from his lawn tools. But even though they themselves cling to familiar patterns, older couples cannot avoid watching the changes around them.

Many of them have strong feelings about what they could have done differently—of what they have missed—even though they know it's too late for them to change those things. They may react to their children's marriages with amazement, admiration, or just as likely with disapproval. They may even feel envious of the younger generations' newfound freedom. One partner may accuse the other of refusing to change and accept new, more liberating patterns.

LATE-LIFE ROLES

Change may be a matter not of choice but of necessity in late life. No matter how rigidly they have held on to long-established roles, Bill may be forced into the kitchen if Jane becomes disabled. Jane, in turn, may be forced to mow the lawn, clean the gutters, and cope with the bills when Bill is incapable. Caregiving for both partners in the past may have involved merely pitching in and nursing through an acute illness for a matter of weeks. One of them may have to assume the role of permanent caregiver for the other if a disabling condition becomes chronic and irreversible in late life.

Parenting, often a central, absorbing role in the relationship of a younger couple, shifts in late life to a grandparenting role and a filial relationship with grown children.

Each of these roles—parent, grandparent, provider, caregiver—will be discussed at greater length in later chapters. This chapter focuses now on two key roles that may have the most profound influence throughout marital relationships today and that may change dramatically or take on special significance in late life: the roles of sexual partner and emotional supporter.

ARE YOU STILL LOVERS?

"Mistresses we keep for the sake of our pleasure, concubines for the daily care of our persons, but wives to bear us legitimate children and to be faithful guardians of our household." So said the Greek statesman Demosthenes more than two thousand years ago. As time passed, however, such arrangements went out of favor in most places, in public at least. The wife alone was expected to serve in all three capacities. Sexual gratification in our society traditionally has been supposed to be confined to marriage.

While their passionate sex life may be the driving force monopolizing the thoughts of young lovers—and older ones too—it is questionable whether sex continues as the dominant force in marriage. A poor sex life is not necessarily the chief reason for marital dissatisfaction or unhappiness or divorce. A good sex life does not necessarily hold a marriage together. A couple whose sex is unsatisfying may stay together because other bonds are strong and gratifying, while partners who enjoy great sex may break up because other crucial elements are missing in their relationship. A good sex life, one expert claims, narcotizes but does not wipe out other problems.

Sex may not play a major role in the lives of some couples. They may maintain a perfectly satisfactory relationship over the years without much. Or sexual activity may be of great importance at one stage but diminish in intensity with age.

Until recently, open sexual relationships outside of marriage were considered immoral in our society, and they still are by many. Heterosexual unwedded partnerships, however, are now more visible than ever before—among the elderly as well as younger relatives. Grandchildren and grandparents alike have live-in partners. Homosexuals, to some extent, have come out of the closet. Although there is no denying that discrimination because of sexual choice still exists, gay couples in many places are accepted members of their communities.

As homosexual couples grow older, they may suffer a double dose of discrimination—ageism and homophobia—yet many of these couples sustain satisfying relationships for forty years or more, just like their heterosexual counterparts. Lesbian women have two special advantages: the partners have the same life expectancy and, as they grow older, their world becomes increasingly female, a situation many heterosexual women find painfully difficult.

There is no denying the sexual revolution. Even so, sexual activity remains an integral part of the marital relationship and to a greater or lesser extent can be a source of gratification to both partners. The pendulum seems to be swinging again and stricter monogamy may be back in favor in the near future as a direct result of the AIDS epidemic. (The number of AIDS patients over sixty is on the rise.)

Sexuality was once shrouded in mystery and misunderstanding. Scarlett O'Hara and her friends were not the only girls who worried they would get pregnant if they kissed a boy. Old wives' tales, myths, and taboos were passed on from one generation to the next. Many mothers were unable to approach the subject at all. If they told their daughters anything, it was that sex was a necessary evil that men seemed to enjoy, but since it was the only way to have a baby, it had to be tolerated. Included in Victorian mother-to-daughter sexual education were such suggestions as "Close your eyes and think of England" and "Nice ladies don't move." While it is true that there was an undercurrent of sexual,

even pornographic, material circulating clandestinely in certain Victorian circles, that undercurrent has today become an overt tidal wave,
with experts trying to pinpoint legal boundaries separating a frank
portrayal of sex from pornography.

Although there were many earlier studies of sex, Alfred Kinsey and
his colleagues have been credited with making sex a subject for open
public discussion. *Sexual Behavior in the Human Male* in 1948 and *Sexual
Behavior in the Human Female* in 1953 described, after thousands of
interviews, the great varieties of "normal" sexual behavior. In the 1960s
sex therapists Masters and Johnson sent out the word that age does not
limit sexual responsiveness and that an ongoing and satisfying sex life
can continue into the seventies, eighties, even nineties. Innumerable
how-to books, manuals, and articles have probed the subject of sexuality still further to such an extent that one young woman, faced with a
mountain of reading matter on her desk, complained to her grandmother, "I thought I was supposed to have fun!" and added that she had
more required reading for her sex life than for her college courses.

Only a few years ago Grandma had nowhere to turn for advice on
how to step up her sexual satisfaction or deal with any sexual problems
she might be having with Grandpa, or her live-in lover. The sexuality
of the elderly received little attention in all the proliferation of studies
and how-to books or from gerontologists themselves, the very people
working with the elderly. A recently announced national survey on
sexual activities and lifestyles in Britain planned to interview 20,000
people aged sixteen to fifty-nine. Obviously, the researchers assumed
that no one in Britain's over-sixty population of more than 8 million
had any sexual activities, or none worth studying.

Robert Butler and Myrna Lewis's *Love and Sex After Sixty,* published
in 1976, was one of the first books dealing specifically with the sexuality
of the elderly, but even with this breakthrough book and many others
that came after, the old myth still holds in the minds of many people
that sex over fifty is unbecoming, unlikely, or unnatural. For all the talk
of the sexual revolution, there has not been much interest in the sexual
liberation of the elderly. The climate of opinion has not changed much
since Simone de Beauvoir wrote many years ago that the desires and
feelings and requirements of the old are no different from those of the
young, yet the world responds with disgust.

The "world" is not completely to blame, because the myth of the "end of sex" is often perpetuated by the elderly themselves. Even though plenty of older couples can report from personal experience that sex can indeed go on indefinitely, too many others have been brainwashed to believe that something is a little wrong with them if they still have sexual urges and, worse yet, if they actually give in to these. The brainwashing also goes in the opposite situation: if either partner suffers any dysfunction in sexual performance, the immediate assumption is "Well, I guess it's over for us." If such couples could suppress their embarrassment long enough to consult a knowledgeable doctor, they might find a remedy for a situation that may be merely temporary.

The young also help to perpetuate the myth. Despite their own freewheeling sexual activity, many younger people still find it hard to believe that there is no age limit for an active sex life and, therefore, dread their own aging. A liberated son might well react with total disbelief if anyone were to suggest that his seventy-six-year-old widowed mother might be happy to find a new sexual partner. An equally liberated daughter might be equally disbelieving if she discovered her old parents were consulting a sex therapist. But an encouraging indication that a change in public opinion is in the wind comes from a recent *People* magazine poll in which sixty-year-old Sean Connery was voted the sexiest man alive.

Ignorance is probably the main culprit responsible for keeping the scary old myths alive. Young and old alike are generally ignorant about their own bodies and how these function, or cease to function, as they grow older. Gerontological professionals—doctors, social workers, etc.—do not do much to counteract this ignorance. Some of them are just as hesitant or embarrassed as their aging patients about discussing sexual matters; others assume these matters are no longer relevant. No one needs to be told that all parts of the human body—including those involved in sexual functioning—change with age. What they need to learn is that although some conditions put an end to sexual activity, most changes need not interfere with the ongoing sexual enjoyment of any reasonably healthy couple. They also need to find out what the changes mean, what to do about them, and how to adjust to them.

Flora Capp redecorated the bedroom when she and her husband Ben were in their sixties. Neither of them had been sleeping well recently, so she convinced Ben that twin beds would be better for them than their old double bed. She did not add that they didn't have much of a sex life anymore so giving up the double bed was no big deal. They both used to enjoy sex, but in recent years it was not much fun. Ben took longer and longer to get an erection, making Flora wonder if she'd lost her sex appeal and putting a damper on her enjoyment. When he did finally get an erection and was able to penetrate her, she began to find intercourse increasingly painful. Her pain, in turn, affected Ben and he started to have long periods of impotence, which added to Flora's sense of rejection. Neither talked to the other—or to their doctor—about their problems. Eventually, supposedly because Ben's snoring kept her awake, Flora moved into the guest room and they both moved into a sexless old age.

If they had been able to raise the subject of sex with their doctor and if he had been able to discuss it with them, they might have found out not only some simple basic biological facts but also that their sexual problems were perfectly normal and could be easily remedied. Ben might have learned that, in general, erection comes more slowly with age. Older men need more time and usually more penile stimulation, tactile or oral. They have increased control over their ejaculations, but the force of these is reduced. More time is needed before the next erection can be achieved.

Impotence is not part of normal aging. Temporary impotence, experienced by many men of all ages, can be caused by drugs, alcohol, prostate surgery, and organic disease or by such psychological factors as fatigue, tension, unusual stress, fear, anger, or disappointment. Ben's performance was perfectly normal, although he did not understand this. No one had told him.

Flora did not understand that a vaginal lubricant, making for easy penetration, is produced by younger women in response to sexual stimulation. She did not know that intercourse was painful for her because secretion of this lubricant is delayed in postmenopausal women, resulting in vaginal dryness. Pain may also come from the thinning of the vaginal walls because of lack of estrogen. A water-soluble jelly or vaginal suppository—both available over the counter at any pharmacy—or estrogen therapy, which requires a prescription, can help to alleviate these problems. Flora did not know about these—no one had told her.

Nothing succeeds like success, and this is certainly true for the sexual functioning of older couples. Those whose activity continues without interruption know this and those whose problems can be remedied discover it. The hot passion of their youth may cool down, but this may be replaced by an emotional depth that carries them right through their late life together. There is increasing evidence to support the belief that aging is no bar to sex. "All you need to have sex in old age," according to a current saying, "is good health and a partner." The sad reality, however, is that neither of the two requirements is always readily available as people grow older.

ARE YOU STILL THERE FOR EACH OTHER?

Miss Lawless somehow envisaged her (Betty's rival) as being blond with very long legs and also as being very self-assured. "Not a bit of it!" Dr. Fitz said, and described a woman who was not at all svelte, who wore ordinary clothes, who had never been to a beauty parlor in her life and was overweight. "So why did he run off with her?" Miss Lawless asked, genuinely mystified. "She makes him feel good," Dr. Fitz said.
—Edna O'Brien, "Lantern Slides"

"She makes him feel good." Or, "He makes her feel good." These may be simplified translations of a variety of more technical terms: ego enhancement, emotional satisfaction, self-esteem. Human beings have so many different kinds of emotional needs to be satisfied and these vary in intensity from one individual to the next. Fearful individuals need to feel safe, the lonely to feel cared for, the insecure, strengthened. The unattractive need to be reassured about their looks. The gifted need confirmation of their talents. Narcissists' emotional demands are harder to satisfy. They need constant reaffirmation of their beauty, their brains, their talents, their bodies, their sexual prowess. A one-sided need for endless flattery and ego-boosting can wear down a relationship.

Most of us want to feel that our achievements are admired and our strengths appreciated. Most of us also need to know that our weaknesses—in character, ability, or accomplishments—are accepted within our most intimate relationships, that we are no less loved because of them. People usually put on some form of public mask in facing the outside world and only those closest—usually husbands, wives, or other close companions—are allowed to see the private selves stripped of disguise. Even if they have plenty of applause for public performance, approval in private is also needed, particularly by those who do not believe they merit their success. If there is little worldly success outside the house, a compensating sense of personal value can be provided within the home by someone who cares.

Philosopher Bertrand Russell spoke of love as the antidote to "the deep-seated fear of the cold world and the possible cruelty of the herd"; the same could be said of emotional satisfaction. This is now considered to have such a high priority that for many couples it looms as more important than any other element in marriage. In the 1970 movie *Lovers and Other Strangers,* a son tries to explain to his family that he and his wife are getting divorced because they are no longer happy with each other. "What's happiness got to do with marriage?" bursts out his bewildered Old World father. No one is especially surprised anymore when a couple divorces for "emotional incompatibility." Even in the absence of divorce the absence of ego-stroking can result in permanent dissatisfaction.

> When Max made vice president at thirty-eight, everyone was thrilled. Max hoped that this would finally convince his wife Ginny that he was going to be as successful a man as her father. But Ginny couldn't stop reminding Max that her father had been younger when he made VP. From then on Max knew he would never live up to Ginny's standard. Their marriage continued "for the good of the children," but they gave each other little emotional satisfaction or nourishment as they grew older.

It is also currently acceptable—another form of "emotional incompatibility"—for marriages to break up when there is a conflict between traditional marital roles and one or both partners' need to satisfy other significant personal drives.

> Jeff always raved about his wife's cooking, her talents as a homemaker, a mother. "Oh, yes," he sometimes remembered to add almost as an afterthought, "she paints a little, too." Painting was vitally important to Marilyn. She grew increasingly resentful

that Jeff belittled her talent and undervalued something that meant so much to her. Eventually, she rented a separate studio. Before long she found herself spending more and more time there or with other artists and less and less time with Jeff. One day when they were both close to seventy, she moved there permanently.

Way down deep in some corner of our being, most of us want to feel like King Tut or the May queen to some special person, and then we can feel good about ourselves. When partners learn how to satisfy each other's deeper emotional needs—if they can ever figure out what these are—this may be the glue that bonds their relationship indefinitely.

REMARRIAGE AND RECOUPLING

Since women outlive men by six years on the average, men are more likely to continue their marital roles until death. Population figures speak for themselves: most older men are married and living with their wives—80 percent at age 65–74 and 66 percent at 75 and over. By contrast, 37 percent of women are widowed at age 65–74 and the majority are widowed from 75 on. It is estimated that by the year 2000 there will be 350 women for every 100 men over 85. Older women, therefore, have to assume by themselves roles and responsibilities that were formerly carried by two people. Older women, therefore, are usually alone just at the time when they are the most vulnerable. Noted gerontologist Robert Butler writes that "the problems of old age are the problems of women."

HIS CHANCES, HER CHANCES

The figures showing that men remain married longer than women do not necessarily refer to their original marriages. These may have been disrupted more than once at earlier times by divorce or death. While some remarriages take place in younger days, the lure of wedding bells still continues in later life. In 1985 an estimated 71,000 people over sixty-five remarried—25,000 women and 46,000 men. Although an increasing number of couples are singing the song "Love Is Better the Second Time Around," the statistics are contradictory. They show that the success rate for second marriages is even lower than for the first.

Recent sociological studies seem to suggest that those who have been widowed after happy marriages are more likely to remarry, but some widows, survivors of happy marriages, may avoid another one, refusing to risk second widowing. Many women never even get a chance to remarry. The fact remains that more men remarry than women, perhaps because men find it harder to be widowed than women.

It is also partly due to the reality that men have a much larger pool in which to fish for a new bride. Not only do they have their single, divorced, or widowed contemporaries to sift through, but also a whole range of women in different age groups, some young enough to be their daughters or even their granddaughters. Although the combination of younger men and older women is not as socially unacceptable or as uncommon as it used to be, the odds for remarriage still favor men.

The aging newlyweds can make a new start in life just at the time when their long-married contemporaries have settled into comfortable but unexciting routines. Albert Schweitzer once wrote of this new start:

> *At times our light goes out and is rekindled by a spark from another person. Each of us has cause to think with deep gratitude of those who have lighted the flame within us.*

HIS PAST, HER PAST

For those who have endured long but stressful marriages that have finally been ended by death or divorce, a new marriage offers a blessed second chance at happiness before it's too late. A long marriage looks back on years of shared history—good and bad events lived through together. Couples newly married in old age do not have this history. They have no fond memories of good years and no resentments built up over bad ones. Looking back together, they see only blank pages.

But each partner has a lifetime of experiences to share with the other.

Their new life can now be one of mutual exploration as well as a race against time as they hurry to build up their own stock of memories. One new bride, fully aware of her new husband's unhappy previous marriage, still wanted to wipe the slate clean of all traces of her predecessor. Bit by bit she managed to banish to the basement valuable souvenirs collected by her husband and his first wife over years of travel and to replace them with her own things collected during the two years of her marriage.

A different problem, particularly for the widowed who remarry, is the ghostly presence of the previous partner, who may have handled the marital roles with greater efficiency. This haunting, sometimes referred to as the "Rebecca" syndrome, can be dangerous to the marital health of the aging bride and groom.

Older newlyweds must cram a lifetime of shared experiences into what is likely to be a relatively short time. They must also work through the intricacies of the marital roles that their long-married contemporaries had figured out years earlier, for better or for worse.

HIS FINANCES, HER FINANCES

The new couples face the same hazards of aging as the older ones but in addition have special problems to deal with: his home versus her home, his children versus her children, his finances versus her finances. When it comes to dollars and cents, the couple may decide that marriage will cost them too much in cold cash. A widow's Social Security payment will be reduced if she remarries; a divorcee may lose her alimony. When it also dawns on them that each will be financially responsible for the other's medical and nursing-home bills, wedding bells may have a sour ring. They may decide to live together instead, combining their lives, their loves, but not their bank accounts. Thanks to the ever-changing sexual mores of this century, there has been a growing acceptance of these "live-in" relationships not only for the young but for their grandparents, too.

HIS CHILDREN, HER CHILDREN

While there are no surefire formulas for the success of any marriage at any age, experts suggest that late-life marriages are more likely to succeed when the newlyweds have known each other for at least ten years, when there is an adequate income, and when the children of each partner offer their blessings. *His* children and *her* children can make or break a relationship. They may voice their disapproval openly if they feel someone is taking advantage of their parent, or if they are convinced that parent is behaving foolishly, or out of worry about threats to their inheritance.

They may also resent the union out of loyalty to the parent who is dead or divorced. One elderly man, aware of his own shortcomings as a husband to his dead wife, was determined not to make the same mistakes again. He became a devoted husband, catered to his bride's every need, and kept romance alive by celebrating their wedding anniversary every month with a gift, flowers, or at least a card for the next five years. He received in return adoration from his wife but total resentment from his children, whose reaction was, "Why didn't you ever treat Mom this way?"

BREAKING THE TIES

Marital statistics, as noted earlier, project that one out of every five married couples will celebrate a golden wedding anniversary. These same figures can be read another way: four out of five couples will not. These unions will be terminated by death or divorce somewhere along the line between the original ceremony and its fiftieth anniversary.

Because people are living longer, marriages have a greater chance of lasting longer; they also have a greater chance of breaking up. Many couples are not able to cope with the renegotiations and readjustments demanded by the different stages of life. One or both sides may be rigid or inflexible, refusing to change or grow. Divorce is more likely to split couples apart in the earlier years; nevertheless, there is growing evidence that a relationship of many decades may break up, too. The absolute number of divorces over the age of sixty is not large—one study reports around 30,000 annually—but the rate of divorce was two and a half times greater in 1988 than in 1983. This rate is expected to rise.

LET'S **NOT** GROW OLD TOGETHER

When an elderly couple breaks up, everyone wonders, "How come?" "Why now after all these years?" Then comes the inevitable question, "Who's to blame?" Possibly neither of them is to blame—or maybe both. Perhaps they lost touch with each other years ago and only stayed together until the children were grown, until retirement, or until one just couldn't stand the other a minute longer.

"Darling, let's grow old together," goes the old song. But what if one partner merely grows old but does not mature? What if the partners grow in different directions? What if one outgrows the other? This can happen in the third year of marriage or the thirtieth.

The interests, tastes, skills, and ambitions of a couple may mesh beautifully at one stage of their relationship but become increasingly incompatible at another. Anthropologist Margaret Mead, when asked once to comment on her three failed marriages, was reported to have replied that none of her marriages failed. She had three successful marriages, each one satisfying the needs of a different period in her life.

REJUVENATION AND RENEWAL

Even in late life, wives and husbands may be "swept off their feet" into rejuvenating romances and be determined to spend what little time they have left with the new love object.

All the reasons we've mentioned for late-life breakups are logical, but some further, more compelling reason is missing. When the question "Why now, when there's so little time left?" is asked, perhaps the answer is *"Because* there's so little time left." Late divorce may have more to do with late life itself than with anything else. A long-standing marriage may symbolize to one or both partners the inevitability and closeness of death. Did they not both vow "till death do us part?" Breaking that vow may be a reassuring death-defying act.

Some couples can keep on feeling young and renewed in the same old marriage with the same old partner, but for others a staleness sets in—something is needed to put a spark back into the years that remain. This is particularly true for men and women who rage against growing old or fear the process. When they look into the aging face of their partner, they see their own aging reflected, their fears confirmed. The face of a younger partner is a mirror of youth and renewal.

Rejuvenation and renewal, however, do not always come from a new partner who is young. Remarriages after divorce in late life are often to partners of approximately the same age. The very act of renewal may be the cure for staleness and boredom. If this is true, perhaps the same rejuvenation could come from renewing the original marriage contract for one last time?

FORSAKING THE UNBEARABLE

Remarriage or a change of partners need not necessarily follow a late-life divorce. Some marriages may just come unglued because they have become unbearable. Even if there are only a few years left, at least let them be lived in peace.

> Hilda Price was seventy-four when she left her husband. For fifty-four years she had endured life with a man who had abused her physically and emotionally. She had contemplated leaving him but stayed for her children's sake. Once they were grown, she actually did leave several times, but being of the "old school," she went back each time, hoping things would change. But nothing changed—the abuse continued and she knew it always would. So with the support and encouragement of her children, she found a studio apartment in a congregate housing project and left him for the last time. When she was asked what she had gained by breaking up her marriage after so many years, she had a quick answer: "Peace and contentment before I die."

In the past, divorce created scandal even when it occurred in the early years of marriage. The more eminent the couple, the greater the scandal. England's Edward VIII rocked the world in 1937 when he gave up throne and country rather than "the woman I love." But Edward and the twice-divorced Mrs. Simpson were in their thirties. In 1989, over fifty years later, Andreas Papandreou, the prime minister of Greece, gave up his thirty-eight-year marriage and the leadership of his country because of the love of a woman not his wife. Involved in this public ordeal in addition to the seventy-year-old Papandreou were his sixty-five-year-old wife and the "other woman," thirty-five. A bulletin announcing the impending divorce of sex therapists Masters and Johnson shocked the country in 1992. Although Dr. William Masters, seventy-six, and Virginia Johnson, sixty-seven, advised clients to take time to nurture their relationship, they apparently were unable to nurture their own.

Such geriatric dramas make headlines today because of the prominence of the players but many others go unnoticed, with half of the couple—usually, but not always, the wife—bearing the heaviest burden. Older couples today must be contemplating divorce, or actually getting divorced, in sufficient numbers to prompt the American Association of Retired Persons to put out a how-to guide titled *Getting Divorced After Fifty*.

THE LIBERATED WOMAN

Though it is generally assumed when a marriage fails in late life that the man is the one behind the breakup and the woman the unwilling victim, this is not always the case. Contributing to the rising divorce rate among older couples is the changing status of women, many of whom long ago shed the role of dependent "little woman" themselves or who have learned from the example of their daughters or younger "sisters" that working women can take care of themselves. They know something their mothers might not have believed possible: they can make it on their own.

This is not true of *all* women—witness the millions of needy women, old and young—but many are far better off financially through their own efforts than they were in the past. Millions return to work during or after early child-rearing years and, if fortunate enough to be in the right place at the right time, can start contributing to pensions. These, combined with their Social Security checks, can help them feel secure—financially at least—about growing older. Such women are less likely to feel forced to stay in an unsatisfying marriage as they grow older simply for the security of bed, board, and financial benefits.

THE FAMILY CIRCLING

Most couples do not live in a vacuum isolated from the rest of the world as they grow older. How they accommodate to aging depends to a great extent on the relationship they have with close family members. And, conversely, the relationship they have with close family members depends on how the couple accommodates to aging.

When the emotional climate with children and other relatives is warm, the relationships positive and caring, older couples receive immeasurable support. When feelings are uncaring or abrasive, couples are denied that support. The result is often the further erosion of their well-being, emotional and physical. How couples relate to each other in late life depends to a great extent, as this chapter has discussed, on the history of their past relationships. The exception to this are the newlyweds who start with a clean slate. The same is true of families. Relationships developed in younger days are likely to have a strong effect on relationships in old age with adult children, grandchildren, older parents, and other close relatives.

Where does a couple stand in the family circle? What kind of interaction goes on between the generations? How much giving is there? How much receiving? How much pleasure lies ahead? How much pain must be expected? Who gets the most? Who gets the short end? These questions will be raised in the next chapter, but there will be no universal answers, since partners can only answer for themselves.

4

Were the young knights—his sons—catching up on him? Overtaking him? Grasping at his crown? Did he gaze with anxious eyes at his princess, fearful that one day she would become like her mother—a woman he despised?

And she? Did she walk the empty halls of the castle looking in vain for her children long grown and gone? Did she yearn for other loved ones, brothers and sisters, uncles and aunts, far away in distant kingdoms?

THE FAMILY
CIRCLE

Bill and Claire Stone researched retirement homes carefully for over a year, weighing the pros and cons of each one they visited. Finally, they settled on the *perfect* place, a parklike complex in Arizona. "It's got everything!" they reported ecstatically. "Golf, tennis, health clubs, lectures, dances, concerts! It's even got a nursing home attached if, heaven help us, we need one. We're set for life." And so they were for seven years. But when Claire's lung cancer was discovered, it was not long before they moved back to Cleveland. Their friends in Arizona could not understand. "You've got everything here!" they kept repeating. "What's in Cleveland?"

Claire's answer came in one word: "Family!"

*F*ew marriages exist in a vacuum, totally self-sufficient. Most couples are connected beyond their own private twosome to other family members. These connections may be limited to a child here, a brother, sister, aunt, or niece there. Or they may include a crowded network made up of three or four generations of close or distant relations known in some parts of the country as "kinfolk."

Bill and Claire are a couple. They relate to one another as husband and wife. But they have other roles to play, too. They are parents to their children and grandparents to their grandchildren. If they still have living mothers and fathers, they have filial roles to play. There may be other connections requiring less demanding roles: siblings, cousins, and the growing number, thanks to the prevalence of divorce and remarriage, of step-relations, many of whom are likely to become involved in the lives of older couples. These people can be vital sources of strength and support, but they can also be sources of conflict and strife, because wherever there are relations, there are bound to be relationships. These can be negative as well as positive. Like marriage, the family unit is fertile ground for a mixed bag of strong, often ambivalent, frequently contradictory emotions:

> love . . . compassion . . . sympathy . . . empathy . . .
> understanding . . . forgiveness . . . altruism . . .
> admiration . . .
>
> as well as
>
> hate . . . resentment . . . jealousy . . . hostility . . . rivalry . . .
> rejection . . . vindictiveness . . . or plain dislike . . .

When emotions are generally positive, they can provide vital support for older couples, helping them to negotiate the rocky terrain of aging and adding to the meaning and continuity of late life. Surprisingly enough, negative emotions do not necessarily act as handicaps. For some people hatred or anger or resentment can act as life-giving forces. Cantankerous old people, sometimes referred to as being full of "piss and vinegar," often seem to keep on going forever, suggesting that their very orneriness gives them a reason for living. It might even seem as if *any* strong emotions are more sustaining than none at all. The family is a gold mine for every kind of emotion.

THE ''BEANPOLE'' FAMILY

Today's older couples, in contrast to earlier ones who were members of two- and three-generation families, may belong to four- or five-generation families. Fifty percent of couples over sixty-five are members of four generations. Twenty percent of women over eighty who died in 1988 were great-great-grandmothers, matriarchs of five generations.

Offsetting the proliferation of surviving elderly relatives is the steady decline in size of each succeeding generation. As the birthrate declines, with fewer children per family, and life expectancy rises, experts talk pessimistically of the weakening of the extended family which, in former times, had strength in numbers. In its place has appeared a shaky vertical structure aptly named the "beanpole" family.

This beanpole may not be as precarious as some fear. It may provide opportunities, rarely enjoyed in the past, for longer periods of shared experiences between the generations. Older couples today can often look back on fifty or more years of life with their children and frequently twenty-five years or more with their grandchildren and other valued descendants. This coexistence of several generations can be bewildering. One woman delighting at the birth of her first grandchild suddenly realized that even though she was now someone's grandmother she was also someone's granddaughter. Her own grandmother, matriarch of five generations, was still going strong at ninety-five!

Gerontologists refer to the "shared biography" enjoyed by the various generations. There may be fewer members in each age group, but they overlap for much longer periods and have time to establish strong bonds shaped by weathering the ups and downs of life. As Matilda Riley explains:

> *My daughter and I have survived together for forty-five years of which only eighteen were in the traditional relationships of parent and child. Unlike our shorter-lived forebears, my daughter and I have been able to share many common experiences. . . . She shared a major portion of the historical changes I have experienced. She also shares my early experience of sending a daughter off to college, and will perhaps share my experience of having a daughter marry and raise children.*

Thanks to the beanpole structure, many couples have the opportunity to connect with their past through their aging parents, with their present through their children, and with their future through their grandchildren. The opportunity can also be enjoyed through interaction with other older and younger relatives. These relationships in and of themselves are vital to some couples in weathering the late-life crisis.

YOU AND YOUR AGING CHILDREN

In most marriages the husband's chief source of support is his wife, and vice versa. But next in the pecking order are their children, or one particular child. Older couples turn to their children not only for help in times of trouble but for pleasure and companionship when life is moving along smoothly. Among the many myths still to be put to rest about old age is that the younger generations in the United States have little involvement with the older ones and care only minimally about them. Even though this myth has been proven totally untrue, the old accusation that children neglect parents and grandparents still enjoys wide circulation. While younger people admit they prefer to live by themselves with their own children in their own homes, this preference is generally shared by their older relatives. They want to live alone, too. But separate homes are not synonymous with separate lives. Researchers studying the elderly keep on rediscovering how much involvement there is between the generations and how close it often is.

A couple's involvement with their children may remain close even without face-to-face contact, although it will be less spontaneous and require more thought, effort, and planning. Geographical proximity works wonders, but so do frequent visits, leisurely phone calls at off-peak hours, videotapes—and that other, often-forgotten art, letter-writing. Summer or winter vacations, not infrequently paid for by the older generations, combined holiday celebrations, and weekend visits all make ongoing interaction possible. Many airlines, seeing profit in these intergenerational ties, are offering coupons to older travelers that can cut flight costs by close to a half.

THE TWO-WAY STRETCH

Much emphasis has been given in recent years to the question whether the younger generations are willing or able to help when the older ones run into trouble, but little has been given to the reverse question: how much help do the older ones give to the younger? The answer to that one is "Plenty!" Help does not run along a one-way street, but flows back and forth in both directions. Many older couples, not rich but enjoying greater financial security than their own parents and grandparents did in the past, are able—and willing—to help their children financially in a number of ways: with advanced tuition fees, down payments for homes, or sometimes regular handouts for clothes, rent, other necessities, and even, now and then, a luxury. When married children both work, their parents, if retired or even if still on the job, may baby-sit, market, garden, make household repairs, cook meals, or stock the freezer. Children may reciprocate in kind on weekends or whenever either of their parents is ill.

BEWARE OF STRINGS ATTACHED

Much of this reciprocal assistance is offered willingly, without any sense of obligation on either side, thereby enriching the quality of life for everyone. Trouble can be predicted when help is given with strings attached or with the implicit message "I'm helping you, but in return I expect you to take my advice"—or "go to law school," or "marry a professional." Trouble is also ahead when one side expects too much from the other. "We *have* to go to Mom and Dad every Sunday! We never get a day to ourselves or with our friends." A father complains, "Sally and Bill think there's no reason we can't drop whatever we've planned and house-sit for them whenever they want to go away. Just because we're retired, they think we don't have anything better to do." In such situations both sides feel martyred and ill used. Neither generation has learned that a gentle "no" with a friendly explanation can work wonders.

STRAINED RELATIONS

The friendly "no" may help some relationships but not all. Quick first-aid remedies may not cure deeper wounds. Serious conflicts between parents and their grown children usually have a long history and rarely appear full-blown suddenly in later years. They are generally rooted in the past and explosions can be triggered anew years later by a seemingly innocent phrase, a gesture, or even a fleeting facial expression.

Daughter: You hate this outfit, don't you?

Mother: What do you mean? I haven't said a word about it!

Daughter: I know. But you gave me that look!

Mother: What look?

Daughter: That look you always give me when I choose my own clothes. You think I have no taste. I love this outfit!

Mother: Okay—enjoy it! Why fight about it? Why do you always have to fight about everything?

This mother-daughter conflict goes back a long way. Notice the use of the words "You always"? It's a simple little two-word phrase, but it speaks volumes. Another revealing phrase is "You never" as in "You never had time for me," or "You never believed in me." "You always" and "You never" imply years of messing up. No amount of denial or explanation can reverse long-standing resentful feelings. These keep on smoldering and flaring up long after children are grown and gone from their parents' home.

DIGGING FOR ROOTS

If anyone were to review all the sources of parent-child conflicts, the litany would be long, but a few are worth highlighting:

• *Favoritism.* " 'Jean says!' 'Jean says!' You always listen to her. You've never listened to me!" Translation: Jean is the older and favorite daughter—at least that's what Beth, the younger, has always felt and resented. She's never going to stop fighting for first place.

• *Disapproval.* "No, I'm not going to get my hair fixed or get a 'real' dress for your party. Ray loves the way I look even if you don't." Translation: Mother has always disapproved of her daughter's appearance and probably of Ray, too. Disapproval is not limited to appearance. Parents may disapprove of their children's choice of careers or work, their choice of mates, their housekeeping, child-rearing, handling of money, behavior.

• *Shame.* "If you'd just as soon I didn't visit this year, that's okay. I get the message. You don't want everyone to know Claire and I are splitting up. We're supposed to be the golden couple, aren't we? People will talk! That's what you're afraid of. That's all you've ever cared about. You don't care about me and how I'm feeling now." Translation: His parents' first priority has always been keeping up appearances, public opinion, and what the neighbors will say. Their son's feelings have always taken second place.

• *And finally—disappointment.* Most parents have hopes, secret or outspoken, for their children from birth or even from conception. "My son/My daughter" the doctor, lawyer, astronaut, athlete, millionaire, and, of course, *president!* Some of these hopes turn into realities, but many parents wait patiently only to realize in their late life that the hopes will never come true.

A special burden is put on children by parents who are disappointed in their own accomplishments or feel they have been deprived of something they deserved—love, admiration, fame, acceptance, happiness. They may hope to live vicariously, basking in their children's glory:

> Be successful *for me!*
> Be beautiful *for me!*
> Be a star *for me!*
> Be happy *for me!*
> Be popular *for me!*

So many dreams—and so often, so many disappointments. These are not limited to career choices. Couples may be disappointed in a daughter's husband, a son's wife, in their children's lifestyles, housekeeping, child-rearing, political affiliations, and sexual preferences.

Disappointments are not necessarily shared by a couple. The mother may be able to admit that her son is gay or her daughter is a lesbian, but the father may be incapable of accepting the situation. He may reject the child who, he feels, has rejected his values. Such a radical break is untenable for the more forgiving and accepting parent, who continues a relationship with the "black sheep" openly and defiantly, or perhaps secretly. Either way there will be an adverse effect on the older couple, putting distance between them.

Adult children may be far less ambitious than their parents were at their age. They may be perfectly happy to settle for careers or ways of life that appear to their parents as failures, for the older couple may have no understanding of their children's goals. Attainment of these goals may offer little prestige, monetary rewards, or power but may give great personal satisfaction.

GROWING UP IS HARD TO DO

"Once a parent, always a parent" is an oft-repeated cliché. Nothing can change that relationship. What can change, however, is the way the older and younger generations interact with each other. "He still treats me like a child!" a forty-year-old son complains about his father. "I'm still my parents' little girl," laughs a grown daughter, herself the mother of four.

Most parents eventually catch on and realize their children have become independent grown-up people responsible, for better or worse, for their own lives. A few fortunate children enjoy the mature filial relationship described by the playwright Terrence McNally in the *New York Times* in 1990:

> *Now I am a man and my parents no longer punish me or try to impose their ethics on me. It is assumed that I have some of my own and, as an adult, I appreciate their confidence.*

Trouble can usually be predicted when parents are completely unable to back out of their children's lives and remain convinced that their sons and daughters cannot fly solo. "I don't want to interfere, *but* . . ." is a familiar opening gambit for a sermon of unwelcome, unsolicited advice. "You didn't ask me, *but* . . ." is another. If they haven't been asked, why have they volunteered?

Sons and daughters who complain that they are still being treated like children often perpetuate this treatment themselves by letting it trigger in them the same old childish responses. "Don't fiddle!" Mother whispers, patting her son's hand as he plays with the silverware on the dining-room table. She has only given him a gentle maternal rebuke and is genuinely hurt and surprised when "her boy" throws down his napkin and stomps out of the room. She is still trying to control him just as she always has done and seems oblivious to the fact that "her boy" is over fifty years old and has just been made the CEO of a large corporation. He has never, however, learned how to behave like a grown-up with his controlling mother.

BETTER LATE THAN NEVER

Since it is so often difficult to achieve a well-balanced relationship, many older couples find life with their children fraught with tension, resentment, and open conflict, producing little pleasure for either side. It is no longer unusual these days to hear of "parenting" classes for mothers- and fathers-to-be before their babies are born, or during the early years of child-rearing. It is a little more surprising to hear of couples enrolling in parenting classes when they are in their sixties and seventies, desperate to learn how to relate to their adult children. But such classes are mushrooming in adult education programs, church groups, and other educational facilities. "I got an A," carols a mother proudly waving her term paper entitled "How I Won Back My Daughter." A more apt title might have been "Better Late Than Never." While courses help some parents, they cannot solve all problems. Other couples may find their solutions by talking to a doctor, a priest, a therapist, or a social worker skilled in dealing with family problems.

GONE FOR GOOD

A small amount of any of these negative elements does not necessarily poison relationships and lead to trouble in the future. As Oscar Wilde pointed out, "Children begin by loving their parents; as they grow older they like them; later they judge them; sometimes they forgive them." All relationships have their ups and downs, but some conflicts are so destructive that they can lead to long or even permanent estrangements. Children who go against the beliefs of deeply religious parents may be written off forever. Devout Catholics may excommunicate from their families a child who has left the church or converted to a different religion. Some Orthodox Jews "sit shiva" and mourn for a child who has "married out" of their faith, as if that child had died.

Political disagreements can shatter relationships. A radical son may prefer to have minimal contacts with his conservative parents because any meeting always ends up in a shouting match. Richard Rusk, son of Dean Rusk, secretary of state under Lyndon Johnson, was so violently opposed to his father's position on the Vietnam War that he moved to Alaska—far away from his parents in Georgia. He and his father had little contact with each other for fifteen years.

Without such dramatic sources of conflict or even without any conflict at all, children may simply outgrow their parents. Mom and Dad may just have no place in Junior's world now that he is grown up and successful. Mom and Dad may know this. They may feel uncomfortable, out of place, in his social, professional, artistic, or monied life. Although he'll never admit it, he's probably ashamed of them. They may have absolutely nothing to say to the woman he has married, and vice versa. The two generations probably no longer speak the same language. Junior may prefer to limit contacts with his parents to obligatory visits at birthdays and holidays or if these are impossible to arrange, convince himself that lavish presents can make up for his absence.

Some sons and daughters find it too painful to continue the old battles and solve the problem by distancing themselves as much as possible from their parents' orbit. This may involve moving hundreds of miles away or simply establishing emotional distance. Either way, the involvement can then be remote and infrequent. Occasionally, the older couples themselves are the ones who feel the need of distance and remove themselves geographically from their children's lives. There may also be resentment when a couple chooses a retirement condo with only one bedroom. Their children, and other relatives, may receive the signal that frequent or prolonged visits will not be encouraged—exactly the signal the older ones intended.

THE NOT-SO-EMPTY NEST

Little did poet Robert Frost know early in this century that lines he wrote then would be taken so seriously by many young people and their parents toward the end of the century:

> *Home is the place where, when you have to go there,*
> *They have to take you in. I should have called it*
> *Something you somehow haven't to deserve.*

Twenty years ago children were less likely to pay attention to Frost's message. The young people of the sixties from affluent or just comfortable families often didn't want to come home to Mom and Dad once they had left. If they needed a roof or temporary shelter, they crashed in a friend's pad. In that youth-oriented society the generation gap seemed too wide, so kids and their parents were brainwashed into agreeing with Thomas Wolfe that "you can't go home again."

Until recently, couples expected to experience the "empty nest syndrome"—the often difficult emotional and physical readjustment that had to be made when children leave home for college, marriage, or just to do their own thing. Couples today—with so many more women working outside the house—are better prepared to roll with the changes in family patterns. But even so, the period when the children first leave can be a critical one for both partners, a time when their roles as parents diminish and the relationship as husband and wife has to be renewed. Even if they do find themselves enjoying the new pattern, it would be dangerous for any couple to assume that this will remain stable forever. It may not. Changes in society and the economy have worked miracles in shrinking that generation gap which only a few years ago was considered too wide to bridge. A few figures confirm this:

• Twenty-two million young adults are currently sharing the same house with their parents, a 50 percent increase since 1970.

• Today's under-thirty generation is living at home and staying dependent longer than any other since shortly after World War II.

• Perhaps because of the sexual revolution (no need to marry in order to have sexual relations) the number of those between thirty and thirty-five who have never married has doubled since 1970.

and perhaps the most crucial figure of all:

• The cost of living has risen 267 percent since 1970.

In addition to those children who have remained for more years than ever under the parental roof are others who, having once fled the nest, are now bouncing back into it. A wry comment on this contemporary happening is that it is only appropriate to extend the upper limit of middle age to 65–70 because adolescence seems to last until at least age 30 for many of today's young people.

Couples expecting freedom in their sixties often find themselves tied down, supporting children aged twenty-five or older through graduate and professional training, or through undergrad schools for sons and daughters who had taken time away from their books when they were younger in order to "do their own thing" or to "find themselves."

In a commencement speech at the University of South Carolina in 1986, comedian Bill Cosby gave his own interpretation of the words "go forth" to the graduates. "All across this great nation people are graduating and going forth. My concern is whether they know where 'forth' is. The road home is already paved. 'Forth's' not back home. We love you and we are proud of you, and we are not tired of you . . . but we could get tired of you. 'Forth' could be next door to us, but you pay the rent."

Not too long ago many children were accused of being too distant from their parents. That complaint is not heard so much these days. The opposite accusation—being too close—is being leveled at great numbers. Nurturing doesn't necessarily end in the nursery. Many parents are now expected to be ready, often with little warning, to nurse grown children through broken romances, divorce, illnesses, job disappointments, financial reverses. Couples complain that the uncertainty is the hardest element to cope with—never knowing what they will be coping with tomorrow, the empty nest or the full house.

The house may become full for many reasons:

• The skyrocketing cost of rents in many parts of the country. Young people—and not-so-young people—ask, demand, expect, or are invited to live at home until they have collected enough money for a place of their own. Getting this place often involves the first month's rent, the last month's rent, a security deposit, and perhaps an agent's fee—sums that can run into thousands of dollars.

• A similar scenario involves adult children saving for down payments on houses, or needing temporary accommodation while a newly purchased home is in the process of renovation.

• A married daughter, now divorced or widowed, comes home to her parents, often bringing along her children and their pets. Sons in the same position may also return, but this seems to happen less frequently.

• Children—single or married-with-children—may be forced to ask for shelter because of financial problems or unemployment—a plant closes down, a company relocates, a business fails, an investment turns sour.

• Serious illness may bring children home to the place where they can expect to find care and concern during convalescence, long periods of recuperation, or even permanent invalidism. Many parents have accepted the tragic responsibility of nursing a grown child through the terminal stages of AIDS.

Added to the numbers of children returning home because of legitimate problems of health, money, employment, or tragedy are the children who have never been able to stand on their own feet, or perhaps have never been allowed to achieve independence. These sons and daughters keep returning home for advice, comfort, handouts, mothering, or to fan the flames of conflict they have never been able to resolve. In such situations the parents have usually played a major role by encouraging dependency and scuttling attempts at independence. Mother and father birds usually chase their babies out of the nest. Their young are expected to take off. This is also true in principle with people, but many human mothers and fathers do not act like birds.

While pushing an offspring out of the nest with one hand they hang on to its tail feathers with the other, all the time asking "Why can't he fly?"

UNEXPECTED TROUBLE SPOTS

After raising their families, couples often breathe a sigh of relief and look forward to devoting themselves to each other in their later years. The relief may be short-lived. To their surprise and dismay many find themselves still embroiled in their children's lives. Sibling conflicts, which parents assume will be left behind once the nursery days are over, do not necessarily die down just because everybody is grown up. Stormy relationships often continue to simmer and flare up all through life. These may be intensified, with more people involved, when brothers and sisters marry and bring in-laws into the picture.

Some siblings who as toddlers fought over possessions or parental favors may learn to share, but others keep the same struggles alive forever. Jealousy about who is prettier, handsomer, more athletic, more popular, more talented, more successful, or richer may also continue. Conflicts are not necessarily limited to those directly involved. Adversaries seeking support may look for reinforcements among other family members. They may keep on trying to line up their parents on "their side." Couples who refuse to take sides, who try to act as peacemakers and mediators, may find themselves under attack by everyone. Where, they may wonder, are those peaceful years together they had earned?

Trouble may also come, surprisingly enough, not from warring children but from oversolicitous ones. Even though most children do respect their parents' autonomy, some caring sons and daughters, concerned for their aging parents, may become too involved and try to direct their lives long before there is any real need for intervention. Though such a takeover is benign, not hostile, the effect can be equally negative.

"I can't stand seeing Mother and Dad still living in that terrible neighborhood. But they won't budge!" wails a well-intentioned daughter, desperately trying to dislodge her parents and move them to a safer, pleasanter neighborhood. *She* can't stand the neighborhood but *they*, who have always lived there, can. They may admit it has deteriorated and is even dangerous, but it's familiar. The stress of adjusting to a new environment may be more hazardous to their health and well-being than all the negative factors in a neighborhood that is familiar. When well-meaning children step in to influence not only where their parents live but how they live, spend their money, occupy their time, socialize, etc., they are likely to undermine the confidence of the older couple just at the point where this confidence may be starting to slip.

WHEN THE BALANCE SHIFTS

Couples can coast merrily along, maintaining a satisfying or even an unsatisfying but workable relationship through the years with their grown children, both sides handling the ups and downs of independent daily living and neither side imposing on the other. A mutual process of give-and-take dominates the relationship between the generations; if the process is uneven, this is most likely to be the result of adult children's overdependence on their parents.

But then at some point the older couple may begin to show signs of deterioration—slowly, with a mother's first symptoms of Alzheimer's disease, or suddenly, after a father's stroke. In general, it is usually one parent who is afflicted, so the other is able to serve as caregiver. But children may worry on the sidelines or feel obliged to pitch in and help out. Parent-child relationships that had maintained a fine equilibrium over the years are now thrown off-kilter. Perhaps for the first time help has to flow in one direction only—from the younger to the older generation. The days of the two-way stretch are over.

When both their elderly parents are in trouble—and this usually happens late in life when the older couple are over seventy-five, often in their eighties or nineties—the support and care their children are able and willing to give may be critical. This may be the deciding factor that makes it possible for a frail pair to remain in their own home rather than enter a nursing home. Studies have shown that the most likely caregiver for a disabled wife is her husband, and vice versa. But next in line as caregivers are the couple's children.

IT'S ALL RELATIVE

Many older couples find their lives enriched, fragmented, or overburdened by other family involvements, not only by children. Thanks to present-day mobility, out-of-town or even out-of-sight relatives may not stay away forever. Elderly ones like Claire and Bill Stone, mentioned earlier, may come back seeking family support after years of absence. Distant cousins may move closer and new intimacy may develop with people whose names had been barely familiar in the past. Family feuds may be patched up and family skeletons may reappear not to haunt but to renew relationships denied them for so long. Black sheep like "Uncle Max who ran off with his boss's wife" or "Cousin Maryanne who abandoned her husband and children and joined an ashram" may return to the fold. Marriage, divorce, and remarriage add and subtract in-laws and multiply step-relations.

Since one out of five of the nation's elderly is childless, quite a number of older couples have a smaller network of relatives. Lacking children, they therefore lack grandchildren and the variety of connections just mentioned resulting from the marriages and remarriages of sons and daughters. But the childless may not be less busy or less involved. While there may be a prevalent assumption that being childless is a pitiable state, couples without children do not seem to report a lower sense of well-being, morale, happiness, or general satisfaction with their lives than their more prolific contemporaries. Denied the pleasures of positive parent-child relationships, they are also spared the pains and strains that are inevitable when these relationships are negative.

When family connections are limited to contemporary or older relatives, who obviously cannot last forever, couples, once these are gone, may be left with a sadly diminished circle to turn to for companionship or support. Those who maintain ties with younger connections as well are usually more safely prepared for the future.

CONNECTED AS GRANDPARENTS

Over the river and through the wood,
To Grandfather's house we go . . .

These familiar lines conjure up an ideal image of traditional grand-parenthood—a tender Norman Rockwell–style painting showing white-haired Granny and Gramps presiding over a Thanksgiving table groaning with mouth-watering foods. Such images may be realities for some families today but not for all. It's just as likely that a family who wants to spend Thanksgiving with Grandma and Grandpa will have to jet down to their condo in Florida or speed along interstate highways to their retirement home in Arizona.

Since projections suggest a steady rise in the numbers of beanpole families over the next years and into the twenty-first century, a family may include several generations of older members—Grandpa and Grandma, Great-Grandfather and Great-Grandmother, and even Great-Greats. Today most couples over sixty-five have grandchildren and 40 percent have great-grandchildren. While the generations at the top may grow increasingly frail and play a less dominant role in family affairs, the younger ones below can still reap great benefits from the older, gaining firsthand knowledge of the past, not only of their own families but of life over a span of nearly a century.

Grandchildren are often the ones who insist that their great-grand-parents, and grandparents, too, recount family history in front of video cameras or into tape recorders, thereby creating a permanent family record that might otherwise be lost when the older relatives died. One fourth-grader found a way to make history more understandable for himself. He classified all events into two categories, not B.C. and A.D., but before and after Great-Grandpa was born. Included in the "before" category were such events as Noah's Flood, the Trojan War, and the American Revolution.

It's impossible to paint a meaningful composite picture of today's grandparents or even of the generation preceding them. They come in all shapes and sizes, with many cultures and traditions, in different states of physical health and—perhaps most important of all—with a wide range of personalities. They also come in many different age groups. One man, a father at twenty-one and a grandfather at forty-one, became a great-grandfather at sixty-one, exactly the age his cousin became a father for the first time. When, if ever, will the latter see grandchildren?

Younger couples have a variety of different styles of grandparenting, but so do older ones. There are no typical patterns. It is safe to generalize, however, about one event. The birth of the first grandchild—and of subsequent ones, too—is almost universally a moment of high excitement sending sparks of joy throughout the extended family and up and down the family beanpole. The new generation revitalizes the family structure and helps to ensure its continuity. A new grandchild is like a blood transfusion and may reawaken for older couples the early years of their own marriage and early parenting. Through their grandchildren they can relive these years without the stresses and burdens of the first time around. Husbands and wives may even find their own relationship to each other enriched by this infusion of young blood. One patriarch of a large family gave his own view of the rewards of grandparenting: "Children are the principal. Grandchildren are the interest."

Parents often discover unanticipated rewards from their grandparenthood. Some report sadly on the fun they have with their grandchildren. There was no time for much fun with their own children, when life was crowded with other demands: career pressures, financial struggles. A successful salesman playing on the floor with his baby grandson looks up at his wife and asks wistfully, "Why didn't I know how much fun this was when Tom was a baby?" Such devoted grandparents can be the mainstays of life for young parents and for their children as well. "My mom and dad are out," announced six-year-old Daniel as he answered the phone. "We've got a sitter." Then he quickly corrected himself. "Well—I mean she's not just a plain sitter. She's my grandma and she's special."

Close relationships between the generations reap benefits above and beyond concrete help and support. Children learn a lot about life when they are involved with people of all different ages. A little boy watching how his parents treat his grandparents may be given a pattern to follow in the future. At this young age he may be learning how he will behave toward his own parents when he is grown and they are old. Children may also gain greater understanding of the life cycle and the continuing process of living and dying. Arthur Kornhaber in his book *Grandparents, Grandchildren: The Vital Connection* offers this statement from a young grandson when his grandmother who lived with his family was dying: "Grandma is here all of the time, but her body is shrinking. She seems to be getting smaller and smaller, a little bit every day. I mean, Grandma's body is getting smaller but Grandma is not shrinking. Just her body."

Grandparents may want closeness, they may try to achieve it, but their own desires are not the only factors determining their relationship with their grandchildren. How they and their children have felt about one another through the years may well affect the interaction with their children's children—how much closeness is encouraged; how much permitted, how much rejected. Experts are convinced that daughters and daughters-in-law rather than sons and sons-in-law act as "gatekeepers" directing the flow of grandparental traffic—moving it ahead, sending it back, or calling it to a halt.

When a couple's relationships with their own children have been generally positive, these are likely to extend also to their grandchildren. Young parents often turn to their mothers and fathers, hoping that years of experience will shed some light on dealing with problems of child-rearing. "I really don't know the answer," sighs Grandma regretfully to her son-in-law's questions about some minor infant behavior worry. "But you *must* know!" wails the young father. "You're a *grandmother!*"

Here again, as in parent-child relationships, trouble may come when advice is unsolicited. "You really should work on their manners!" a critical grandmother hisses to her daughter. "These children eat like savages!" It just may happen that daughter has been trying valiantly to work on her children's manners and now realizes she has failed in her mother's eyes—failed again! But conversely, perhaps she feels her mother's eternal emphasis on decorum has been the bane of her own life and does not want to inflict this on her children. In either case, dinner-at-Grandma-and-Grandpa's is likely to become less frequent or to be endured as a duty and not a pleasure.

In contrast to those couples who are heavily involved with their grandchildren are those who opt for greater autonomy and distance. They may love these children dearly but have no intention of devoting their lives to child-oriented activities. They have their own work, or pleasures. Fulfilling themselves has a higher priority than fulfilling anyone else.

Andrew J. Cherlin and Frank Furstenberg, Jr., authors of *The New American Grandparent*, neatly wrap up the way they see today's grandparents in the book's subtitle, *A Place in the Family, a Life Apart*. As one of the book's respondents explains:

> *When we were raising our children we figured when the children got married and moved to their own locales, we'd be free to do as we please . . . then we find out when we're grandparents they say, "Uh, Mom, Pop, how about baby-sitting?" Once in a while is fine but we wouldn't want to be tied down to that.*

Possibly as a result of increased longevity and the survival or greater numbers of elderly men and women, numerous studies of grandparenting have been made in recent years. More than twenty years ago one of the first studies, made by Bernice Neugarten and Karol Weinstein, described five major kinds of grandparents: distant figures, fun-seekers, surrogate parents, formal, and finally, those who are the reservoirs of family wisdom.

But generalizations are still hard to make even given these rough categories. Relationships cannot be counted on to stay constant over time. The fun-lover may become distant. The formal try fun for a change—won over by a particularly seductive three-year-old. Grandparents may play favorites—so may their grandchildren. Some grandmothers adore the babies—a new arrival becomes the latest favorite, unseating a currently rebellious two-year-old brother who once wore the crown but now is demanding and exhausting. Or there may be a permanent favorite. It could be the child of the favorite, the firstborn, the only boy, the one who takes most after "our" family.

Relationships also change over time as both generations move into new phases. "Grandpa's no fun anymore," a teenager complains to his mother. "All he talks about are aches and pains." Grandpa, on his side, is exasperated by his grandson's rudeness, unkempt appearance, and "unspeakable" taste in music and food. The two, once the closest allies, may have little in common now.

Grandparents who become surrogate parents have a particularly crucial and demanding role to play in their grandchildren's lives because they are involved in an ongoing schedule of caring and nurturing. Stories of addicted babies of addicted mothers are becoming tragically familiar in today's news. Less newsworthy are the stories of grandparents who accept responsibility for the care, or sue in the courts for custody, of grandchildren when the parents are addicted to drugs and alcohol and unable to provide a healthy environment. Grandparents are also forced to step in when parents are unwilling or unable to care for their children or to protect them from physical or sexual abuse. These grandparents—and their numbers are growing—may be senior citizens and long removed from child-rearing routines. A probate judge in one Connecticut town reported that in 1986 he had 40 active files of grandparents seeking custody of their grandchildren. In 1989 the number had quadrupled to 160. The Fort Worth, Texas, chapter of Grandparents Raising Grandchildren has 95 of what have come to be known as "skip-generation" families.

A further disruption in the lives of the older couples can be expected when the parents of the abused or abandoned children are rehabilitated and ready to take over their parental responsibilities. Grandparents who have had to learn how to live with children all over again must now learn to live without them.

Such extreme situations aside, grandparents can often give children a sense of stability and security when life is stressful. They may even act as intermediaries and go-betweens when grandchildren are in conflict with their parents.

Grandparents often provide almost life-giving support to both children and grandchildren who are going through the stress and turmoil of a divorce, offering comfort, consolation, continuity, and sometimes money. But sadly, divorce all too often ends in severed relationships. It is also sad but true that the death of a son or daughter may become a double tragedy for the surviving parents, resulting in the loss of their grandchildren as well. The death or divorce of a son is more likely to jeopardize his children's relationships with their paternal grandparents. The widowed or divorced daughter-in-law generally turns to her own family, or, if she remarries, becomes involved with a new set of in-laws.

"When in trouble, get together with fellow sufferers!" This seems to be the practice these days, so it is not surprising that in many states individual grandparents who have been denied access to their grandchildren because of estrangement or the death or divorce of sons or daughters have banded together to assert their rights. In 1975 grandparents had no legal rights, but there are now laws in fifty states making it possible for grandparents to petition the courts to obtain the legal rights to visit their grandchildren.

"Take a course!" is another familiar suggestion for those who want to improve their skills, their relationships, their habits, etc. Since there are so many older couples surviving into their eighties and nineties these days and becoming grandparents and great-grandparents, some of them are unsure about the role they are expected to play. The world is rapidly changing. So are patterns of behavior and interpersonal relationships. Courses in parenting are now familiar, so why not courses in grandparenting? There must be a need for these, too, because they are on the rise. Arizona State University was among the first to initiate a pilot program, in which two hundred grandparents between the ages of fifty and eighty took part in a twelve-week course, "Becoming a Better Grandparent."

CONNECTED AS IN-LAWS

The old familiar claim, "I haven't lost a daughter, I've gained a son," may ring true for many fortunate parents but may have a hollow ring for others less fortunate. The claim might be rewritten more appropriately as "I've gained a son *and* his family, for better or for worse." The son may be okay, but his family may provide the problems. The same can be said of the daughter and her family. Most couples are aware of the potential hazards of in-law relationships and do their best to handle them gently. This is not always easy. The parents of a daughter may know intellectually that once she is married they will have to share her with their new son-in-law and, to some extent, with his family, but their heads and their hearts may not pull together. Like three-year-olds, they may find sharing a painful process. "When I realized that Judy would be spending Christmas with her in-laws this year, I was heartbroken," admits the mother of a recent bride. "We always had Christmas together. Judy says they'll alternate and come to us next year, but it won't be the same. It'll never be the same."

In-law disagreements, voiced or repressed, can be expected not only over holiday sharing but over anything or everything—over grandchildren's visits, grandchildren's rearing, over housekeeping, religion, vacations, and over the giving and spending of money. Do the in-laws who have the most and give the most automatically earn first place in a young couple's life?

> "Jimmy's folks are renting a house at the beach for all of us this summer."
>
> . . .
>
> "Mary's folks are lending us the down payment for the house."
>
> . . .
>
> "Frank's grandfather is picking up David's college fees."

The other in-laws in all three families may feel they cannot compete with these larger bank accounts and may therefore feel they count for less in their children's lives. They may or may not be correct. On the other hand, although money can buy gratitude and indebtedness, it cannot buy affection, companionship, devotion.

> *Wife:* Look what we do for them. We give them everything!
>
> *Husband:* Too much! I've always told you that, but do you ever listen?
>
> *Wife (ignoring the dig):* And what do they give us back? Nothing!
>
> *Husband (bored: he's heard it all before):* So what do you expect? They've always been like this. Did you think they'd change when we retired?
>
> *Wife:* They hardly give us the time of day. Everything's for *her* folks. And what do *her* folks do for them?

Her folks may have retired on a fixed income with little to spare to help their children. But they may be active, informal, and great fun for the younger couple and their children to be with. *His* parents may be sour, buttoned-down, stiff, humorless, and hypochondriacal. The younger family may be concerned with both sets of aging parents out of duty to *his* and out of genuine affection for *hers*.

It's easy to understand why future in-law relationships are problematic if one set of parents, or both, oppose a marriage. Disapproval or outright dislike of a son's choice of a wife or a daughter's choice of a husband can get things off to a disastrously bad start and determine relationships for years ahead. A revealing indication of a relationship is how a parent-in-law refers to the new family member. If Mother speaks of "my daughter's husband" rather than "my son-in-law," without even realizing what she has done, she has distanced herself from him. Old wounds can heal, but they usually leave permanent scars.

Couples who take all sorts of vows of nonintervention and nonaggression when their children marry may still be drawn into cold-war tensions—or even all-out hot-war battles—with a seemingly innocent remark. Such innocent remarks may be misinterpreted by one side or may not be delivered quite so innocently by the other. "There's a linen sale at Gorham's next week, Mimi. We need sheets, so Dad's driving me there on Tuesday. You probably could use a few, too. Shall I pick some up for you?" Is this a genuinely caring offer to their son's wife? Or did Mimi's in-laws notice when they baby-sat that the children's beds were unmade and the sheets torn? Is the offer a subtle criticism of Mimi's sloppy housekeeping? It can be taken either way, depending on the history of Mimi's relationship with her parents-in-law. If this has always been strained, then Mimi is likely to take the offer the wrong way. She'll probably attack her husband later about his parents' implied criticism. He is likely to argue back and a marital argument may follow because he defends his parents—or he may defend his wife and end up fighting with his mother and father. Mimi may carry things further by complaining about her in-laws' treatment to her own parents who, in turn, may discuss it with other family members. One "innocent" remark can thus send ripples of animosity through a whole collection of in-laws on both sides.

An especially painful situation lies in wait for couples who, because of their own longevity, risk living to see their children's marriages break up. A son- or daughter-in-law who has been loved and cherished over twenty or thirty years, who may have even been a prime source of support, may suddenly be out of the picture, and perhaps be replaced through remarriage with a strange new in-law who joins the family and totes along a whole new set of relatives. If the older couple has managed over the years to maintain a genuinely affectionate and gratifying give-

and-take relationship with their children's in-laws, these relationships are likely to be permanently disrupted or strained when the younger couple gets divorced. One divorce, therefore, can create a series of losses in more than one family. There may eventually be gains, but these cannot be guaranteed.

CONNECTED AS STEP-RELATIONS

Divorce at any stage of life—if it is followed by remarriage—is likely to produce new relatives of step rather than blood ties. Most divorces take place in younger marriages, but older couples are involved in the world of step-relationships, too. If they themselves have been divorced, whether recently or long ago, each husband and wife may have brought to their new marriage children from a previous union. After the new wedding ceremony a man becomes a husband again and simultaneously becomes the stepfather of his new wife's children. A woman, after the same double-duty ceremony, becomes both wife and stepmother. There are so many permutations and combinations in divorce, widowing, and remarriage these days that a formerly unlikely scenario is no longer incredible, though still guaranteed to stun the young couple. Supposing the young groom's divorced mother has recently married the young bride's widowed father after the young couple have exchanged vows and rings, the two become simultaneously not only husband and wife but stepbrother and stepsister as well!

Fortunate couples who enter new marriages trailing along children from previous ones may work out solutions that satisfy everyone. Personalities may mesh well—his with her children, hers with his, and all of them together with each other. A new family unit may emerge that is stronger than the old ones. But this does not always happen. Husbands may have the same conflicts with their own children that were discussed earlier; wives may, too. Each one may be drawn into the conflicts of the other and the stresses multiply.

Even if their own marriage remains intact through the years, a couple are not immune from step-relationships. They become step-grandparents when their children divorce and remarry a partner who has children already. The record high rate of divorce among the young and middle-aged is producing more and more of these mixed-up step-relationships. This situation, although having its own built-in problems, may have its up side, too, and produce unexpected benefits. While the extended family, familiar in the past, may be shrinking, these new relationships help to spread the family in different directions. The new additions may provide opportunities for new friendships and alliances. One couple who kept bemoaning their lack of grandchildren recently learned from their fortyish bachelor son that he was going to get married. His parents were delighted but a little stunned to hear that their new daughter-in-law-elect was bringing along four children from her previous marriage. At the wedding the groom's parents became the instant step-grandparents of four noisy children ranging in age from two to fifteen. Overnight the older couple was brought into contact with the unfamiliar worlds of infancy, childhood, and adolescence.

CONNECTED AS BROTHER AND SISTER

Sibling relationships in the early years have been widely studied by professionals trying to understand why brothers and sisters feel the way they do about each other and how they have interacted from their nursery days.

Until recently, however, experts have shown little interest in probing what happens to these relationships over time. This is surprising, since these can be particularly significant later in life when retirement cuts off regular contact with coworkers, when social networks begin to diminish, and when replacements are harder to establish. Interest in this area intensified in the 1980s and many experts are examining these long-lived sibling relationships. In 1990 the first International Symposium on Brothers and Sisters was held in the Netherlands, proving that sibling bonds at all ages are of interest in other countries as well as in the United States.

Psychologist Stephen P. Bank says, in *The Sibling Bond,* "We are willing, on the basis of greater security, having marriages and careers, to be forgiving of all people, including our brothers and sisters. And as our parents grow older we realize that our siblings are the last limbs of our family tree. As we get older, siblings become among the most important people in our lives. The fact is that the sibling relationship is the longest-lasting relationship in our lives in terms of number of years." Many brothers and sisters would echo the words Thomas Jefferson wrote long ago, "I find as I grow older that I love those most whom I loved first."

Close sibling relationships may remain constant all through life, although marriage and the introduction of in-laws may affect and permanently alter a sister's feelings for a brother and vice versa. Or, as often happens, interaction may be more intense, or less, during certain periods. The majority of people over sixty-five have at least one living sibling and some older couples look to these relations as their most valuable source of support.

Old animosities and rivalries, however, dormant for years, can be rekindled late in life. Old grievances dating from nursery days can crop up again among siblings of eighty or ninety, triggered by major differences but just as likely by minor ones. These episodes can have negative effects on older couples, disturbing the peace of their daily lives. Their own marital relationships may suffer, too, if each berates the other for the behavior or unreasonable demands of "your" sister or "your" brother.

The greatest potential for unpleasantness between older siblings is the decline of one or both of their aging parents. Here tempers and recriminations are likely to fly. New wounds may be inflicted; old ones may be opened up and these may never heal even after a parent's death. Brothers and sisters, even those who have managed to maintain a good relationship with each other and their in-laws over the years, may not enjoy having to be closely involved with each other again as they were in childhood.

Old emotions dating back to those days may rise up, making cooperation difficult or well-nigh impossible just when it's needed most. Brothers and sisters may once again fight battles begun and never resolved in nursery days. "So Chuck and I are supposed to take Mother in, are we? What about you and Joe? You won't lift a finger, will you? You never did—you always left me to do the dishes when you gabbed on the telephone." Is it possible that resentment over childhood chores can rise to affect the welfare of a ninety-five-year-old mother? Apparently it is! Admittedly, this same old mother may still be playing favorites from her wheelchair and fanning the flames of ancient rivalries.

AND STILL CONNECTED AS SON OR DAUGHTER

> In late 1990 Sally and Mort Hoffman were finally able to cele-
> brate their wedding anniversary by taking a cross-country camp-
> ing trip. They had waited a long time for this. Even after their
> last child was married, they had never been able to get away
> because of recurring crises or the need for ongoing care by their
> elderly parents—all four of whom lived into their late eighties
> or nineties. Mort's mother survived the longest and died at
> ninety-seven. After her death Mort and Sally took that long-
> postponed trip to celebrate their anniversary—their *fiftieth!*

Sometimes, as discussed earlier in this chapter, older couples need
help and receive it from one or more of their grown children. But these
days there may be more than one older generation at the top of the
family beanpole. Couples may be parents and grandparents but at the
same time still remain children if their own parents are alive. This
situation may add burdens, although not always. Quite a number of
very old people remain fiercely independent right until their final days.
There may be benefits and rewards, too. Men and women in their
seventies may have never learned what it is to be orphans. They may
have never known life without a parent. "I didn't really feel old," a
seventy-year-old woman admitted sadly, "until Father died and I
wasn't anyone's child anymore."

With life expectancy on the rise, the fastest-growing segment of the
population is the one eighty-five and older. This may sound like a
miracle considering that less than a century ago life expectancy was less
than fifty, but the down side of this miracle is that the over-eighty-five
group is the one with the most serious health problems and therefore
the one needing the most ongoing care. Because life goes on so long
for so many, more couples, and singles, too, will retire with one or both
parents still alive. Ten percent of today's senior citizens have children
who are also senior citizens. How long will the empty nest remain
empty after the last child has left for the last time, before there will be
new demands on their parents' newly gained free time and energy, or
new occupants for the vacant rooms?

According to the House Select Committee on Aging, in 1988 the number of years grown children spend with parents over sixty-five now exceeds the years spent with children under eighteen. In 1960 only 16 percent of people over fifty had surviving parents. This figure is expected to increase to 60 percent early in the next century. It is projected that around the time when the Baby Boomers graduate to the senior class, there will be over a million men and women a hundred years old or older. It's hard to believe, but if this projection actually becomes a reality there may also be several million sons and daughters, probably in their eighties themselves, still calling someone Mom or Dad!

BEYOND THE FAMILY CIRCLE

Kinfolk can be key figures, for better or for worse, in the lives of older couples. Some contribute support; others generate conflict. No one chooses these relationships—they are conferred on everyone by blood or marriage. But for most people a circle of friends lies beyond the family circle. These friends, chosen rather than blood-related, play an equally important, often an even more crucial, role in the lives of the elderly. "I love my sisters and they're very important to Jon and me but"—an elderly woman hesitated before admitting—"Liza and Marc are really the people we're closest to. We depend on each other. I don't know what we'd do without them."

As we grow older, our social world tends to shrink. Death cuts down the numbers while colleagues and coworkers may drift away after retirement. Some die, some are in poor health, others move, or we simply have little to say to each other once our common interest—the workplace—no longer ties us together. Old close friends and the intimacy they offer us have even greater significance. Not only have we been there for each other through earlier years, sharing happy and sad events, but we are still there for each other in late life. We count on our close friends for companionship, amusement, shoulders to cry on, understanding, sympathy, and helping hands whenever these are needed.

Couples have each other to turn to in late life, but friends sometimes can offer support partners cannot. Most of us want to have a confidant—someone we can trust completely with our intimate feelings, someone who listens and does not judge. Recent studies of older couples report that the majority of respondents rated their marriages as "very happy," yet later in the interview when asked to name a confidant, a large number named friends rather than partners.

The death of a valued friend can be a tragic blow at any age, but particularly for the elderly, who have neither time nor hope of finding anyone else to fill the empty space in their ever-shrinking circle.

Couples are fortunate if they find other couples they both enjoy. When this happens, strong friendships are born and may continue through decades. In some cases, however, if one partner cannot abide the other partner's friends and complains about every meeting, eventually, for the sake of peace and harmony, the friendship will be dropped. Conflicts also can be expected when partners differ in their social needs. *She* may be a people person thriving on social interaction. *He* may be a loner needing few human contacts. What law demands that couples should be evenly matched in sociability or that every twosome has to be a foursome when it comes to friendships? No such law exists, and many couples are discovering that their relationship will not suffer—is actually more likely to flourish—when each partner has a few friendships independent of the other. They are likely to discover this pattern will add variety to both their lives.

Although a couple tend to function as a twosome in late life, the partners are better insured for the future if each one has a few friends independent of the other. If they have always socialized in tandem, what will happen when one of them dies? The widowed partner often feels out of step. "We were all so close," a recent widow sighed. "The six of us—Jim and Marie, Frank and Tess, Carl and me. Now Carl's gone and we're five. It's not the same! It'll never be the same!"

Husbands and wives growing old together these days when one century is ending and another about to begin, when life expectancy is inching upward, may feel they are living in the best of times or the worst of times. They may see the glass as half-full or half-empty.

Couples who are convinced they are living in the best of times feel lucky to be alive now at the turn of the twenty-first century. Their marriage, which a hundred years ago would have ended at middle age or before because of the death of one partner, can now continue for decades. Those who remarried late in life can still believe that they have some future together. And their marriage is not the only relationship that has lasting duration. They are now able to grow old along with a varied collection of relatives—siblings, in-laws, step-relations, aunts, uncles, cousins. But what may amaze them most is that they have a chance to see the younger generations grow up. They may see one grandchild graduate from college, watch on television as another walks in space. They may even be able to dance at a great-grandchild's wedding, to hug the groom and to kiss the bride.

Those who cling to the view that it's the worst of times point to the fact that by living longer they may contract one or more of the seriously degenerating physical or mental diseases that occur most frequently in people over eighty-five. Or they may bewail the sad truth that by living longer, although still healthy themselves, they have to watch treasured family members—people who had been their pillars of support and companionship—succumb to illness and dependency. They may have to endure the tragedy of outliving their closest relatives, even their children and grandchildren. One day there may be no one left alive who calls them Mother or Father, Aunt or Uncle, Grandma or Grandpa. There may be no one left who even knows their first names. Such couples may be justified in echoing Truman Capote's assertion, "Life is a moderately good play with a badly written third act."

*"Well, old girl, this is the third act. What,
if anything, do we have up our sleeve?"*

5

Did he, his warrior days at an end, now enjoy once again the favorite pastimes of his youth, the tourney and the hunt? Did he find his long-forgotten dulcimer and pass pleasant hours playing melodies? Or did the endless days of hunting weary him? Did the music sadden him?

And did she, her children grown, find joy in creating new tapestries and satisfaction tending the sick, feeding the hungry, comforting the bereft? Or did she stare out of her castle window with blind eyes, seeing only that life had passed her by?

RETIREMENT
MYTHS

Faye: I want to help Cliff, but he won't let me. Ever since he retired, he's changed. He acts like life's over. I can't make him see that it's not. So he doesn't have an office to go to anymore? So what? We've still got each other, haven't we? We've got plenty of money. We're not sick—we even look pretty good, too. I know he's hurting, but I can't reach him. I try, but he keeps moving further and further away. How can I get him back?

Cliff: She keeps saying "I understand." I know she means well, but I wish she'd quit. How can she understand? She's got her life together. Nothing's changed for her. Can't she see what's happened? I was a good manager—people respected me! I loved my work. I used to be somebody. What am I now? Nobody!

THE THREE FACES OF RETIREMENT

Retirement! We use the word all the time, but what does it mean? In its strictest sense "retirement" refers to giving up one's career or business because of age. But it has taken on many different meanings. Like old age itself, it is also surrounded by myth and misconception. Try discussing retirement with any three friends and you are likely to get three different views.

The first may rely on facts and figures with no emotional overtones and tell you matter-of-factly that retirement comes at age sixty-five when you stop work, and draw Social Security and—if you're lucky—pensions and investments. From then on it's up to you to fill your days.

Another friend waxes ecstatic, describing retirement as paradise, crowing about "the best years of our lives," telling you how great it is to be out of the rat race, free of stress, pressure, and bosses. "I go where I want to go—I do what I want to do."

Your third friend, like Cliff, tries to convince you that retirement is the end of the line, the time when active, productive years are over, when you're a "has-been." You're put out to pasture, put on the shelf, thrown on the scrap heap.

You may agree with one of these views and disagree with the others. You may be surprised to learn that none of the three views is correct and that each of your friends has accepted as gospel one of the popular myths of retirement. Most myths stay alive if they include an element of truth, and there is a germ of truth in each one of these views of retirement. But none of them has a universal application. Each one may apply to some of the people some of the time. Furthermore, partners may disagree completely in their views of retirement, and this may cause new conflicts in their relationship.

MYTH 1: AGE SIXTY-FIVE

This retirement myth arose when the concept of "retirement age" was introduced by Germany's Chancellor Bismarck in 1889 and then adopted throughout the industrialized world. Bismarck set 65 as the age when workers could start receiving a pension. He arrived at his figure by adding another twenty years—around 50 percent—to the life-expectancy figure current at that period—age 45. The average worker had little hope, therefore, of living to receive a pension, so the nation had little concern about bankrupting itself. If the same formula were used today in the United States, when life expectancy is 75, we could expect pensions and Social Security to start rolling in when we are around 113! But for some reason Bismarck's old figure—65—still retains its symbolic if not realistic significance.

There is nothing magic about the number sixty-five. Nowhere among the Ten Commandments is one that states "Thou shalt retire at sixty-five." Furthermore, mandatory retirement is no longer legal except in certain specialized professions where it has been raised from sixty-five to seventy-five. People are forced to retire, however, when departments are eliminated, when plants close down or relocate, when companies merge, or when businesses go bankrupt.

Despite the lack of uniformity in the retirement age, that sixty-fifth birthday is still ingrained in the minds of many people as the great dividing line separating men and women from active living and beyond which they acquire the label *senior,* even though there is nothing different in the way they feel, behave, or function. The only point they have in common is that they can now draw full Social Security benefits. By the year 2000 this age will be raised to sixty-seven according to the Social Security amendment of 1987. Sixty-five is also the dividing line in other Western countries, too. Witness the French, who speak of *le troisième age,* and the British, ever blunt and direct, who still refer to "old-age pensioners."

Some lively couples ignore that man-made dividing line and blithely cross over it, still gung-ho for the future, like Peter and Trisha Vellen, in their seventies, who are looking around and trying to figure out "what we want to do when we grow up." Others are like the character in Arthur Miller's play *Clara* who expected when he grew old "to sit looking at the ocean somewhere wondering where my life went." But some have little to agree about—one partner sees the half-full cup and the other the half-empty one.

So sixty-five, once the age of mandatory retirement, can no longer serve as a meaningful definition for the age of retirement. Men and women *do* retire at sixty-five. One or the other may retire at a much younger age or at a much older age. There is as much a growing trend toward early retirement as there is toward later retirement. There are more options, so now we can pick and choose. Thanks to improved health practices, serious physical disability for many has been postponed until the eighth or ninth decade. People are living longer and are capable of working longer. No more are they at the mercy of one birthday. Slowly, reality is eroding the "sixty-five myth."

The theme of the nineties echoing throughout gerontological circles is "tapping the resources of an aging population." This theme does not yet have widespread acceptance in society at large, but more and more older people are spreading the word. Slowly, very slowly, society is looking at its older citizens and realizing that fewer men and women sit in rocking chairs—more and more are on their toes. Some of them are even dancing!

MYTH 2: THE BEST OF TIMES

Some partners *some* of the time do indeed feel that their best years come with retirement. During their working years most men and women have had to concentrate heavily on earning a living, supporting a family, paying those bills. For some, just staying afloat and making ends meet was a heavy enough responsibility. For others, "getting ahead" was the goal, so sacrifices had to be made, usually at the expense of family, recreation, and anything detracting from the demands of the office.

Retirement for some people offers a release from drudgery, monotony, and boredom as well as from pressure, stress, and competition. If they have prepared for it, or know how to make use of it, fortunate people welcome this release and the freedom now available to try out all sorts of new experiences unrelated to their working years.

It's not surprising that people who have had dull, physically taxing, or monotonous work are relieved when their labors are over. It's more surprising that plenty of others are just as eager to retire even though their work was once their major source of stimulation, challenge, or enjoyment. "I loved making money. It was exciting—it charged me up!'' one recently retired businessman explained. "Now I get charged up spending it or giving it away." He went on to admit that it was time to quit when he realized going to work was not a pleasure but merely a habit. Before it was too late, he was determined to find that pleasure again somewhere else.

"It's only taken sixty-eight years, but I've finally become an aristocrat!" a new retiree announced one night at dinner. He went on to explain that through history, and even today, most men and women earned their living at work that was backbreaking, tedious, monotonous, unrewarding, even hateful. Only the aristocrats, endowed with inherited wealth, had the luxury of doing whatever stimulated them, challenged them, broadened their horizons, enriched their lives. Retirees, assuming they have adequate incomes, have the same luxury. Since he had a small pension and a few investments, he was now an aristocrat and planned to devote his next years to something he had never had time for earlier—an intensive study of opera and visits to the great opera houses of the world.

Retirement, for one or both partners, gives some couples a second chance—to rediscover each other, to live for each other, to concentrate on each other without the dizzying distractions of work or child-rearing. Some grab this opportunity and make the most of it. For them this second chance is truly a blessing and their late-life togetherness comes close to surpassing their earlier togetherness. But this blessing eludes many couples completely or comes after a struggle.

Ellen Gladstone lay in bed late on a Friday morning, leafing through the newspaper and half watching a morning TV show. At ten o'clock Linc, her husband, looked in on her with concern and asked in a whisper, "Are you sick?"

"No—I feel great," she answered, yawning and stretching deliciously.

"Then what are you doing in bed?" he asked in bewilderment.

"Nothing special. I've just decided to retire," was her answer.

"What the hell does that mean?" he snapped.

"Well, you tell everyone *'We're* retired.' So that means I'm retired, too. So I've just retired: from cooking, cleaning, marketing, laundry, and breakfast, too!"

Linc got the point and soon was trying to share in the work Ellen had done all their married life. Many such couples work out a full-time partnership after one or both retire. When this happens, it's no wonder they talk about "the best years of our lives."

"We haven't missed a game yet or a rehearsal," the grandparents of a Little Leaguer and a ballet dancer say proudly. The grandfather, a former furniture salesman who spent his life on the road, probably secretly hopes that his present devotion will make up for his past absence at his son's baseball events and his daughter's dance recitals, both of which his wife always had to attend alone.

Those who subscribe to the best-of-times view follow no formula. Some revel in discovery, adventure, trying something new together. Others find equal gratification in the opposite direction, their rewards coming from serenity, contemplation, introspection, life review—internal rather than external exploration. An ex–foreign service officer, tired of always being asked how he and his wife were surviving retirement after their glamorous life, developed a stock answer, "Oh, I've got a little desktop publishing business started and we've each got new adventures brewing." He did not go on to explain that his wife's adventures involved learning needlepoint and improving on her pie crust. He himself did just enough desktop work to justify his idleness and found adventure in what he never had time for: puttering around his house and garden, fixing things, improving things, helping things grow—plants, pets, and grandchildren.

The example set by these happy few is treasured by younger people because it helps to diminish their own dread of aging. This example may rouse envy in contemporaries whose late life drags tediously along or sinks into outright misery. The best-of-timers live positively and think positively, but their lives are not risk-free. Convinced they have the know-how for successful late life, these couples may forget that things will not go on forever this way. They may be totally unprepared for the adversity that is inevitably in the cards for everyone. When serious illness, or problems with children, or financial catastrophe strikes, they often feel they have been robbed, betrayed. Contemporaries who have learned to demand and expect less of life may accept adversity with better grace.

MYTH 3: THE WORST OF TIMES

Some partners *some* of the time do see retirement as the worst years. This myth is truly insidious because it has the power to depress their relatively healthy-minded partners and to shatter less sturdy ones. Furthermore, even though we do not feel useless, finished, today, many of us allow the myth to convince us that we soon will be. In a nationwide survey conducted in the 1980s by Lou Harris Associates, respondents still in the work force were asked when they expected to be old. A large number replied, "When I stop working."

When retirement is paired with unfortunate realities—poor health or financial hardship—the combination can be understandably hazardous to the well-being of any couple. But even good health and plenty of money do not guarantee contentment in late life for everyone.

Like Cliff in the opening dialogue, many men and women feel that retirement is almost a death sentence. Without their roles as breadwinners or contributors they are nonentities—nonpersons. They feel that they no longer have a purpose in life—no worth, no value, no place. For some these are temporary emotions. "I understand. I know you're having a hard time, but you'll get used to it!" one partner, like Faye, may repeat with loving concern in the early days of retirement, but later her understanding may wear thin. "Come on! Snap out of it!" or "Do something! You can't go on like this!" Some people do indeed snap out of it and refocus their lives, finding new friends to replace the gang at the office and new interests to replace the rat race.

An unhappy few—often those whose only sense of self or satisfaction came from their work—never readjust. They feel stripped of any identity when this work is over. They can only look backward at what they used to be; they are disconnected from the past and unconnected with the present and the future. When they ask themselves, "Who am I?" or "What am I?" there is only one answer: "Nobody" or "Nothing." Some new retirees age dramatically in the first year. Their depression, according to some experts, provides fertile ground for deterioration, disease, premature death, and even suicide. The suicide rate for men is four times higher in retirement than in any other stage of life.

A special and somewhat contemporary problem comes from the

growing trend for women who entered the work force late to want to continue to work after their partners retire. These women may have to keep on working for financial reasons, or they may be at the peak of their career, or they may simply have learned to love being out of the house and the apron. They and their husbands may go through painful months readjusting schedules, priorities, and emotions until one or the other partner capitulates—the woman stops working or the man finally discovers he can get through the day without her.

Individual retirees from any walk of life—the lowest to the highest— may suffer ongoing malaise, but the ones most commonly afflicted are those who have grown accustomed to power, admiration, and applause. These are dangerous drugs, and it can be torture when they are withdrawn. There is no "quick fix" to replace the power of the CEO commanding the boardroom, the surgeon commanding the operating room, or the trial lawyer commanding the courtroom. Standing around in the wings is no substitute for center stage and the spotlight. Retired titans are often bitterly shocked to discover they no longer inspire the same degree of awe or reverence they once expected as their due.

A postretirement slump into chronic depression suffered by one can cast a pall of gloom over both partners. This can drive a cruel wedge between them at a time when closeness is needed more than ever. Or the malaise may be contagious and result in two depressed, bitter people, unable or unwilling to help each other or themselves. Their despair becomes compounded when it extends to other family members and friends, who eventually back away from couples who keep singing "those retirement blues." Instead of wallowing in permanent gloom, a more positive move is to consult a therapist or marriage counselor.

REALITY VERSUS MYTH

If the myths just described give false descriptions of retirement, what's the true story? Probably "diversity" is the best word to apply to this as well as every other stage of life. The millions of couples over sixty-five are doing a lot of different things in a lot of different ways. No one pattern can suit such a multitude. For the majority, late life is neither

the best nor the worst of times. Their earlier years were probably full
of ups and downs and their later years, barring serious illness and
incapacity, follow the same pattern.

It's important to repeat here that of the 30 million men and women
over sixty-five, only 5 percent are in nursing homes at one time.
Another 10 percent are as incapacitated as those in nursing homes, and
these with serious incapacities tend to be in the over-eighty age group.
The rest, with variations, are managing to carry on quite normal lives.
Their well-being depends not only on their health but on how they see
themselves and the world around them. The words psychologist William James wrote earlier in this century seem even more true today:

> *The greatest revolution of our generation is the discovery that human
> beings, by changing the inner attitudes of their minds, can change the
> outer aspects of their lives.*

People who carry some sense of adventure into retirement are more
likely to find gratification in these years. The adventure need not be a
physical one like mountain-climbing or deep-sea diving. It can be a
mental one—learning something new, making something new, even
thinking something new. The words "creativity," "vitality," and "cu-
riosity" can carry the same weight as "adventure." When couples
maintain these qualities, growing old will not only add years to their
lives but life to their years.

Any radical change in life is likely to demand a period of adjustment
before the new stage, even the most joyous, can feel right. Some
dislocation is inevitable. Even the most streamlined ship needs a shake-
down cruise to make sure that everything aboard is operating smoothly.
Retirement is no exception. Couples are often surprised—and often
resentful—at how much time, patience, understanding, and insight are
demanded of each of them before they are settled down comfortably.

THE RETIREMENT SHUFFLE

It would seem safe to bet that an easier adjustment would follow a
voluntary rather than a forced retirement. But even when retirement

has been carefully planned and anticipated with joy, the early days may be unsettling—even disturbing—not only for the retirees themselves but for their partners as well. Familiar routines and patterns are eliminated and no new ones have yet filled the vacuum. Few of the newly retired know that retirement is like any skill—it has to be learned. Until they have mastered the basics, they often feel out of step, uncoordinated, discontented, irritable, confused. Doug Bedloe in Anne Tyler's novel *Saint Maybe* felt all these emotions, and this was surprising to him because

> *he was accustomed to the schoolteacher's lengthy summer vacations and he'd never found it hard to fill them. But retirement, it seemed, was another matter. There wasn't any end to it. Also it was given more significance. Loaf around in the summer, Bee [his wife] would say he deserved his rest. Loaf around in winter, she read it as pure laziness. "Don't you have someplace to go?" she asked him. "Lots of men join clubs or something. Couldn't you do Meals On Wheels? Volunteer at the hospital?"*

New retirees, male or female, may revel at first in newfound freedom. "Such a joy! I can sleep late every day!" "Thank heavens! No need to shave every morning!" "No more high heels! No more girdles! What a relief!" But after a short time it may dawn on them that there's nothing to get up for, no one to shave for, and no one to dress up for. "I don't miss the office," one recent retiree complained. "What I miss are weekends and vacations." Others agree, complaining about the sameness of the days.

The term "newly retired couple" is actually a misnomer because two people do not usually become an evenly matched unit. One partner may retire, the other keep on working. If they retire simultaneously, their attitudes toward their move and what they want to do with it may clash. One thing is sure, however. Whether one or two partners retire, both must readjust their own individual clocks and timetables. And perhaps just as important, they must readjust to each other. Even though couples think themselves totally prepared *before* retirement, they may find they are ill-prepared to handle the intense togetherness that comes *after* retirement. With thirty or forty years of life together behind them, two people probably assume they know each other so intimately there could be few surprises left. Even those who married later in life may make the same assumption. But there may be plenty of surprises in the early retirement days, the greatest one probably being that they do not know each other quite so well after all.

After years of knowing how to spend weekends and holidays together, two partners may seem virtual strangers to each other on weekdays. "Is that what you eat for lunch?" a husband asks his wife as she spoons out yogurt. Married for nearly forty years, he may not have the slightest idea what she normally eats for lunch or what goes on in their house for eight hours or more every weekday.

As for her, she darn well knows everything that goes on in that house and is in command of it all. Or at least she used to be. She had nobody intruding on her kaffeeklatsches, invading her kitchen, or monitoring her telephone conversations. "Two of us is one too many!" she may mutter to herself in his early postretirement days.

"How can one person take up so much room?" an exasperated wife asks, explaining that her house seems smaller since her husband retired and is home all day. Overnight there seemed to be less air to breathe, less space to move around in. Her solution was to find a part-time job that guaranteed her time out from togetherness for a few days a week.

Another desperate wife relates: "What I used to love about Nicky was that even at his busiest he was always so interested in me—what I was doing, what I was wearing, what I was thinking. But now that he's retired, he's my shadow—he kibitzes on everything every minute every day. I'm starved for privacy. Can't he let me have just a few hours just for *me?*" Still a third reports that when she grabs her coat to make a quick getaway she's never quick enough to escape the same barrage of rapid-fire questions her husband shoots after her—"Where are you going? Who are you going with? Why are you going with them? What are you going to do?"—and then one final salvo—"What d'you want to do that damn-fool thing for?"

Men and women who over the years have single-mindedly focused on breadwinning or career advancement often redirect that intense focus after retirement onto their personal relationships. Their partners, having had to do without their husbands, wives, or companions over time, may have worked through their loneliness and settled into satisfying lives with their own interests and friends. Having learned to do their own thing, they may have no desire to share them every minute of every day with formerly absent partners who are now home.

"Always intruding!" or "Always interrupting!" are complaints often voiced by both partners as they struggle with their new togetherness. Philip Roth in his book *Patrimony* offers an apt description of a retired husband—his own father:

> *His obsessive stubbornness . . . had nearly driven my mother to a breakdown in her final years: since his retirement at the age of sixty-three, her once spirited housewifely independence had been all but extinguished by his anxious, overbearing bossiness. For years he had believed he was married to perfection, and for years he wasn't far from wrong. . . . But then my father retired from one of the Metropolitan Life's big South Jersey offices, where he'd been managing a staff of fifty-two people, and the efficient, clear-cut division of labor that had done so much to define their marriage as a success gradually began to be obliterated—by him. He had nothing to do and she had everything to do—and that wouldn't do. "You know what I am now?" he told me sadly on his sixty-fifth birthday. "I'm Bessie's husband." And by neither temperament nor training was he suited to be that alone. So . . . he settled down to become Bessie's boss—only my mother happened not to need a boss. . . .*

A relationship may suffer when one partner retires but the other does not. Usually, but not always, if the wife is younger than her retired husband or has entered the working world later and is reluctant to leave it, she is the one who goes off to her job while her husband stays home wondering what to do with himself until dinner. "John and I are like those colorful little men and women in the Swiss weather vanes," one working wife admitted sadly. "When one of us is outside, the other moves back in. We never get a chance to connect with each other anymore. How can we ever get back in step?" Stormy weather can be predicted for such couples, but eventually, with enough patience and understanding, they're likely to stop shuffling around and fall into step with each other.

RETIREMENT: PLANNING FOR IT VERSUS DRIFTING INTO IT

Although it's likely that most couples need time to adjust to retirement, it is safe to predict that those who do some advance planning usually find late life more satisfying than those who just drift into it. Drifters run the danger of losing control of their lives. Planners are more likely to keep control of theirs.

As they move into their late fifties or early sixties, couples who are determined to take control—and keep it—need to look squarely at the years ahead and ask plenty of questions. The first cover basic needs: "How will we manage financially?" "Where will we live?" "What if one or both of us gets ill?" These questions will be examined in the next chapter, but another crucial question perhaps almost as basic remains: "What kind of life will we have?"

The answer, of course, is very often determined by income and health. Couples struggling with physical or mental illness or with severe financial problems have little chance to worry about quality of life. Getting through each day is challenge enough. Health and money alone do not guarantee contentment. These are blessings indeed, but are only the means to an end. Fortunate couples who have both blessings still have to decide for themselves what this end shall be.

Since life expectancy is so much higher now than ever before, couples are likely to have plenty of quantity—more years ahead—but what of the *quality* of these years? What will make them contented in later life? What is likely to bring pleasure and meaning to them—as a couple or as individuals? Can they make their preferences mesh smoothly together?

PLANNING TOGETHER OR SEPARATELY

Most workers—white-collar or blue-collar or laboring—have a fixed pattern for their lives: five days a week, forty-eight or fifty weeks a year, decade after decade. The pattern, while providing structure, may seem like a stranglehold to many who are convinced that life would be blissful without it, like the woman in her early sixties who kept on saying, "I can't wait till Jake retires. Then we'll have all the time in the world to do everything we've always dreamed of doing." But when asked about specific details, she had to admit that she and Jake hadn't done any concrete thinking about how to make these dreams come true or whether they were even realistically possible. She and Jake were in danger, therefore, of drifting into late life still dreaming and, like children when school lets out, might one day ask each other, "What should we do now?" If they had done their homework, some advance planning, they would have a better idea of what to do next. Homework could involve a series of steps.

STEP 1: THE RETIREMENT QUESTIONNAIRE

If no questions are asked, no answers will be forthcoming. When couples begin to ask questions of each other and of themselves about what lies ahead, they are likely to focus more clearly on the kind of life they would like. Examples of such questions are:

• Do I like where I'm living now and hope to stay here?

• What changes would make me happier? Do I want to move? If so where? Far away? Nearby?

• How important are my relatives? Sisters, brothers, in-laws, children, grandchildren?

• What do I like doing now and want to continue?

• What do I hate doing and would like to give up?

• What would I like to do that I've never done before?

• What bores me? What excites me?

• What makes me feel good about myself?

• What do I like doing alone?

- What do I like doing with my husband (wife, partner)?

- How much social life do I really want?

- What gives me the greatest satisfaction?

- How does my husband (wife, partner) answer these questions? Do we agree? If not, what kind of compromises can we work out?

Answers to these questions must be honest and they must be realistic. There's no point in dreaming of living in the White House or becoming a tightrope walker.

STEP 2: KNOW YOURSELF

All those questions involve the feelings of one individual. It may seem paradoxical when speaking of couples planning for their late life together to ask each one to "stand back and take stock of yourself as a person." But this is actually very logical, because how can you begin to plan for your future together if you yourself don't know what you want? Think about the wife who says, "Sol has always dreamed of living year-round at our place on the lake. He loves it so much and he's so happy there! I guess we'll move when he retires." But is it enough for her that Sol be happy? What about her feelings? Will she be happy, too? If she raises only mild objections—"I'll miss my friends"; "The children won't come much"; "The church is seven miles away"; "It'll be sad to sell this house"; "I'll have no one to talk to"—he'll pooh-pooh her objections and won't ever know her true feelings about moving. But if she's willing to be honest, maybe she'll admit she really dreads the thought of being stuck out there alone with him all through a long dark winter. If she can show him how strongly opposed she is to moving, they may find a solution that works for both of them. They might settle on six months at the lake—or even eight—a compromise, but one they both can live with.

Self-understanding carries special significance at this stage of life since it is almost inevitable that one partner will die, leaving the other to grow old alone. If surviving partners have little understanding of their own feelings and have always lived according to the wish lists of other people, they will be ill prepared for solo living or for forming new relationships. The more couples know about themselves as individuals, the more likely they are to work out a satisfying pattern for late life together and for late life alone.

STEP 3: KNOW YOUR PARTNER

Who is this person you are living with? Do you know this man? This woman? Is this the same person you have lived with all through the years—or even for just a few, if it's a recent relationship? You may think you know, but your emotions, or old habits, or the way you both have always interacted with each other, may interfere. When two people live closely together, neither may notice changes in the other. Even physical changes may be ignored when there is little distance between them. Interior emotional changes are even harder to pick up. So it's not surprising that couples often make decisions based on a wrong assumption one has about the other. Or an assumption may have been correct for an earlier time, when both were younger and had different needs, but is no longer valid. False assumptions about another person's wishes and fears can cause as much trouble in late-life relationships as they do in early life. (See Chapter 2.) Consider a few such false assumptions:

> "I made that new vegetable garden to surprise Millie on the day she retired. She was surprised, but she didn't seem happy about it. I thought she'd be real happy. She always loved gardening and forever kept complaining she didn't have enough time for it. What's wrong with her now?" *Millie did love to garden—once. It was a great release from the tensions at her office. But she had no intention of spending her retirement gardening. In the back of her mind she had her own wish list of things she'd never had time to do. Being tied to a vegetable garden wasn't one of them.*

> . . .

> "Before Pat retired, I got us involved in a book group, a bowling league, all sorts of activities. I filled our life with people. I was so afraid he'd miss the office. He's always loved being with

a crowd. I don't understand why he doesn't seem to enjoy anything." *Pat always did love being with people—once. But as he got older, he needed them less and less. He looked forward to doing more things alone or with his wife after he retired. He only agreed to her arrangements because he assumed she enjoyed them.*

. . .

"We keep talking about all those faraway places we've never seen, but every year it's the same old trip—miles of driving to visit relatives. His relatives, my relatives. Can't we ever skip family and do something different? We're not getting any younger. But these reunions mean so much to Zach. How can I ask him to give them up?" *Zach felt exactly the same way about their annual pilgrimages, but he thought they meant so much to his wife he couldn't ask her to give them up. So they made the same trip year after year carrying their false assumptions with them.*

The subject of aging is somewhat taboo for many couples. Even though two people may share many intimate secrets with each other, they may be unwilling to voice their feelings about growing old to anyone, even to themselves. One person's reluctance to deal with aging can thereby stymie retirement plans for two.

The Lockharts never talked about what their life would be like after Jack retired. He was willing to talk about plans for the year ahead but no further. "Let me alone!" he'd growl whenever Frieda broached the subject. "We'll deal with it when it's time!" His wife knew he dreaded the day when he would have to retire from the plant that had been his life for forty years. So Frieda tried a new tack. She talked about the past instead, asking him what he felt he had missed during all those busy years at the plant. What would he have liked to do that he'd never had time for? Before too long Jack surprised Frieda and himself by talking about the future as well as the past.

STEP 4: KNOW YOUR MARRIAGE

Remember the types of marriages discussed in Chapter 2? Together forever, parallel tracks, separate routes? These patterns may have developed during earlier years, when daily life was crowded with work, household demands, children, and family responsibilities. Couples had little time to spend with just each other, and what time they did have may have been precious because it was so infrequent. With retirement comes a chance for plenty—possibly a surfeit—of togetherness. Each partner needs to decide—within limits—how much is enough, how much is too much. Each one may have a perfectly legitimate plan for their late life, but the two scenarios may contradict each other. His may lead south to the sun and sports; hers may depend on the artistic excitement of a city in a colder climate. Neither scenario is wrong, but they pull in opposite directions. Once again it's time to renegotiate and find a middle course pleasing to both.

Patterns that worked for decades may move smoothly into late life and continue unchanged. But some may need to be renovated to adapt to new circumstances—or even completely reversed. The together-forever couple may wonder if their very closeness, so important to them, could lead them into trouble.

> Aggie and Peter Furst spent as much time together as they could during their early years, but it was never enough. Peter's work as an oil engineer kept him traveling, so Aggie pursued her own interests with friends—concerts, museums, shopping. Once Peter retired, they were both thrilled they could finally do things together. It seemed ideal, but one day they realized they had almost written other people out of their lives. If anything happened to one of them, the other would be dangerously alone. Reluctantly, they decided they had to modify their togetherness and let other people in as insurance for the future.

Parallel-track couples, by contrast, may find themselves turning more to each other in the later years because of declining health or fading interest or loss of friends.

> Everyone who knew the Richters through the years admired— even envied—them. They seemed to have such boundless energy and such an array of talents that took each one in different directions. When Jules Richter's Parkinson's disease began to incapacitate him in his seventies, and he became housebound, no one expected Gina to give up her interests, or that she would be able to cope with such a limited existence. To everyone's

surprise she coped well. She and Jules, for the first time in the same place at the same time, finally had a chance to get to know each other in new ways. They liked what they found. The two had to give up something, but each one, in turn, found surprising satisfaction in their new relationship.

STEP 5: KNOW YOUR LIMITS

Successful planning needs to include choices that are possible—within the reach of physical and emotional energies. Fear of aging, and dread of emptiness in late life, sometimes drive people into hectic activity. The Auerbachs could not be accused of drifting—they made plenty of plans and when retirement came they were ready for it. They enrolled in courses, arranged frequent trips, joined discussion groups, took up golf, volunteered in local politics. Within a few years they found themselves exhausted, dissatisfied. They had never asked themselves, "How much is too much?" or "What are our limits?"

Making choices according to what our friends are doing, or what the children try to tell us to do, can lead to trouble. So can continuing some activity because "we've always done it" or because it's expected of us even though it has become burdensome or is no longer gratifying. The Potters, for instance, talked endlessly about their grandchildren and how they hoped one day to move closer to them. But before it actually came time to move, they leveled honestly with each other and admitted the tension they had felt during recent visits with three preadolescents and their hot-tempered son and daughter-in-law. They decided to move to Florida, instead, choosing hot weather rather than hot tempers.

Long-standing patterns that have worked for years may not work indefinitely. The Wrights had always been theater buffs. Every year they renewed the same Friday night seats with the Butlers. When both couples were in their seventies and Paul Wright's vision was deteriorating, Dale Butler suggested they switch to Saturday afternoon. "No way!" Paul snorted angrily. "We're not the kind of people who go to matinees!" He changed his tune, however, when his wife pointed out to him that his poor night vision made him a menace on the road, that she was terrified to drive home with him, and, furthermore, that he routinely fell asleep during the second act. His own physical limits turned him into a matinee kind of person.

Knowing limits also means evaluating activities in terms of the organs they depend on. Music lovers, lecture-goers, and discussion-group members are dependent on hearing. Readers, game-players, art-lovers, handicraft hobbyists, and woodworkers are dependent on sight as well as dexterity. Walkers, cross-country skiers, athletes of all kinds are dependent on mobility. Impairment of any of the senses or deterioration of bones and joints can interfere with, or even completely halt, activities that have given thousands of hours of pleasure over the years. Some of these impairments and deteriorations can be helped by special appliances or with rehabilitation (see Chapter 7), but the possibility of such limiting disabilities occurring in late life needs to be considered. Once faced, they can be followed by contingency plans and alternate routes. The couple who claim "We'll be fine as long as we have a bridge game!" might be wise to wonder what will happen if either—or both—of them cannot see the dummy anymore or cannot hear the bidding.

The disability of one partner often comes to be shared by the other because they can no longer do things together. If the husband, with his vision and hearing intact, continues with his bridge games, what will his wife and former partner do while he's playing? She'll need a substitute activity, or they may find something new to do together.

Admitting limits and considering substitute activities to fall back on can be crucial steps in the whole process of planning ahead. Another crucial step is to become familiar with personal computers and fax machines. These are boons to the handicapped homebound, giving them access to material beyond their doors. If they cannot go out into the world, these machines can bring some of it to them.

LOOKING FOR ROLE MODELS

There's something intimidating about watching supermen and women in action. How could we ever follow their lead? Impossible! So why bother to try? When we see an eighty-five-year-old run a marathon, we know we'd never be able to be like him—we probably don't even want to. But when our neighbor, equally old, keeps his body in shape by taking a brisk two-mile walk every day, or keeps his mind in shape by going back to school to learn Italian, or keeps his hands in shape by making miniature furniture in his basement, we see someone whom we might copy—a role model. Few people in late life can hope to become creative like Picasso, or active like George Burns, or involved with others like Mother Teresa, or thin like Nancy Reagan. But many people of the same age, with a little effort, can become more creative than they used to be, more athletic, busier, more involved, and thinner!

The stars are beyond the reach of most average American couples. They are made of "different stuff." They certainly aren't "just plain folks" like the rest of us. So it doesn't help much to ask how the stars do it. We should be asking, instead, as King Arthur asked in *Camelot,* "What do the simple folk do?" Plenty of just plain folks are finding late life a very satisfying stage, perhaps even more satisfying than some that came earlier.

So, the first step for us to take as retirement approaches is to look around and see all the millions of people like us who have not retreated from the mainstream of society. They are living proof that F. Scott Fitzgerald was wrong when he wrote that there are no second acts in American life.

These are the people whose self-image and self-esteem are not completely dependent on the work they once did. They do not see themselves as "used-to-be's," for example, "I used to be a teacher" or "I used to be a foreman." Even though it's normal to have some nostalgia for the past, these sixty-, seventy-, and eighty-year-olds are less likely to look backward with regret. Rather than seeing themselves only as retired *from* teaching or *from* the factory or *from* civil service, they are more likely to see themselves as retired *into* new ventures.

THE MENU OF "RETIRING-INTO" VENTURES

The menu of ventures is as long and varied as the menu in a Chinese restaurant, with enough choices to suit almost everyone, even those who are no longer as vigorous as they used to be. Couples may choose from the menu together, finding ventures that appeal to both partners alike. Or they may prefer some variety—something from column A and something from column B—sharing some and pursuing others individually. If their relationship needs greater distance, life is likely to move along more peacefully when both do their own thing. The Retiring-*into* menu falls into five basic groups:

RETIRING *INTO* NOT RETIRING

Attorney Jesse Vickery had a fatal heart attack right in the middle of a five-way intersection, stopping traffic in all directions. He had been on his way to interview a witness in an important case he was handling. Vickery was eighty-nine. Some people just won't give up. They intend to die with their boots on, doing the work they chose decades earlier. They reject, hands down, the whole concept of retirement. It's not for them. They have no intention of retiring *from* anything *into* anything else. "Keep It Up!" is their motto. Late life is no different from early life. They may, under pressure from wives or husbands or children, slowly cut down—fewer hours each day, fewer days each week. Money is one motivation for continuing, but equally important is self-fulfillment. Their self-image and their egos cannot be separated from their work. When retirement is suggested, they probably wonder, "Who would I be if I closed my office (my practice, my studio, my business)?" The answer that comes is "Nobody."

Nonretirees are to be found among business owners, the self-employed, professionals: physicians, lawyers, therapists, CPAs, architects. Creative artists also are likely to keep on going: painters, sculptors, musicians, actors, designers.

Pitfalls

• Men—and women, too—can become workaholics, sacrificing everything else to the Great God Work—their marriages, their children, friendships, hobbies.

• If any disability forces them to retire, they are unprepared and have nothing to fall back on—no plans, no skills, no ideas, and probably few companions.

RETIRING *INTO* PAID WORK

When a telephone interviewer conducting a market-research survey asked seventy-one-year-old Tillie Gustavson whether she and her husband worked, Tillie answered, "Oh, no! We're unemployed! I mean, we're retired." Her first answer was correct because that was the way they really felt—unused. That day she and Gus decided to reemploy themselves and started looking for paid work.

FULL-TIME, PART-TIME, AND TEMP

The picture of retirement depends on which report is being featured and which statistic is being headlined. Statistics reveal that more people are retiring earlier—only 16 percent of men remain in the labor force after sixty-five and most women enter later and retire earlier. Department of Labor statistics estimate that by the year 2000 only one in four over-sixty-five men will still be working. These figures give one view of retirement, reinforced by retirement-community ads featuring portraits of contented couples who seem to get younger every year.

Other reports highlight two different views: that many retirees—about 25 percent—continue working or go back to work, full-time, part-time, or as "temps," and that there is a growing trend among some innovative companies and employers to hire older men and women. (The trend is hardly a tidal wave, and ageism, though illegal, is still widespread. Many employers, believing the negative myths about aging, are nervous about hiring older workers.) Part-time, temporary, or seasonal work is particularly attractive to older workers because it fits best with their physical energy and their finances. By earning less, they can still collect full Social Security. Benefits are reduced for workers under sixty-five if they earn more than $6,840 and for those sixty-five and over if they earn more than $9,360. After seventy the sky's the limit.

A postretirement job may not have the same prestige or clout as the preretirement job—some employees seem surprisingly overqualified for the positions they accept. They probably see gains compensating the losses. Gone is the stress of competing for the next promotion, the corner office. A recent study commissioned by the Commonwealth Fund reported that older workers are more flexible, learn new technologies as quickly as younger ones, and are better salespeople. They are less likely to switch jobs and are absent less often. Employers report that their back-to-work retirees, sometimes referred to as "gold-collar workers," definitely earn their keep.

Some women who have never worked before are now taking paid jobs for the first time, mostly in low-paying clerical positions. "Sure, we can use the money, but I've got my own reasons, too," giggled the checkout woman at a supermarket register. "I get a break from Tim now that he's retired. I love him, sure, but who can love a man twenty-four hours a day! Thank God for the A&P." Another admitted, less cheerily, "This job is a lifesaver for us. It buys the groceries. We thought once our two boys grew up, we'd manage fine on our pension—no mortgage and only two mouths to feed. What a laugh! This one's out of work—that one didn't get a raise. Guess who's coming to dinner half the week?"

Pitfalls

• Older employees are usually underpaid and have little job security. They may not receive benefits.

• They may feel patronized by fellow workers, even discriminated against. Slips of memory or illnesses that are tolerated in younger employees may be seen as signs of approaching senility in older ones.

SECOND CAREERS

In a newspaper account of a local wedding, the bridegroom, marrying for the second time, was described as a sixty-one-year-old painter. The account went on to report that he had retired several years earlier as vice president of a large accounting firm. He no longer saw himself as a CPA—he was already well into his second career as an artist when he started his second marriage.

Second careers offer retirees a chance to retool and start again at a time when, in the past, no such renewal seemed likely. They also offer couples opportunities to pool resources, to work together after retirement, in their own businesses, outside or inside their homes. Some of these careers are planned and prepared for through courses or special retraining. Selma Duncan had been a secretary and Fred, her husband, a draftsman. Both were familiar with computers but far from expert, so they took a variety of specialized courses in their preretirement years. When it came time to retire, they were prepared to set up their own small desktop publishing business right in their own apartment. This turned out to be an ideal decision because Selma was becoming increasingly deaf and Fred painfully arthritic. Neither handicap prevented them from conducting a business from home.

Second careers can come about without such planning through an unexpected chance encounter—a long-standing hobby may turn into a moneymaking venture. Sally and Glen Bloom satisfied their love of travel and flea markets by going to Europe twice a year. They reveled in browsing for bargain treasures year after year even though they never bought much—just a few things for themselves and their children. But then friends began asking them to find lace pillowcases "just like yours" or antique linens or embroideries. The requests multiplied, and soon after Sally and Glen retired from their first careers, they were established in their second career as importers. After a stroke left Glen partially paralyzed, he managed the business while Sally went off on buying trips.

Pitfalls

• It's not easy to keep a small business profitable, especially in current times. Cash flow is a perennial problem.

• With a staff of only two people, if one partner becomes seriously incapacitated the full burden of the entire business falls on the other one, as well as the responsibility of caring for the invalid.

RETIRING *INTO* VOLUNTEERING

Work does not have to be rewarded by money. Volunteering involves work paid for in a different but often equally valuable kind of coin. Many older volunteers, who have plenty of available time and no need to supplement their incomes, report that the work they do keeps them feeling young or at least takes their minds off their aging bodies. It keeps them active, gives them a sense of purpose and involvement. "I spent my whole life in the rat race! Now I have time for the human race," said a retired executive trying to explain to his amazed family why he and his wife were applying to the Peace Corps when they were nearly seventy. He probably was not the oldest volunteer. In 1987 there were twenty-three Peace Corps volunteers over seventy.

Volunteering in late life may simply be a continuation of working for pet causes, but before retirement many people, because of multiple demands on their time, were unable to find extra hours. In retirement they are freer to pick and choose among programs that appeal to them. They may make use of experience gained in their former work: retired teachers with literacy programs, retired doctors with clinics, retired athletes with coaching. They are just as likely, instead, to plunge into a totally new venture like Will Snyder, former copywriter, who had never before had any contact with children except his own, now grown up. Just to keep busy after retirement, he took a training course given by the school system in his small town and began to work one-on-one with slow readers in the early grades. His volunteering turned out to be more than busywork. It gave him excitement and stimulation he never had anticipated.

Volunteer programs are not usually as adventuresome as the Peace Corps, which sends recruits into Third World countries, or VISTA, a government-sponsored assistance program in the United States, nor can they guarantee for everyone the rewards Will Snyder gained, but there is a great variety to choose from, locally and nationally, enough to suit the interests and talents of almost everyone: religious institutions, museums, zoos, philanthropic organizations, cultural groups connected with theater and music, political parties, hospitals, libraries, schools.

A number of programs designed to help the disabled elderly are staffed by their healthier and more fortunate contemporaries: food programs like Meals on Wheels, transportation programs, telephone reassurance and friendly visiting (companionship) programs. Foster Grandparents, organized by the Department of Health and Human Services, provides a vital service, training volunteers to work with children in hospitals, schools, and day-care centers.

The Volunteer Talent Bank of the American Association of Retired Persons (AARP) has been set up in order to match people with specialized skills with appropriate volunteer programs. Retired Senior Volunteer Program (RSVP) also depends on the expertise of each community's retired citizens. Some corporations have organized volunteer corps for their retirees. Local Area Agency on Aging offices can usually offer information and referral on volunteer possibilities in each local community. A few programs are more than volunteer. Some pay minimum wage; others provide insurance, travel expenses, or meals.

Pitfalls

• Activities are not always well organized.

• Responsibilities may not be clearly defined.

• Hours and schedules may be irregular.

• There is a generally negative view of volunteering as "busywork" because it is unpaid.

RETIRING *INTO* NEW WORLDS

"Settling into a rut!" was the answer one about-to-be-retired pilot gave when asked what he and his wife dreaded most about the years ahead. Their fear is a common one and the antidote is to try something new: learn new ideas, explore new places, create new things.

LEARNING

Nicki and Foster Welsom met on registration day as they were poring over their college catalogues and arguing over which courses to take.

Fifty years later they were back at their old school, once again poring over catalogues and arguing over courses.

School days are no longer the exclusive property of the young. Parents and grandparents have a share in them, too: a seventy-year-old makes it through law school; an eighty-year-old finally wins a high-school diploma. But older students are not only interested in degrees or specialized training. They are crowding back to schools of all kinds to learn something new they never had time to study before or to sharpen their wits or to challenge themselves as well as to meet new people.

An ad placed by Fordham University in a 1991 issue of *New York* magazine was headlined "College at 60" and went on to describe a program for older people "seeking new friends and new ideas as an alternative to retirement."

Some kind of continuing education can now be found nationwide, ranging from a limited program of adult courses offered in a local school to a full university curriculum geared to adult interests. Brown University's president, Vartan Gregorian, even went so far as to suggest Brown's graduates be allowed to return to their alma mater to take courses free of charge for the rest of their lives. Prestigious universities abroad, including Oxford and Cambridge in England, have summer programs to offer visiting older students.

Over fifteen years ago five New Hampshire colleges opened their classrooms and dormitories for one- or two-week sessions to students over sixty who wanted to learn, to enjoy campus life again, or to experience it for the first time. That small pilot experiment has now mushroomed into Elderhostel, an educational system involving colleges and universities across the United States and in forty other countries. In 1988 nearly 200,000 students signed up.

Pitfalls

• Disappointing or incompatible fellow students.

• Boring or ill-prepared teachers.

• Loss of interest and motivation.

• Disappointing accommodations and food.

EXPLORING AND/OR TRAVELING

She: What have you got against Tibet?

He: Nothing. It's just too far away and I don't want to sleep in a yurt! That Tibet trip's strenuous.

She: So was the China trip. We did that fine last year.

He: But we're a year older now. You just won't accept the fact that we're not as young as we used to be. That's your problem!

She: You've just lost your sense of adventure! That's your problem!

That mild marital argument between Cissy and Nick Sarton about their annual trip ended in a compromise. They did not go so far away, but they still found adventure—rock-climbing in Nova Scotia. In recent years they have been to China, the Soviet Union, Indonesia, and to several Elderhostel courses in such distant places as Australia and Greece. He is eighty-four and she is eighty-two! The average octogenarian may not be as adventurous or as affluent as the Sartons, but there's no denying older Americans are on the move.

"They're always on the road!" complained a daughter about her newly retired parents. "Now that they've bought their Winnebago, their game plan is to visit every one of the fifty states! I bet they don't even get home for my birthday." A son anxiously traces the map trying to follow his parents' itinerary—last year down the Amazon, this year into Indonesia. "Other people worry about their parents' health. I'm worried that mine will be killed by bandits somewhere or get caught in a revolution."

The travel bug is biting millions—single individuals and couples alike. They're buying campers and camping gear. They're taking buses, planes, trains, or driving their own cars, visiting relatives, national parks, ancestral homes in "the old country," wherever that may be. Hotels, restaurants, as well as airlines and railroads, aware of the profits from their senior customers, offer tempting discounts. (Discounts on airfares usually have restrictions. These should be looked into carefully before making bookings.) Tours, cruises, and packaged trips vary in cost, and accommodations range from the simple to the luxurious. They are not designed only for the active and adventurous. Some are specially tailored to the needs of those who are less spry and have diminished energy levels.

Pitfalls

• Getting sick before leaving (trip insurance is a safeguard).

• Getting sick en route.

• Quality of arrangements, accommodations, and guides not living up to brochure descriptions.

CREATING

The list of artists who continue to be creative and productive right through late life is a long and familiar one. Grandma Moses, who started painting in her seventies, is the prime example of a late-blooming artist, but many people discover it's never too late to try to find out whether they have any artistic or creative gifts. They are often surprised in late life to find that they actually have talents they never knew about earlier. The talents may not be particularly outstanding, but they're strong enough to provide hours of enjoyment at first and possibly even deeper satisfaction later. Aging artists, writers, sculptors, musicians, even actors in amateur theater groups, may never become rich and famous, but they may thrive on their own creativity as well as through relationships with others devoted to the same passion.

> When Henry Grumman, an engineer, was forced into early retirement, he became increasingly depressed as he tried unsuccessfully to find other work. Estelle, his wife, worried constantly, but nothing she did seemed to help until she happened one day to notice Henry's workbench in the basement. She remembered how much he had enjoyed making small wooden pieces years ago and urged him to get his tools out again. He did this reluctantly and begrudgingly just to "get her off his back." But he gradually spent more and more time in the basement and

turned out more and more boxes, mirrors, stools, plant stands, and what have you. Eventually, again at Estelle's urging, he took a table at a craft show and sold most of his pieces. From then on he entered craft shows all over the country. He didn't earn a fortune, but enough to pay for materials, tools, and travel for himself and Estelle.

Pitfalls

• Expecting talents to surface too soon; the first classes are unlikely to produce masterpieces.

• Expecting recognition or financial gain.

• Inability to accept disappointments.

RETIRING *INTO* SPORTS AND HEALTH

When sixty-six-year-old Ellen Hermann woke early one morning just as it was getting light, she glanced out of her window, expecting to see nothing. Instead, she saw her normally quiet suburban street alive with people, her neighbors, walking or jogging past her house. Some of them were older than she was. "My God!" she gasped. "Is that what I'm supposed to be doing?"

The message is everywhere: Activity is *In*—Inactivity is *Out!* Medical science has sent out the word: activity leads to health and vitality; inactivity leads to weakness and disability. These assertions apply to people of all ages. Sports, once reserved for the young or the middle-aged, have now been passionately embraced by the aging and even the very old.

Seventy-three-year-old Pat Dunlop plays two sets of tennis and then later takes a five-mile walk. His wife, a few months younger, keeps telling him he's crazy, but he has an answer. "Who's crazy? What about you, swimming fifty laps in the Y pool every day?"

Marge Tilson and her husband race-walk each other three miles a day. But walking is not enough for them: he's on a volleyball team and she's in a bowling league. Both are nearly eighty.

Men and women in all parts of the country, in all walks of life, and all above sixty-five are devoting a substantial percent of their normal routines to one form of physical activity or another, and not just to fill up their days, either. Each sport has incentives to offer in addition to good health: fun, stimulation, excitement, and challenge. Each one has a special meaning to each participant and sometimes that meaning is shared by couples:

"Jack and I live for golf."

"We both *have* to swim every day."

"Running keeps us alive."

"We'd be crippled with arthritis if we didn't play tennis."

For those who continue to need competition, there's plenty available. There's built-in competition attached to every sport—against one opponent, a team, or simply trying to beat one's own record. Sixty-nine-year-old Gary Ickes had thrived on competition all his life, struggling to rise to the top of the company ladder. After retirement the fizz went out of his life—he had no one to compete with. He found the solution in running marathons—once again he had people to beat, to get the better of, to win out over!

An athletic activity can be simple, solitary, and require little or no equipment. Just plain vigorous walking is the frequent choice, or following an aerobic tape on the VCR. Other people need the stimulation and sociability of a group, or a team sport: volleyball, bowling, softball, soccer, ice-skating.

Sports, with or without competition, can be enjoyed in the backyard, or in a local school or Y. But sports can take people out of their own communities and into broader competition. The U.S. Tennis Association, sponsors of the U.S. Open, has leagues all over the country that include women seventy-five and older and men eighty-five and older. The ultimate competition for older athletes is the Senior Olympics held at different sites every second year.

The value of exercise and physical activity is now considered so essential for older people that some companies, among them Campbell

Soup and Bank of America, have started fitness centers for their retirees and about-to-be-retired employees. Follow-up studies have revealed improved all-around health for those who use the centers regularly.

Pitfalls

• Pushing too hard.

• Starting up vigorous activities without a prior checkup.

• Omitting a warm-up period.

• Letting sport become a religious experience. What happens when you cannot play anymore? What's the answer to the question "Is there life after golf?"

• When one partner cannot participate any longer, what happens to the other?

BUY SOME GREEN BANANAS

"Follow your bliss," said Joseph Campbell, the noted mythologist, in a 1988 interview with Bill Moyers on Public Television. Campbell explained his words by describing how important it has been over the centuries and across differing cultures for human beings to be true to themselves, to do their own thing collectively or individually.

Campbell's motto might be applied to the ways people live as they grow older, even though "bliss" may be a strange word to use in connection with late life. But except for those who are seriously disabled mentally or physically, or desperately deprived financially, men and women can continue to do their own thing, assuming they know what this "thing" is and can find the way to do it. If their lives are to be satisfying, men and women need to work out patterns that mesh with their own individual personalities. Couples need to adjust their relationship according to each partner's needs and limits. No formula can be used across the board—your bliss can be your partner's misery. Compromises are usually inevitable unless one of you is too rigid to change—or too angry.

Bliss for one couple can come from retreat and relaxation, enjoying relationships with relatives up and down the "family beanpole" described in Chapter 4. If that's what you enjoy, go to it. Don't let public opinion or your children or the next how-to book tell you that you're wasting your golden years. You may be one of those people who breathe a sigh of relief when all the stresses, strains, struggles, and competition of the early years are over. Peace at last! "What a joy it is to hear my son rave about white-water rafting and to know I'll never have to do that again!" says one seventy-nine-year-old sinking comfortably back into his hammock.

For your friends next door such flagrant self-indulgence is shameful, limiting, even suffocating. This couple may need the stimulation of work, church and charity, active sports, and travel. They may need to feel actively involved in the world, that they are still needed. Being on the sidelines doesn't disturb your ego at all. What's important is that both you and they are satisfied with the way you have chosen to live.

Minimal or no satisfaction comes to couples who, without legitimate reason, such as illness or poverty, believe the old negative myth of retirement and decide to live according to it: withdrawn, resentful, bitter, isolated. They allow themselves to feel that society has denied them the chance to do their own thing, that they have been cheated and discriminated against, cast aside, rejected. This is very often the attitude of older couples when one or both have been forced to retire before they felt ready to and therefore before they had done any advance planning. While it's never too late to look through the vast menu of retirement ventures and to improve their lots, their bitterness may blind them to possibilities.

There is no denying that late life is a final stage and that all sorts of frightening possibilities lie ahead the later it gets. Death is ever in the wings. But planning has a place for, and in, late life. Although long-range projects may be unrealistic at this time, there's still time for short-range ones.

There once was an old man who focused so intently on death and was so sure it would come any minute that he never bought any green bananas. There are plenty of green-banana buyers among this country's elderly millions—couples and individuals willing to gamble that they will still be around when their bananas are ripe and ready for eating.

CHAPTER

6

Did he grow anxious about the heavy cost of maintaining his kingdom? Did he fear losing control of his subjects? Of himself?

And she? Did she come to hate the drafty old castle where her bones ached and her teeth chattered? Did she beg him to build a cozy palace for their old age?

INSURING FOR
THE FUTURE

Myra: I never believed life could be like this! When people talked about the "golden" years I used to laugh, but it's true—they are golden. Irv and I are closer than we've ever been. Look at us—sixty-nine last year and acting like a couple of kids—even in bed! We dance a lot. We love our life! But all of a sudden Irv's started talking about getting old and all those awful things that could happen. I don't even want to think about them. But I can't make him stop. Why does he have to spoil everything?

Irv: Myra's been a great wife. She was a great mother, too. And she's right. These last ten years have been the best yet. And we're still having fun. But I know it can't go on forever. We ought to be looking ahead. What if one of us gets sick—really sick? Who will help us? Our kids have their own problems. What if our money doesn't hold out? What if I die? How will she manage? I *need* to talk—she won't listen.

LET'S NOT TALK ABOUT IT NOW

There are plenty of couples like Myra and Irv: one side dwelling constantly on the potential perils of aging, the other side denying the passing years or refusing to face them.

Avoiding unpleasantness is a natural human impulse. "Stop lecturing Junior at the table about his report card. It's ruining dinner." Or "Forget about the office—you're spoiling the vacation." In *Gone with the Wind,* Scarlett O'Hara gave us one of the most-quoted avoidance phrases: "I'll think of it all tomorrow. . . . After all, tomorrow is another day."

Some fears can be avoided. If we're lucky, we never have to face them. Afraid of snakes? Avoid the woods. Afraid of heights? Avoid the mountains. But growing old is a reality that cannot be avoided except by the unwelcome alternative—dying young. It's not unreasonable or unrealistic to have occasional fears about what might lie ahead—fear of illness and pain, fear of loss of beauty, money, independence, fear of loneliness, and ultimately, for most of us, the greatest terror of all—death. The best way to handle these fears and future negative possibilities is to face them, discuss them, and start thinking about the best way to deal with them if and when they become realities. Experts recommend that financial planning for the retirement years start ten to fifteen years before the fact. One of the reasons membership in the American Association of Retired Persons opens at age fifty is to stimulate middle-aged working Americans to start thinking seriously about their overall retirement life—which may still be years ahead—and not just the financial side, either.

It's ironic, however, that very often the greater the need for discussion and planning, the greater is the avoidance. The very events that most need to be anticipated may be so frightening and upsetting that they result in a paralysis that thwarts planning. People who may have been realistic and organized earlier in life may turn into ostriches when it's time to contemplate their old age, burying their heads in the sands of time. Prime examples of such ostriches are those so incapable of contemplating their inevitable death that they never make wills and die leaving their affairs in chaos for their heirs to unscramble.

An added complication thwarting planning is that many couples—like Myra and Irv—do not see eye-to-eye about growing old. So much depends on how each partner faces late life. Remember the four *R*'s of aging—resignation, resistance/rage, relaxation, and renewal—described in Chapter 2? The resisters may be chasing after the bluebird of youth and happiness, the impossible dream; the resigned may see nothing but doom and gloom ahead, a prophecy that may be self-fulfilling. "You brood all the time," Myra keeps on berating Irv. "You're poisoning the years we have left."

Couples who disagree on the approach to late life may practice deliberate sabotage. Whatever one partner suggests, the other immediately vetoes. The rift may be so serious that some couples come to realize they really have no future together. They may decide to break the tie that binds them.

Those who have opted for the relaxation or the renewal *R,* or both, seem the most likely, according to the experts, to find health and happiness. Since they accept, perhaps even welcome, growing old, finding positive as well as negative possibilities, they are more able to work through plans for their future together, and in the process find their relationship stronger and closer than ever.

IT'S NEVER TOO LATE

"All my friends are into retirement planning. Not me!" laughed Mac Denton when he was in his late forties. "No Denton man has lived past fifty. I've got everything wrapped up for Jinny and the kids—they'll be okay. So I don't worry about anyone's future." That's what he thought. But he beat the odds, escaped the "Denton curse," and stayed alive and well. In his late sixties he had to unravel the carefully woven plans he had made for his family's future and make plans for the future he and Jinny would have together. They are now in their mid-eighties.

Impossible though it may seem, it is rarely too late to make plans for the future, although it does become more expensive the longer you wait. It's naturally impossible to secure a healthy retirement income once your working days are over unless some long-lost relative leaves you a fat inheritance or you discover oil in your backyard. The older you are, the harder it is to find good low-cost health or life insurance. Take a look at all the promotional pamphlets flooding your mailbox announcing those "wonderful" policies for health and life. "You Can't Be Turned Down," their headlines proclaim in bold type—"No physical exam needed and age is no barrier." They sound wonderful until you check the monthly premiums required if you are over sixty. They are so expensive that few people of that age and older—except the very rich—need apply. Furthermore, the older you get, the higher the premiums.

Planning can be delayed when partners are in disagreement—the raging versus the relaxed—on how to approach their old age. But what if both partners agree? Suppose both are enraged or both resigned? Then neither wants to focus on the future. They drift on through the years. Sometimes these couples are jolted out of their fool's paradise when a formerly vigorous relative goes into a serious decline or when the family next door, friends for forty years, sell their house and move to the protection of a retirement community. Their neighbors may finally see the handwriting on the wall and admit, "If it can happen to them it can happen to us," and wonder if it's too late for them to start thinking about the future.

Even in their seventies and eighties couples can still make plans. The future may seem limited, but there may be quite some time ahead. That seventy-year-old retired couple reveling in the birth of a grandson could live long enough to watch this baby grow up, get married, and have a child of his own, turning the grandparents into great-grandparents at ninety-five. In those intervening twenty-five years that seventy-year-old couple may also turn from being vigorous, independent, and helpful into somewhat frailer, more dependent family members. At seventy they could not change their finances or insurance, but they could still plan for the way they wanted to live in the years remaining to them.

Some plans may be even more appropriate once late life has arrived. As they grow older, couples may change their attitudes toward life and death, and have different personal needs and altered relationships with other family members. We're all familiar with older people who constantly rewrite their wills as their feelings blow alternately hot and cold about one relative or another. Sixty-year-olds who settle on the "ideal" retirement complex may find the place less ideal when they are in their seventies and less wedded to golf.

DON'T CLOSE ANY DOORS

> *The best laid schemes o' mice an' men*
> *Gang aft a-gley;*
> *An' lea'e us nought but grief an' pain,*
> *For promis'd joy.*
> —Robert Burns, "To a Mouse"

Ideally, anticipating the future and thinking through possible solutions should begin before there's any trouble. Planning cannot be counted on to prevent all problems from happening, but it can make some easier to deal with and prevent others from becoming overwhelming. While it's good to have some of the answers ready before the questions are asked, in general answers need to be flexible, open to change and revision, because the future is rarely clear or predictable. It's impossible to plan for every eventuality—some may arise that you've never dreamed might happen. The "sure thing" that you bet on may be the horse that comes in last, or not at all.

Take the Laughtons—Bill was twenty years older than Flossie. When he was in his late fifties and she still in her thirties, he started worrying about what would happen to her after he died. To prepare for her widowhood he kept paying huge life-insurance premiums that he could ill afford. No one could say that Bill was not a careful planner. But no one could have predicted that Flossie's breast cancer would cause her death at fifty-two. Life has a way of sabotaging even the most carefully laid plans.

WRITING THE RETIREMENT SCENARIO

Planning for the future—negotiating the late-life crisis—depends to a very great extent on financial planning, which must consider most aspects of late life, not just assets. Money does not guarantee happiness, but much of what goes wrong in late life can be traced to the lack of money. Couples without financial resources find their choices severely limited.

"Money, money, money!" Jessie complains. "Whenever I want to talk about what's going to happen to us, all you talk about is how much money we'll have. I don't care about that. I care about quality of life."

"One of us has to be sure we have enough quantity—without that we're not going to enjoy much quality," Floyd mumbles, barely looking up from the bank statements on his desk. Floyd realizes that the pitfalls of old age, particularly health problems, can drain even lavish resources.

Each of the two has a valid argument. Floyd is right that financial planning is a significant part of overall retirement planning. It includes saving and investing as well as securing a steady income and health insurance for the years after paid employment is over. Jessie is right in worrying about quality of life. Retirement planning is not limited to finances anymore. Other important conditions can jeopardize a couple's well-being in late life and serious thought needs to be given to them: the choice of housing, where to live; provisions for health care, including medical and supportive help; preventive health measures and decisions involving death and dying.

In planning for their future together couples should also contemplate their future alone and raise the question "How will I get along without you?" since it is likely that at some point one partner may have to function alone if the other dies or is disabled. But even though it is so important for each one to have some areas of individual independence—like the separate-track couples—this is sometimes the hardest and most painful eventuality to face. Many couples, particularly the inseparables, suppress the possibility completely and then end up ultimately defenseless against loneliness.

STARTING A DIALOGUE

It can be hard to get going. There's a future full of all sorts of possibilities ahead. Who can plan for them all? It's impossible to cover all bases. A good way to begin is with the "What if" or the "Suppose" question, a game writers often play when developing their plots. They set up hypothetical problems and then try out different solutions. Assuming couples answer honestly, they can keep trying out different scenarios for their future life stories until they finally hit on one they both like. The following questions can serve as openers:

• What if one of us dies or is incapacitated? How will we manage financially? Is our money limited?

• Suppose one of us becomes seriously ill and incapacitated. Is each of us prepared to take care of the other?

• What if we're both incapacitated? Who will take care of us?

• Suppose we have more leisure time together. What steps can we take to make this enjoyable for both of us?

• What if we have separate interests? Should we try to combine them, or should we each continue to do our own thing? Is either of us willing to give up something to accommodate the other?

• What if our sex life becomes unsatisfying to one or both of us? What can we do to improve things?

• Suppose our children and grandchildren still need us. How much can we expect to do for them?

• What if we want our adult children included in our future plans? How much input should they have? How do we involve them?

All these are questions that need to be answered by both partners. But another set needs to be considered by each partner individually and separately:

• What do I want to do about my own health?

• How do I want to die?

• Who do I want to care for me if my spouse cannot?

• Suppose we don't care enough about each other to make planning worth the effort. What do we do about our relationship?

While these questions can only involve the wishes of one partner, the answers can be conveyed, verbally, on paper, or by innuendo, to the other and—it is hoped—will then be understood, respected, supported, and implemented when necessary.

Contemplating the future, together or alone, can be a painful process whether it begins early or late in life. It forces two people to face squarely certain dire realities they'd rather ignore and to consider the possibility that something dreadful could happen to either or both of them one day. It's not surprising that plenty of couples find it rough going. One weary wife complains, "John keeps saying we have to have 'cool, calm, sensible planning sessions.' Who can be sensible? We start fighting before we get a chance to start planning." In ancient times bad tidings were so unwelcome that leaders were known to kill the messengers who brought them. Couples may not kill each other off, but it's not surprising that the tension between them may mount whenever they sit down for one of their emotionally charged summit meetings.

EXTENDING THE WEALTH SPAN

"How are they feeling?" or "How are they fixed financially?" These are logical questions often asked by those concerned about the welfare of older friends and relatives. Security in old age revolves around the two poles—money and physical condition—termed by gerontologists as the "wealth span" and the "health span." These two spans go hand in hand with the life span, which lasts from cradle to grave.

Although lucky breaks and good heredity do play a part, few people can count on easy living in their late years without sensible health and financial habits, preferably developed in their early years. These habits, unfortunately, are not universally practiced. Furthermore, whenever saving for the future is suggested, a chorus of outraged young voices is likely to be heard: "How can we be expected to save for our old age? We're hardly making it through our young age!" "Look at our mortgages!" "What about those college tuition bills?" "Look at our grown kids who still need help!" Many of them, however, are saving for their futures almost without realizing it, through their Social Security and pension-plan contributions on the job.

While it is true that older men and women fare much better these days than ever before, no one will deny that there are still too many people—old and young as well—living out their lives in dire need. A small percentage of older people, particularly women lacking the advantage of work-related benefits, still remain below, or close to, the poverty line. The wealth span hardly has meaning to them any more than the health span has for those suffering from irreversible chronic disease. But the majority of older couples—and the single elderly, too—continue to live relatively healthy lives well into their late years, sustained financially not only by Social Security checks but by pensions, investments, and property. These couples would never think of themselves as rich. The great majority are in the middle-income range. They would probably be surprised to hear that they have a wealth span to consider just as the affluent do. The latter, obviously, deal in greater numbers. Those who have designed the structure of their wealth span early seem to be in the best shape.

Financial planning and money matters seem to be on everyone's mind in the nineties. Even the young with their entire careers still ahead of them are confronted on their jobs with decisions about pension plans. There is a nationwide interest in Social Security and its future. Older people are doubly challenged when it comes to their assets. First they are told to "save" for their old age. Then they are told they have to learn how to manage these assets—no easy task. An army of consultants, financial advisers, and estate planners, formerly involved only with the affluent, are now interested in guiding those who have only modest assets. (Advice on financial planning is far beyond the scope of this book. Helpful references are listed in Appendix D.) Here again, with or without the help of a financial consultant, certain questions need to be considered:

• How much do we need for basic living?

• If there's anything left over, how much do we want to invest? To buy? To sell?

• How much do we need to set aside for our health care?

• How much should be set aside to support the one of us who survives the other?

• What do we want to give to our children? To our grandchildren? To other people? To place in trust for them or to leave to them?

• How much do we want to leave to our favorite charities?

The questions seem pretty straightforward, don't they, and much easier to talk about than disease and dying. We shouldn't have much trouble with them. They involve some addition, subtraction, and division but hardly higher math. Once we start, however, we're likely to find that much more than dollars and cents is involved here—our emotions, our personal relationships. We may be forced to realize that we do not think alike on one or more of the issues that need financial agreement: retirement, lifestyle, children, health costs.

COMMUNICATION AND RESPONSIBILITY

Experts generally agree that money is one of the two prime sources of conflict between partners. (Sex is the other.) Because of this, many couples try to avoid the subject and quickly establish patterns for handling money that continue throughout their relationship. There would be problems enough if couples disagreed merely about how to spend money or how *not* to spend it. But money is more than cash on hand or in the bank.

An angry husband may cut a housekeeping allowance. An angry wife may shop extravagantly, knowing the best way to wound a skinflint husband. Money can be a symbol or a replacement for things even more valuable. It can replace love or tenderness or caring. It can be used to buy sexual favors, or these favors may be withdrawn when money is withdrawn. Money is power. When the husband is the sole breadwinner, his wishes usually dominate. "I make the money, so I carry more weight." A less chauvinistic husband, but one with a yet-unliberated wife, enjoys repeating "I make the dough and Mary spends it." But is he really open with her? Does he give her *everything* he earns? Or does he reserve some portion for playing the stock market? The horses? For his girlfriend? And does she pad the bills or steal from the housekeeping allowance to buy luxuries he denies her?

One partner, the one with the best head for figures—not always the male and not necessarily the breadwinner—often takes over as family accountant, paying bills and managing assets. This is more likely to happen in relationships where tasks and duties have been divided between two people and little collaboration or communication is expected.

Couples may coast along well into late life with one partner or the other blissfully ignorant of the joint finances, and as long as there is plenty of money, this one-sided relationship can work. But there are hazards ahead when assets dwindle, when health costs skyrocket, when inflation rises. No one can really afford ignorance—life itself can be put at risk.

Many husbands among today's elderly saw nothing wrong in singlehandedly, without consulting their wives, charting out the course of their joint financial future. The "little woman" was often perfectly willing to remain in the dark about everything, comfortably assuming, since she had "no head for money," that he would take care of everything. Too many women have lived to discover after widowhood or divorce how wrong their too-trusting assumption had been. A financial officer in a major insurance company reports that his most difficult moments come when he has to tell an elderly woman, recently widowed, that her husband has made no provisions for her in his pension plan and that it has died with him. She is left with nothing but her Social Security to support her. Every day she gets the same message from the grave: "I never cared about you!"

Even when they are left with plenty of money, women who have never learned to handle it may face life as widows or divorcees feeling more helpless, confused, and abandoned than ever. Since current statistics show that wives on the average live seven years longer than husbands, ignorance of financial matters is a luxury no woman can really afford. No man can afford this either if his wife, the family accountant, dies or is disabled. Each partner should be informed of, if not closely involved with, the overall financial picture. Some couples sit down at least once a month for an informal business meeting to ensure that both partners are up to date. These meetings may be stormy but nevertheless informative.

> Dick Gammond was an absentminded inventor. Laurel, his wife, learned early in their marriage that if they didn't want to be evicted or let insurance lapse she would have to pay the rent and everything else. When Dick's inventions began to take off, Laurel learned about investments and money management. As they grew older, she drew up their wills with their lawyer and figured out how to set up trusts for their children.
>
> Through the years she kept Dick informed about everything, and when she developed the first symptoms of Alzheimer's disease, he was able to follow along the financial path she had carved out.
>
> Although no one could prove it true or false, the rumor circulated that Laurel had even thought ahead to Dick's remarriage in the event of her death and had made sure that his financial picture was clear enough for the second wife to understand.

THE LIFESTYLE FACTOR

A couple's priorities—quality of life versus money—are very likely to clash headlong when it comes to making decisions concerning their lifestyle—where and how to live. Here the old fable of the hardworking ant versus the playful grasshopper is played out over and over again.

> "Will you look at this fabulous cruise! Let's sign up for it this winter," carols the grasshopper, waving a colorful brochure.
>
> "Will *you* look at the cost!" growls the ant, barely glancing at anything except the fare.
>
> . . .
>
> "We don't need to move south as long as we get away for a few of those bad winter months," announces the grasshopper.
>
> "Can't afford that," asserts the ant, closing the subject.

The feeling that one can or cannot afford something may have little legitimate basis in fact and bank balance. Ants and grasshoppers very often maintain their personalities all through life, including old age, the one still saving for the rainy day that may have already come and the other still spending as if the supply would last forever.

Individual preferences may block a reasonable partnership in financial matters. One person's pattern of spending may not mesh with the other's. Their personalities play a part, too. She may feel secure only if she can keep up with the Joneses in material possessions. His security may depend on the growth of his investments and his bank account. The conflicting priorities need to be brought into line as a couple grow older or they may be in serious trouble.

> Les learned his penny-pinching from his Depression-scarred father. He saved string, bought day-old bread, and turned out lights almost before people had left the room. Each time a light went off Zoe, his wife, muttered under her breath, "You're going to be the richest man in the cemetery." She stayed with Les while the children were young, expecting to leave him when they grew up. By that time she had taken up weaving, first as a hobby, but then she began to sell. Soon she had a paying business and was finally able to buy some of the luxuries she and the children had been denied. She took them all on trips, bought concert and theater tickets, reupholstered furniture. Les shared willingly in the luxuries she provided, but when Zoe's arthritis crippled her fingers, she could not work. Her business failed and she had to be dependent on Les and his penny-pinching once more. Their relationship became even more bitter, and now as an old woman she could be heard muttering almost inaudibly whenever a light went out, "He's going to be the richest man in the cemetery."

THE RETIREMENT FACTOR

The timing of retirement is not only determined by company pressure or questions like "When do I leave?" or "Do I want to retire?" or "Will I be happy?" discussed in Chapter 5, but by another—"Can I afford to retire?" A number of couples postpone retirement because one or both partners get so much gratification from their work and want to keep on going indefinitely. Working also provides an escape or a distance from an unsatisfactory relationship and couples can postpone the day when they will have to spend more time together. But the wealth span plays a part, too. Early retirement may be chosen if a company offers a lucrative retirement package. "I can't afford *not* to retire!" an ex-executive may say when asked why he is vacating his corner office at sixty. Other contemporaries may feel they can't afford retirement, which normally reduces income, or they keep on postponing the day because they simply *want* more money. Some organizations point out to their prospective retirees that they can maintain their living standards with less money after retirement, perhaps five-sevenths of their former salary, since theoretically expenses are less when there are no commutation costs, no lunches out, no need for an extensive wardrobe. Retirees may be able to manage well with their Social Security and pension checks.

The theory does not take into account the likelihood of rising health costs as couples grow older or of the rising cost of living. So careful consideration must be given to hard-nosed financial realities.

> Bill Berry at sixty-eight had already postponed his retirement as a patent lawyer in a small firm even though his wife and family nagged him to stop working. He knew he could count on a good pension, but as he looked over his financial situation, he was worried that he had too little saved or invested. There was no pressure on him from his firm to retire, so when his wife begged him to "stop working and enjoy life," he would reply, "I'm enjoying life right now and we'll both enjoy it more when we retire with a lot more money in the bank."

Even though mandatory retirement is no longer in force except in certain areas of employment, many people have no choice about when and how to retire. Those who have a choice are more fortunate—it's up to them to set their own departure date. It's also up to them to think of the future beyond the "gold watch celebrations." Are there assets enough—a pension, a deferred-income Keogh plan, investments or savings—to give them financial security? After all, there may be another twenty, or even thirty, years ahead. Once these sticky financial questions have been tackled, quality of life can be determined more realistically.

THE CHILDREN FACTOR

"Life was a constant struggle for us financially. We want our kids to have it easier than we did," explained one retired father who was still putting money aside for two rainy days—his own and his grown children's.

. . .

"We made it on our own—no one helped us. So can they," insisted another father as he polished a speck of dust from his newly purchased camper. On the back was a bumper sticker reading, "We're spending our children's inheritance."

The two statements represent diametrically opposed views of that eternal triangle: parents–children–money. Couples may subscribe to either one or to any of the many variations lying in between. Their attitudes may not reflect their actual assets—the richer may withhold their largesse and the poorer may be lavish with their limited funds.

Older couples generally find late middle age and early late life—with no children to support—the most affluent years of their lives. More of them now than in the past have moved into the middle-income range—they can cover their own expenses and have something left over. They are able to make a decision on whether or not to help their grown children. A husband—and a wife, too, if she works—is likely to be earning his top income and enjoying the results of good investments and accumulation of property. Some parents are in a position to help their children, if they want to, with tax-free gifts. (The limit on these varies from year to year: it was $10,000 per child in 1991.) Gifts are not limited to children alone but can go to grandchildren and even great-grandchildren. One couple, now in their nineties, are thrilled to be setting aside money for the education of newborn twins, their great-grandson and great-granddaughter, who will not enter college until the year 2010.

Some parents think less in terms of outright gifts today than about how their assets should be distributed, and suffer the least taxation, tomorrow—after they die. In addition to making bequests in their wills, they may establish trust funds for children, grandchildren, and great-grandchildren. Many of these financial arrangements are complex and require the help of financial experts skilled in the ways of tax avoidance.

Children and money can be another source of conflict for their parents, particularly those who are habitually in financial disagreement. They may be in full agreement that children should be helped in an emergency, but they may totally disagree on what constitutes an emergency. Father may feel help is warranted for a down payment on a house, for financial support in times of unemployment or illness, for tuition; Mother may agree on these, but since she hates to say "no" to her children, she may want to cover the cost of purchases he sees as "idiotic, senseless luxuries."

You may be forced to learn how to say "no" if you are barely covering your own expenses because rising inflation and escalating medical bills are eating away at your fixed income. That "no" may be your shortcut to security, although it's hard to say and, unfortunately, often just as hard for grown children to hear. There may be resentment when the Mom-and-Dad Bank, once taken for granted as a permanent institution, closes its doors or severely curtails handouts, allowances, loans, and gifts. If you further deplete your limited finances by giving in to your children's requests for financial help, you will ultimately harm rather than help them by creating an even more serious burden for them in the future. When you look carefully at the bottom line, you are likely to find it easier to say "no" than "yes."

THE HEALTH-COST FACTOR

"You're so lucky to be old enough for Medicare. I can't wait till I'm sixty-five! Then I won't have to worry about these doctor's bills!" one sixty-year-old kept repeating enviously to an older friend. The younger one blithely assumed that Medicare would cover his health costs through late life. He labors under a giant misapprehension, and so do plenty of others like him. Medicare will *not* give him the blessed relief he expects. If he's wise, he'll anticipate having to shoulder plenty of his medical costs out of his own pocket and plan accordingly.

Since it is the rare person who moves through late life without ever needing medical attention, health care is perhaps the most central concern of financial planning. You can debate the wisdom of giving money to your children, or buying stocks, or setting your retirement date. But if you need a doctor, there's rarely room for debate, and furthermore, the older you get the more medical attention you are likely to need. Moreover, the lifestyle of both partners in a couple can be seriously affected even if only one of them runs up the medical bills. To make things more difficult, health costs keep on rising much above the average yearly inflation rate. One expert estimated that if the annual health costs for a sixty-five-year-old in 1990, including insurance premiums and out-of-pocket expenses, were $2,100, they will probably rise to $5,447 by the year 2000.

Medicare, the federal government's universal health-insurance system established under Social Security, can be seen as a blessing. It *does* provide tremendous financial relief for the elderly in the area of health costs. Presumably, it covers hospital stays, surgery, outpatient visits, as well as other medical needs and emergencies, but its coverage is far from total. There are still an endless number of conditions and procedures not covered at all or only partially covered. *The Medicare Handbook,* published annually by the U.S. Department of Health and Human Services, is an excellent guide to understanding the limits of the coverage. (See Appendix D for other helpful information.) Anyone thinking ahead to future health costs should be aware of the limits and certain financially threatening facts:

• *Fact 1:* There are deductibles and copayments attached to Medicare that can result in considerable out-of-pocket expense.

• *Fact 2:* Some conditions, procedures, and treatments are not covered at all.

• *Fact 3:* Prescription drugs and dental work are not covered.

• *Fact 4:* Most prosthetic devices, including hearing aids, are not covered.

Many couples, well aware of Medicare limits, hope to bridge the gaps in coverage with private insurance. A number of companies offer similar policies under such names as Medicare Plus, Medigap, or Medicare Extended. These, with some deductibles of their own, usually pick up some of what is still owed after Medicare payments. But there are dangers even here. Some companies will not write their most comprehensive policies for anyone with preexisting conditions, and most older people have something that ails them. Other policies are available, but these usually will not contribute to anything that Medicare does not cover. Take, for example, a retired couple who seem to be aging remarkably well. Life still goes on for them pretty much as it always has. They are covered by Medicare and a private policy. If anyone asked them a few years ago how they were doing, here's what they might have answered:

> "Can't complain!" Jack used to say. And he didn't have much to complain about. Sure, he needed to watch his blood pressure and his cholesterol, and his hearing was not what it used to be. But no real problems.
> "Could be worse, considering," was Eva's usual answer. She was happy that she had nothing more than an occasional asthma attack to worry about and some dental problems.

But talk to Jack and Eva now! They may not be so cheery. Jack's blood pressure and cholesterol level have risen alarmingly. He's been put on two new and effective drugs, each of which costs around a hundred dollars a month. Eva is getting dangerous asthma attacks and is put on another expensive drug. They both have dental problems: each one needs a couple of root canals and Eva needs a bridge. Their dental bills will come to well over five thousand dollars this year. Finally, Jack has to have a hearing aid, perhaps two. Another eight- to fifteen hundred dollars.

Jack and Eva are fortunate. Neither of them is seriously ill with a life-threatening condition. They are still quite a healthy, independent, vigorous old couple. But in a short period of time their medical expenses have more than quadrupled, and show no signs of receding. Since Medicare does not cover drugs, dentists, or hearing aids, their supplementary insurance policy won't either. They will have to pay all those unexpected bills—thousands of dollars' worth—out of their own pockets. "There goes our vacation!" sighs Jack as he looks at the bills piling up on his desk. These aging couples and millions like them fall through the cracks in Medicare coverage, and their lifestyles as well as their bank accounts suffer. But the most devastating disappointment of the entire Medicare program is the fifth fact of Medicare limitations:

• *Fact 5:* Coverage for rehabilitation and long-term care is severely limited.

This fact can spell financial disaster for millions of couples. Anyone with an incapacitating illness cannot hope for much more than a few months of coverage from Medicare for rehabilitation. Stroke or fracture patients often require much longer periods if they are ever to regain independent functioning. There is also little assistance for the cost of a nursing home or home health care beyond a limited number of months. There is talk—but as of 1992 it remains just talk—of extending Medicare or developing reliable private insurance to cover long-term care. Private insurance policies now in existence are limited in coverage and so expensive as to be prohibitive to all except an affluent few.

A final awesome fact to be remembered is that there is no surefire safeguard protecting older people, or anyone else, from the escalating and potentially crippling costs of long-term care. These costs can cancel out the benefits of a lifetime of saving. The only solution is to sit it out until assets are all but used up and then to apply for Medicaid—the federal-state-local program for those who must carry the label "medically indigent." Applying for Medicaid assistance, although often essential, is a desperate step that may symbolize to once proudly self-sufficient older men and women that they have given up their last shred of personal independence and autonomy.

EXTENDING THE HEALTH SPAN

"And do you, Grant, take Martha as your lawful wedded wife? Do you promise to love and honor her and *to obey the rules of good health?*"

Although this vow has no place in the traditional wedding ceremony, it might as well be included. These days a wave of health consciousness—almost a health morality—has swept across the country. Good health habits are now seen as virtues while bad ones are considered sins, the former promising satisfaction, the latter producing guilt.

Medical science is constantly searching for new cures for illnesses, many of which are lying in wait for anyone who grows old. The vow to care "in sickness and in health" *is* usually included in the wedding ceremony. Couples must often devote their final years to helping each other cope with serious or chronic illness. (See Chapter 8.) But good health is not limited to curing and treating disease. Preventive care is the watchword of the day.

Modern medicine has proven that preventive measures, especially if begun early, seem to pay off in late life. Women who when young drank plenty of milk have less osteoporosis. Those who never smoked have less lung cancer. Regular testing for breast and colon cancer can prevent the spread of the disease. Men and women who exercise regularly tend to have better cardiovascular systems.

Newspapers, magazines, TV, and radio fill columns of space and hours of airtime with the newest medical findings, leading the way to good health. Spas and health clubs nationwide are booming. A veritable epidemic of self-help groups promoting good health is spreading across the country. There's always a market for the newest diet program or diet book. Manufacturers keep on designing better sportswear and footwear to encourage everyone to keep moving.

Couples who have always been involved in healthy living and who have avoided life-threatening habits—smoking, drinking, overeating, and sedentary living—are more likely to be rewarded with a satisfying late life. But it's never too late to start. Even if that health vow was not included in their original ceremony, older couples everywhere are learning to live by it and to support each other's efforts. We see them featured together in magazines and on television, decked out in the latest sports togs, jogging, race-walking, swimming, golfing, playing tennis; or they may be in their bathrobes eating calcium-enriched cornflakes, drinking skim milk, or spreading fat-free margarine on their seven-grain toast. No longer do long-stemmed roses or imported chocolates represent romantic gifts. Romance these days seems to be encouraging your true love to eat more bran.

WHO'S IN CHARGE?

Self-help groups often use the motto "Take Charge of Your Life!" Their members are sometimes able to do just that and learn to give up long-standing habits detrimental to health. But all too frequently someone will rewrite the motto to read "Take Charge of Your Partner's Life." This seemingly insignificant revision can have major negative effects on the couple's home life and on their formerly evenly balanced relationship. One partner becomes the self-appointed health czar, the tyrant-in-residence. A wife's dictatorial behavior may come from fear. She may be terrified that whatever ails her husband will kill him. Love and fear motivate her behavior. But perhaps she's always been the submissive one in the partnership and he the dominant one. Finally, she has a chance to reverse the roles and give the orders. He, in turn, is not likely to knuckle under easily. A power struggle is almost inevitable and may be hazardous to the health of both.

"He's got to stop smoking and *you* have to make him," an internist, oblivious to the consequences of his words, says to the wife of a smoker. The wife takes the order literally. She starts cracking the whip, barking out orders. Her endless nagging creates such tension that her husband's only outlet is to smoke even more. He's not given a chance to do things *his* way, to be in charge of himself. If the doctor were to say *"Help* him" instead of *"Make* him," the smoker could retain some autonomy. His wife could be his partner rather than his keeper.

THE "JACK SPRAT" SYNDROME

> *Jack Sprat could eat no fat,*
> *His wife could eat no lean.*
> *And so between them both, you see,*
> *They licked the platter clean.*

Things seemed to work out pretty compatibly for the Sprats despite their differing food habits. But not every couple are so lucky.

Incompatible habits of all kinds—eating, sleeping, exercise—can cause conflict at any point in a relationship. If Mr. Sprat were alive today, he'd know the dangers of a high-fat diet. What if he kept coaxing Mrs. Sprat at every meal, "Come on, dear, try a little lean! It's so good for you!" or shouting, "How can you eat all that fat? It'll kill you"? Pretty soon Mrs. S. would be less likely to reform her eating habits than to snap, "Get off my back!" and flounce away from the table.

Those who are allergic or diabetic have less freedom of choice in what they eat. Their dos and don'ts are more clear-cut. They know they will suffer immediately if they eat forbidden foods. But for the obese and people with high cholesterol or high blood pressure, the consequences of sinning are not immediate. A chorus of "Just this once!" or "A little can't hurt!" or "Oh! I shouldn't!" can be heard at many dinner tables when the beef Wellington, or the chicken paprika, or the baked Alaska is served. If they are not already convinced that dietary sinning can have dangerous long-term consequences, their partners become their watchdogs.

Preparing a healthy diet involves three steps—the buying, the preparation, and then the serving of food. Buying healthy food is a first step, but how is this going to be cooked? If it's fried instead of baked, you'll lose points. If it's healthfully steamed but served with a dollop of sour cream, you'll lose points. Care, concern, and cooperation are involved in the three steps. If agreement is impossible, a workable compromise is better than nothing. When both partners are aware of the value of healthy eating and are willing to help each other to accept certain dietary limits, meals can become a challenge and a pleasure, too. When one partner resents the regime imposed by the other, the dinner table usually becomes a battleground or a place to be avoided whenever possible.

> As Fred and Florence Brad entered their sixties, Florence became increasingly concerned about Fred's weight, particularly because of his high blood pressure. She knew enough not to lecture him about overeating and lack of exercise. Instead, she was very careful about the food she bought and prepared. The meals she made were always Jane Brody specials. Fred never rebelled; he simply escaped whenever possible. He looked forward to going to his office, where he had a Danish and coffee every morning, beef-and-potato lunches, and, whenever he had

a chance, bourbon and a cigar after dinner out with a client. What a joy it was when he could go off on a business trip! He missed Florence, but oh, that was his chance to indulge himself! He was tired of toeing Florence's health line—the daily walk she prescribed and the one glass of wine she allowed. When both met up again together on home turf, he would guiltily assure Florence that he "tried to watch himself!"

Florence's anxiety about Fred's welfare led to her controlling behavior. Fred's excuse for overindulgence was a need to rebel. She became the good mother and he the bad little boy. The result was that Fred kept on gaining while Florence lost weight out of frustration, worry, and all the low-calorie food she continued to prepare.

A similar scenario can be written around exercise. Convinced by reports that exercise is helpful in slowing down osteoporosis, Clint Minor keeps after Marge to take a daily two-mile walk. As his resentful wife goes off every morning, she yells back over her shoulder, "Okay, I'm taking your ——— walk for you." Since Marge is not motivated by her own welfare but by Clint's nagging, she's soon likely to rebel against exercise and against Clint as well. Perhaps if he cared enough to go along with her, she'd find exercise—and Clint—less irritating.

STEPPING ASIDE, LOOKING AWAY

Finding the right balance between overinvolvement and underinvolvement with someone else's well-being is tricky. Too much interference can wreck a relationship, but no interference at all can damage the health of both people. All too often, one partner gives up on the other. Think of the number of times you've heard these complaints:

"I can't do a thing with her!"

"He doesn't take care of himself."

"She refuses to get a physical."

"He won't do a thing about his weight."

"Go ahead, keep on smoking. It's your funeral."

One partner may step aside in order to keep the peace, or may simply not care enough about the other. The asthmatic husband who ignores his wife's smoking may have already given up on the relationship. By giving tacit approval to her nicotine addiction, he not only supports it but allows passive smoking to jeopardize his own health—a no-win situation for both.

In such scenarios both partners are losers; they are also losers in another scenario that unfolds when neither partner will give up unhealthy habits. Both are able to deny their mortality. In these situations naked fear may step in and succeed where nagging, coaxing, stepping aside, or denying fails.

> Ed's heart attack came as a total shock to him and everyone else despite his age—seventy. He'd always been in top physical condition even though he worked hard, chain-smoked, and ate and drank as he pleased. His wife, who also loved high living, went right along with him. They totally ignored all their doctors' pleas to exercise more, cut down on fats and alcohol, and quit smoking. Their doctors got nowhere, but Ed's heart attack succeeded where they had failed. The terror he felt at his brush with death shocked him into healthy living. "I went into the hospital a three-pack-a-day unfiltered-Camel smoker and never picked up another cigarette after that," he told everyone proudly. The terror his wife felt at her brush with widowhood and the reminder of her own mortality shocked her into giving up high living along with him.

WHO CARES?

When illness or disability strikes, it is usually taken for granted that couples will take care of each other, the well partner becoming the caregiver for the disabled one, obeying the "in sickness and in health" vow. Most of the time this happens. Research studies show that among most older couples, caregiving is provided by the spouse.

Premarital contracts prepared when older couples remarry have been known to include a clause stipulating that neither partner will be the caregiver for the other and that funds should be set aside for nursing-home or home care. In such a marriage the traditional vow should be revised to read "until death or nursing home do us part." Some widows, particularly those who have already nursed one husband through years of illness, may not remarry precisely because they never want to become caregivers for another one. To them being a lonely single is preferable to being a married caregiver.

Space needs to be considered, too. A one-bedroom garden apartment may give a couple all the room they want but if one, or both, of them need ongoing home care, where will this caregiver live? A sofa bed in the living room is fine for a temporary stay but not for a permanent one. There is hardly enough space for two invalids much less a caregiver, too.

WHEN BOTH NEED CARE

In some cases plans don't work out in life as they do on paper. Neither partner may have a chance to care for the other because both become disabled and dependent almost at the same time. They may need help with some, or all, routines of daily life and personal care. They may be forced to turn to children or other close relatives who may be willing to help out—for a time. Much depends on the relationships between the generations. But even in families where the feelings are warmest and closest, the younger ones may not be able to provide permanent caregiving. They may have their own health problems, their children may need them, or they may be retired, with less physical energy themselves. Long periods of caregiving can lead to emotional or physical burnout.

If there are sufficient funds as well as space, disabled couples may be able to stay right where they are, hiring outside help as their caregivers. If they lack funds and space, or if there are few caregivers for hire in their communities, they may have to consider moving to a nursing home or a child's home.

CONSULTING THE CHILDREN

If you are counting on help from your children, it would be wise to discuss your expectations with them in advance of a crisis, when heads are cool and emotions more stable. "How much will you be able to help?" "With caregiving?" "With money?" Opening up such a discussion with children can be painfully emotional, but when parents take this step, they are likely to reduce future family tension. Sometimes these "family conferences" are wonderfully productive and give both generations a feeling of greater security about their future.

> Louise and Larry Luft, in their early seventies, were determined they would never burden their children. They were able to reserve a special fund to pay for caregiving if they ever needed it. They outlined their plans to their son and his family, explaining that the only help they might need would be supervision of the outside help. The children willingly accepted their parents' plan and their own part in it.

The outcome is not always so positive. Parents may not hear what they want to hear. But at least they know what to expect and can make decisions with or without their children's cooperation. In families where the subject is never raised, rational planning is unlikely.

Even if a couple does not expect caregiving help from their children, it is wise for them to discuss their plans in advance. Sons and daughters may avoid the subject for fear of upsetting their aging mothers and fathers or because they themselves cannot bear to contemplate their parents' decline. But some may jump the gun and start imposing their own plans on the older generation, urging faraway parents to move in with them or close to them or to enter a retirement home. "The city's a jungle now—you'll be so much better off out here in the country with us."

KEEPING YOUR AUTONOMY

The couple who anticipate the possibility of a protracted caregiving situation and agree together on a plan should review it with their family. This will prevent children and other relatives from stepping into the breach and making unwelcome decisions at the time of a crisis.

> Kathryn and Bob were healthy until their late seventies. They figured that if one of them became ill or disabled the other would step in and take care of things. They had enough savings to pay for help. Even as Kathryn's eyesight deteriorated because of macular degeneration, they felt they could manage. When Bob suffered a stroke, the two were helpless because Kathryn became very depressed. Her children had to take over their care completely and made decisions that greatly upset Kathryn. She felt that both she and Bob had lost control over their lives.

One of the greatest fears that older people have is of losing their independence and personal autonomy. The best way to allay these fears is to plan ahead, set clear goals, and let others know what these are.

THE HOUSE WE LIVE IN

> "Will I still be able to visit you a lot when you move?" six-year-old Timmy anxiously asked his grandmother.
> "Who said we're moving?" answered Grandma.
> "Well, Jason's grandma and grandpa are moving to Florida and Maria's went to California last year and—"
> "Stop your worrying, Timmy," Grandma interrupted, patting his hand reassuringly. "We aren't moving anywhere. We're staying right here in this old house that keeps falling down on us."

One of the most important decisions an older couple can make is where to live: what region, what community, what type of house. This decision has implications for all the factors considered so far in planning for the future: extending the wealth and health span, leisure time and work activity, caregiving, independence. The options open to a couple, depending on their financial resources, are numerous. Whole industries are being devoted now to providing suitable housing, with special safety devices, for older people. All have their advantages and disadvantages.

A PLACE IN THE SUN

As condos and retirement complexes multiply all over the warmer states, it might seem that older people *do* want a place in the sun for their late years. But in actual fact the exodus south is not as widespread as it seems—the majority of the elderly are "aging in place." They are remaining right in their own communities where they have lived for many years, placing greater value on a long-standing social network, with valued relatives, old friends, and familiar community activities, than on an endless summer in an alien environment. It takes a long time to grow new roots once the old ones have been broken.

Many couples—but far from all—are able through good fortune or their own efforts to carve out new lives for themselves in sunny communities, never looking back to the lives they left behind in the snow. Others feel forever out of step. One ex–New Jerseyite, when questioned about her life in Florida, replied without much enthusiasm, "Have we made new friends? Well, I guess so. We have our tennis friends, our golf friends, and our bridge friends."

The affluent can have the best of both worlds. By escaping to warmer climates for part of the year, they can also keep their home fires burning. This move may even provide the extra benefit of protecting their estates. For example, a couple from Connecticut, which has high inheritance taxes, can save their heirs thousands of dollars by living for six months and a day in Florida, where inheritance taxes are lowest.

Decisions must be made and questions asked whether couples move far away or stay put. There are more issues involved than weather and taxes. Both partners should consider carefully what kind of living situation they are likely to need, together or individually, as they grow older. A move to a plush sunny retirement community may satisfy the tennis player or the sailor, but what if the other partner is a painter who thrives on the museums and galleries of a big city? The two need to work out a compromise.

AGING IN PLACE

In a survey conducted by the AARP, 86 percent of the elderly respondents replied that they wanted to stay where they were for the rest of their lives. In spite of the intensity of such a desire, the pros and cons should still be examined. A couple hoping to age "in place" need to ask: What does our community have to offer? Does it have a variety of services to assist the elderly? Doctors? Hospitals? Nursing and home-maker services? What about transportation? Is there a good bus service, or will we have to drive ourselves to shopping, doctors' appointments, and social activities? What if our eyesight deteriorates and we can no longer drive? Is our house (or apartment) convenient if either of us is disabled? Are there neighbors around?

How these questions are answered may tip the scales in favor of moving. The old house on the hill may be filled with loving memories but have three flights of steep stairs and an uphill driveway. One couple reluctantly gave up a historic house with four levels of charm after the husband's bypass surgery. At this stage of their lives and in their physical condition, what they needed was the convenience of a one-floor ranch house with no stairs, good lighting, and easy maintenance. Although accessibility, safety, and convenience have the highest priority in late life when disability is more likely, many of the elderly are convinced that a house without memories is not a home.

THE RETIREMENT COMMUNITY

Residential facilities that provide for the ups and downs of late life are now available in increasing numbers for those who can afford them. They are located not only in the sunny climes but in all states and many communities. Some older people, who choose this type of housing near their old homes, are fortunate enough to be almost "aging in place." Others may choose retirement housing to be near family or for the climate.

The advantages of these facilities are such that some couples move away from their home communities or live far away from other family members. Built especially to suit the needs of older persons, these facilities offer living units that are accessible and easy to live in, with built-in supports if needed. Very often they have a dining room for one or two meals a day and planned recreational activities. Nursing-home care and medical care are usually available.

These retirement facilities can consist of several buildings or comprise an entire community. Planning ahead is usually required if a couple desire to enter such a facility. There is often a waiting list, and couples are much more readily admitted while in good health.

The pros and cons must be weighed. On the plus side is the knowledge that care is readily available in the case of illness or disability. The opportunities for making new friends and socializing can be antidotes to the loneliness some couples experience when they opt to age in place. Structured and accessible recreational opportunities can be an advantage. Not to be overlooked is the advantage to a widow or widower who can remain in relatively safe and familiar surroundings after the death of a spouse. Couples who enter a retirement community together often have this contingency in mind. On the negative side is the loss of living among people of all ages and the feeling of being segregated. If the retirement facility is far away from old friends and family and other things familiar, the loss may be intensified.

MOVING TO THE CHILDREN

Check real estate ads in your local paper. There's sure to be some wonderful house for sale with the tempting selling point "granny-flat over garage" or "in-law cottage adjacent." Real estate agents have jumped on this bandwagon. Living close by loving children rather than under the same roof may be a great solution for both generations, but love is not enough to justify a move.

The move should be carefully evaluated, with answers provided for questions such as: Do we have other friends in the area, or will we be dependent on our children for sociability? Are shopping, the doctor's office, and church or synagogue in walking distance? If we cannot drive, will we be shut in unless someone takes us everywhere? Is there help available in the community—nurses, homemakers, home health aides—or will our children have to be our caregivers in times of illness or disability? Finally, can those of us who are city-bred learn to love the country or the suburbs at our age?

Beware the promises made by children. They may be eager to have you nearby because they love you. It may also ease their anxiety not to have you far away. Their assurances that your life will be rosy near them may be made with the best of intentions, but they may not have thought through what it would be like having you nearby. Are they ready to substitute for lost friends and activities? Are they really ready to change their lives and give up some of their privacy? They may be ready and willing, but it should be thought through in advance.

Older couples should also keep in mind the possibility that their children may move away! It has happened that an older couple move to be nearer their children, only to have them move away in spite of assurances this wouldn't happen. A son-in-law may lose a job and need to move. Sons or daughters, no longer young, may need to move for the sake of their health. Remember that when you are eighty-five, your children will probably be entering late life and making their own plans.

A WORKABLE COMPROMISE

It's not unusual for aging couples to dig in their heels and ignore pleas from their children to move to more convenient quarters, or even safer neighborhoods. For some any move at all can be traumatic. The personal preferences of both partners should carry almost equal weight when making decisions on how and where to live. Both partners should have a voice in the outcome. "Should we stay put or move? If we move, where do we go?" "Far away or close by?" "To a warmer climate or closer to the children?" A workable compromise can serve if agreement is impossible. The submissive partner may have a history of giving in to the dominant one, but this can be the high road to disaster in late life when there may be little time left to make changes again.

> Mimi Jemson's depression totally baffled Tony, her extroverted contractor husband, who spent his first retirement year building a one-floor dream house for his bride of forty-eight years. She kept telling him she didn't want a new house, but he kept telling her she'd love it. He won, as he did always, and then kept asking, "What's wrong with her? All she does is sit there and cry!" Mimi couldn't explain what was wrong except to say over and over again, "How could he make me move so far away?" Far away was actually three miles across town, but for Mimi it might as well have been Siberia. Tony had never understood her terror at leaving the neighborhood where she had lived for seventy-two years. She gave in to him and then spent her next months in tears and on antidepressants.

MEASURING THE COSTS

Money plays a major role in making decisions about where to live, as it does in every other area of late life. You may keep repeating, "The only way we'll ever leave this house is when we're carried out!" This conviction is held by many couples who want to die right where they have always lived. But is this a luxury you can afford? Or if you can today, what about tomorrow?

> The Griffins were deeply attached to their house, which they had bought soon after they married for $22,000 and where they had raised their children. When Bud retired in 1985, he and Marci planned and projected carefully and decided that with Bud's pension, their Social Security, and a few investments they could stay in the house comfortably. After all, the house, with its paid-up mortgage, was a gold mine, now worth $298,000. The future looked good. But Bud and Marci did not count on an annual 4 percent rise in the cost of living. Six years of inflation ate up a frightening chunk of their fixed income. In addition, their local real estate tax almost doubled, both of them had heavy medical expenses, and—the final straw—the house was ailing, too. In one year it needed a new septic system and a new

roof. They could not cover these unanticipated expenses with current income, so they had three choices: secure a home-improvement loan, deplete their limited savings, or what they'd vowed never to do—sell their house. No matter which choice they made, it would hurt—financially or emotionally.

THE MISSING PIECE

When all the plans for living through your later years together have been considered, one last piece of the puzzle needs to be fitted in before the picture of your future is completed: your plans for dying and the feelings each of you has about death. This subject, once hidden under wraps, now out in the open, has such special significance for the elderly that it requires a separate chapter. Chapter 9 will discuss living wills, medical power of attorney, euthanasia, suicide, and other controversial issues making news in the nineties.

Completing the puzzle and putting all the pieces in place for the future cannot, unfortunately, guarantee that all plans will work out success-fully. The future holds too many mysteries. Every aspect cannot be insured. A couple may get an A in planning and yet these plans may be undermined by some event they never anticipated. However, when two people plan for rather than drift into their late life together, they may avoid some of the calamities lying in wait for everyone who grows old or may be better prepared to deal with them if they do descend.

Did his armor weigh heavy on his limbs? Did pain one day stab at his chest and fill his heart with terror? Did he withdraw from the tourneys? Were her fingers stiffening, her eyesight dimming? Did she put away her tapestry, sadly and forever?

Did they both lie awake at night fearing what tomorrow might bring, or that there might be no tomorrow?

FACE-TO-FACE
WITH ILLNESS
AND DISABILITY

Travis and Flo Martens lucked out in 1988. They sold their big house for the asking price and paid no capital gains tax, so even after buying a terrific, efficient condo they still had a sizable amount left over to invest. It was also the first year they didn't have to support any of their three children. "I can't believe it!" Travis used to keep repeating. "All the money coming in is just for *us!* No more college dues, no more loans, no more handouts. We can live it up!" And so began the best years of their lives.

In their late sixties they were still in good health, able to laugh off whatever minor normal problems either one had—Travis's elevated blood pressure and Flo's arthritic pains. There was nothing to stop them from going anywhere or doing anything. And they did! Their relationship was as close and intimate as it had been forty-six years ago when they got married. But when Travis was sixty-nine, he was hospitalized for chest pains. He spent one night in the intensive care unit, and tests revealed that his pains were caused by a partially blocked artery. Flo took him home in a few days. It was a frightening episode, over quickly, but it took its toll on both of them. Their daughter commented sadly, "I don't know what's happened to them. A few months ago they were strong, affluent, sociable, active, enthusiastic people. Now they're scared, gloomy, irritable, withdrawn hypochondriacs."

There are plenty of couples like Travis and Flo. Free of domestic and financial burdens, they were having the time of their lives, almost smug about their ability to cope with their minor infirmities and impatient with friends who allowed themselves to feel and act old. "It's all in your mind!" they loved to say. But those few days in the hospital changed the picture. Suddenly, they saw the handwriting on the wall and were forced to believe that these "golden" years might end one day.

EARLY WARNINGS

The previous chapter reviewed ways to get ready for late life. Preventive health care is an important safeguard against health problems in late life: good nutrition, weight control, exercise, avoidance of substance abuse, physical checkups at intervals. Couples, thinking ahead, may also consider options for health care in case of illness or disability and plan in advance on how to pay for this care. Postponing these issues until a time of crisis will only compound difficulties.

Chapter 6 was a form of dress rehearsal for late life. This chapter considers episodes of acute illness and the onset of physical impairments, examining the effect these may have on couples and their relationships. Admittedly, these illnesses may sometimes be fatal, but they are just as likely to respond to treatment, leading to recovery if not to complete cure.

For healthy sixty- and seventy-year-olds, like Travis and Flo, the first brief encounter with an acute illness or a dreaded diagnosis usually delivers a terrifying shock. As they grow older, they are likely to receive many such messages, and they may or may not eventually take them with greater equanimity or acceptance. Mitzy Connover is a good example. She had been close to hysteria about an operation on a cancerous kidney when she was in her early seventies. She convinced herself, her husband, and everyone else that she had been given a death sentence. Instead, she made a complete recovery. Ten years later when she faced bypass surgery, her husband prepared himself for hysteria. But she surprised him. "I've outlived my mother by fifteen years and my father by twenty," she told him. "We've had a good ten years since that cancer. I'd like a few more, but if it ends now, so be it!"

Lack of information about their own bodies accounts for much of the panic that people experience when a health crisis comes. Out of ignorance new patients may beg for answers: "What's happened to me?" "Is it serious?" "Could it kill me?" Information is a powerful weapon, but it needs updating at every age since older bodies cannot be counted on to respond the way younger bodies do.

Too often, older people simply do not know enough about their bodies, do not want to know, or are misinformed by old wives' tales and myths. The more they know, the better-armed they are likely to be to deal with a crisis when it comes. Partners, both the sick and the healthy, will ask better questions if these are based on some rudimentary knowledge of what's happening. It's reassuring to know what changes are likely, what diseases are frequent, what conditions are normal, what can be treated, what can be arrested.

POOR HEALTH IN LATER LIFE

The elderly are prone to all the common or garden-variety ailments that afflict younger people, plus a number of others that become more frequent as the years go by. An increasing number of conditions once thought to be a normal part of aging can now be attributed to specific diseases. A reasonable question to ask is, "What's the difference? If you're sick, you're sick." It is important to separate normal aging from disease, because not much can be done about aging but a lot can be done about disease. Diseases have the potential of cure. Aging does not. Too many older people—and their physicians, too—attribute health problems to old age. They fail to look further and take corrective action. Medical technology is making great strides, and no condition should be ignored because it once was seen as inevitable. If there's no treatment today for a given condition, there may be one tomorrow.

NORMAL CHANGES

What we do know about normal aging is that there is an overall slowing down as the years go by as well as specific changes in the body's organs. In general, the aging system has less backup reserves and resiliency, and cannot compensate as readily as it did earlier for poor nutrition, fatigue, even the common cold. It is more susceptible to acute diseases, such as the flu, and requires longer periods of recovery from illness and accident. It's not unusual for an older man or woman to complain, "My bounce is gone!" after a bout with flu or gastritis. Thus, the "frailty" observed in the very late years is sometimes a function of normal aging but also may be the result of disease. There is a plus side to this slowing-down process because it benefits the cancer patient. The growth of tumorous cells slows down along with everything else in aging bodies, so the diagnosis of a cancer in an older person is not quite as ominous as it is for someone younger.

If older convalescents understand what is going on in their bodies, they may be more tolerant and less frustrated with a slow recuperation after an acute illness. Their partners may be able to convince them they are not sinking into a permanent decline.

> Seventy-five-year-old Harry Jacobs was in despair weeks after his heart surgery. Everyone had told him he'd be back to normal in no time, but he wasn't. He slept a lot, felt sorry for himself, required great amounts of sympathy, and was full of complaints. Jenny, his wife, wore herself out catering to him, reassuring him, and comforting him. Eventually, Harry surprised himself and did bounce back, but by then Jenny was exhausted and their relationship strained. She in turn became more anxious and worried about the future and this affected her own health. Soon he was the well one and she the sick one.

Their doctor had not made it clear to Jenny or to Harry that no one recovers according to any set timetable and we all have to follow the schedule our bodies set. Fortunately, or unfortunately, there is no built-in computer program determining when any changes in the body will begin, how fast they will move, and how much damage, if any, they will do. There is tremendous individual variation and no two people are likely to follow the same schedule. Some seem to show little if any deterioration with the years, although changes are usually more pronounced in the very late years, over eighty.

Every organ system of the body, including the brain, is made up of millions of cells, and each system loses cells with advancing age. We can even watch this process taking place, since it is visible in the progressive wrinkling, drying, and sagging of the skin and the whitening of hair. This aging process is a boon to the cosmetic industry and to plastic surgeons whose skill with lifts, tucks, and sucks translates into billions of dollars a year.

Each of the sense organs suffers some loss. Most older people experience vision changes; the lens of the eye loses elasticity, making it difficult to focus clearly. We have all seen older people trying with difficulty, when they come in from the dark, to recover from the glare of a brightly lit room. Some of us can even remember the eighty-year-old Robert Frost, at John Kennedy's inauguration, trying to shield his script from the glare of the winter sun so he could manage to read the poem he had composed especially for the occasion. An older person's eyes may take eight or nine times longer to adapt to bright light than a younger person's.

The ear suffers its own nerve and bone changes, and hearing loss becomes more likely with the passing years, starting first in the higher frequencies. "Speak up! Stop mumbling!" is an understandable request from numbers of older people frustrated by muffled sounds and conversation they cannot quite catch. The sensitivity of the taste buds becomes duller, making it difficult to discriminate among foods. "You call this pepperoni pizza! Where's the taste? Take it away—I'm not risking heartburn for this!" Sensory changes are often particularly difficult for the elderly to cope with emotionally since these losses can so radically affect the pleasures of everyday living.

Aging can also affect the nervous system, reducing sensitivity and perceptual abilities. Reduction in pain response—its exact site unknown but lying somewhere in the brain—makes it harder for some older people to actually feel pain. Other familiar signals transmitted by the nervous system that formerly alerted them to the part of their body in trouble may no longer come through loud and clear. Your partner may have suffered a mild heart attack that went unnoticed some time back. Blame the nervous system for sending out inadequate signals. You may be surprised by bruises on your legs but be unable to remember what you bumped into, or burns on your arm but have no idea what caused them. You just never picked up the pain signal.

The body must adapt to other reductions: the excretory function of the kidneys diminishes, the speed of the conduction of nerve impulses slows, and there is a decrease in heart output, which does not necessarily imply that the heart is diseased. Decrease in muscle tissue may produce a decrease in strength, and lung capacity may be reduced, perhaps because the muscles no longer work efficiently. Digestive functions also slow down: the flow of saliva and gastric juices, the motion of the stomach, and the contractions of the intestines—all factors leading to constipation and indigestion. Never underestimate the psychic effects of these digestive problems. Couples whose great pleasure lay in food— eating, cooking, trying out new restaurants—and who loved entertaining and going out to eat with others may find these pleasures curtailed by their rebellious digestive systems. The midnight snack in bed, a nightly ritual enjoyed by many couples, can become a pallid glass of warm milk or an unstimulating cup of herbal tea.

There is also likely to be some alteration in the overall functioning of the nervous system, which plays an important role in coordinating the interactions between muscles, glands, and blood vessels. This may also account for the decline in muscle strength, and since so many acts of daily life depend on this three-way interaction, when all three do not function smoothly together, older people may find simple, everyday activities affected, such as walking, sitting down, dressing, and housework. When the decline in vision, hearing, and reaction time is added to the equation, it is not surprising that the elderly are more fearful of accidents and more cautious than younger people.

As research into conditions prevalent in late life progresses, more and more conditions formerly attributed to normal aging are found to be rooted in disease. Older people are now being advised not to accept the grim prognosis "Nothing can be done!" The overwhelming majority of health problems in late life have a cause not solely related to aging.

TREATABLE CONDITIONS

Many physical problems afflicting aging bodies can be treated; some are even reversible. Disease and illness must always be separated from the inevitable changes just mentioned, although the latter undoubtedly make the elderly more vulnerable and less resilient. Hope for the future comes from medical advances that have already proved that some conditions once considered part of the inevitable aging process can now be classified as disease and are therefore potentially responsive to treatment, if not now, then in the near future.

Arteriosclerosis (hardening of the arteries), for example, was until recently considered part of the aging process because doctors found it more frequently in older people. It also seemed to become progressively more severe in particular individuals as the years went by. Today, however, it is seen as a complex metabolic disturbance and, thanks to advances in the management of hypertension and diabetes as predisposing causes, is subject to treatment and alleviation.

Cataract surgery, once an exhausting procedure involving days in a dark room with the patient's head immobilized between sandbags, is now performed as ambulatory surgery. Lens replacement has proved very successful in restoring and prolonging sight. Special drops taken at regular intervals each day can keep glaucoma under control. Orthopedic surgery has been increasingly successful during the past twenty years with total joint replacements to offset the devastating effects of crippling arthritis. Total hip and total knee replacements are now routine procedures, while replacement of other joints—ankle, wrist, and shoulder—is under continuing study and evaluation. Heart bypass surgery has become almost commonplace—even on the very old—and an amazing array of "wonder drugs" are available to reduce or avoid the ill effects of coronary heart disease.

Sexual impotence in men, frigidity in women, or reduced libido in both genders used to be written off to aging. "What can you expect at your age?" was a frequent, unfeeling question by doctors in the past if any aging patient dared to admit to any such problems. When these do occur—and they often do not, as the active sex lives of many older people prove—the causes may be physical or psychological. (See Chapter 3.) Seventy percent of cases of impotence in older males are caused by physical problems, some of them amenable to correction. Sexual problems of older women may also respond to treatment.

Some mental conditions that once spelled doom—for example, confusion and memory loss—are being diagnosed with much more discrimination today by physicians who have been trained in geriatrics. Poor nutrition, overmedication, depression, and treatable diseases may account for some of these symptoms. Far less frequently are mental disturbances automatically written off to senility or Alzheimer's disease.

BUT SOME CONDITIONS CAN'T BE CURED

Sad to say for the current generations of the elderly, there are still many diseases for which there is no cure and only stopgap treatment. These incurable conditions are usually referred to as "chronic" or "irreversible." While nothing medically or surgically can be done about them, steps can be taken to control their growth through medication, to ease their symptoms, or to restore some functioning that has been impaired by them.

There is no cure as yet for osteoporosis, for example, a disease that reduces bone strength and increases the likelihood of fractures, and which has received much notice in recent years. As a result, much emphasis has been put on strengthening bones through calcium in the diet, although experts question calcium's usefulness once the disease has taken hold. Some physicians prescribe hormones for postmenopausal women to slow the progress of bone loss. Osteoporosis is suffered by both sexes but seems to affect more women than men. This may be because women live longer and the disease intensifies with age.

Leading chronic conditions among older people are arthritis, hypertension, heart disease, orthopedic impairment, diabetes, and vision and hearing impairment. The occurrence of Parkinsonism, cancer, and strokes is also higher in late life. Rarely do these conditions exist in isolation from other health problems and sometimes they are closely interrelated—for example, untreated diabetes can lead to serious vision problems. (See Appendix C.)

While some chronic or irreversible health problems can be stabilized, others follow an unremitting path of deterioration. Alzheimer's and other related diseases are examples; so is osteoarthritis, a painful inflammation or degeneration of the joints. Many older people suffer the pain of arthritis to a mild degree and receive some comfort from medications and physiotherapy that offer symptomatic relief but not cure. In some cases, however, arthritis can be so severe that it seriously interferes with walking, standing, and the use of arms and fingers. It can, at its worst, lead to total immobility and require ongoing care.

Vision and hearing loss can deteriorate to the point where an older person's ability to socialize or function independently is compromised. Blindness ranks second to cancer in conditions most feared, although few older people with vision impairment lose their sight completely.

Devastating impairments due to disease go beyond the "normal" losses of aging and are not amenable, as are cataracts, to corrective surgery. Laser surgery has been found to be helpful in the early stages of some eye diseases, such as diabetic retinopathy.

More people are living longer—that's obvious—and, thanks to advances in medical know-how, are living more healthily. Also obvious is the urgent need for continuing research, for as the survival rate into the later decades increases, so does the incidence of many chronic physical and mental disabilities. These exact a heavy toll not only in terms of dollars but also on human emotions.

IT CAN HAPPEN BY ACCIDENT

The elderly soon learn to be watchful when they go out—they pick their way carefully along the streets. So many dangers lie in wait for them there—hit-and-run accidents, deep potholes, falls on icy sidewalks, muggings. They may not be as careful inside, yet their homes may be full of death traps. Forty percent of all fatal accidents happen at home, caused perhaps by a polished floor, a loose rug, a slippery bathtub, or a greasy spot on the kitchen linoleum. Old people may fall over their own pets—a playful puppy, or a sleeping cat. Add to these menaces the likelihood of failing eyesight, poor coordination, or weakened muscles, and it's remarkable the accident statistic is not even higher.

Falls do not account for all accidents, however. The kitchen stove may leak gas, frayed electrical wires may send shocks, boiling liquid may spill giving serious burns, or a dish towel may catch fire and ignite the whole place.

The medicine chest has its own disaster potential. An eighty-year-old getting up in the middle of the night looking for a sleeping pill or painkiller may overdose accidentally or even take pills from the wrong bottles. Over-the-counter medications usually list warnings—for example, "Do not use if you have glaucoma (or hypertension)," but in such small print that even young eyes may have difficulty reading them.

Because multiple ailments are frequent, older people often take multiple medications and these sometimes react against each other, causing further problems. "I'm a walking drugstore!" one man complained, intoning a list of daily health measures: patches for angina; pills for heart, blood pressure, and cholesterol; drops for glaucoma. He didn't even bother to mention he also frequently took nonprescription painkillers, antihistamines, laxatives, and cold remedies, any of which might combine dangerously with any other. Close monitoring and medical supervision of all medications, prescription and over-the-counter, are essential.

Almost as essential is learning about the side effects of many drugs. While many people are aware that some medications can cause gastric problems, drowsiness, and emotional or sexual disturbance, they may have no idea that others may be responsible for dry mouth—which can lead to periodontal disease—and hearing, vision, and skin problems. Most medications list possible side effects, but these, like other warnings, are usually printed in microscopic type.

WHAT ABOUT THE MIND?

Problems in and of the mind, coming suddenly or creeping in slowly over time in late life, are frightening for older people. This could be because they see them firsthand when a contemporary's mind deteriorates or because so much public attention has been focused on dementia in the last twenty years. A wide variety of conditions affect the mind and emotions in old age, and they cannot all be lumped under the diagnosis of senility. Any one of us who wears the senior tag probably knows firsthand something about memory loss, when perfectly familiar names of people or things fly out of the mind only to be retrieved later. One couple was well known in their circle for their Memory Bank. Each time they both forgot the name of a person or a place—"Who costarred with Humphrey Bogart in *Casablanca?*" or "Who wrote *A Farewell to Arms?*" or "What's the capital of Massachusetts?"—the one who remembered first became the winner; the other had to put a dollar into the box. When there was enough money in the Memory Bank for a decent meal, off they went to their favorite restaurant.

Mental problems range from mild and serious reactions to physical illnesses and personal losses to conditions caused by substance abuse and diseases such as Alzheimer's. One thing is clear: severe mental problems are not "normal" in late life. They are not part and parcel of aging, as many would assume. Scientific studies reported in 1991 concluded that the aging brain is probably the most resilient of the body's organs. No one would deny, however, that illness can trigger a variety of painful emotions adversely affecting the morale of older people.

DEPRESSION AND ANXIETY

Some emotional reactions are intertwined with certain diseases. Stroke victims are prone to wide and unstable mood swings, sudden fits of unprovoked weeping or fury. Illness and disability can spark rage, anxiety, and fear, and these are often dumped on the well partner, who may admit the dumping is worse than the illness. When the well partner reacts in kind, emotions are compounded.

> Previously a seemingly compatible couple, the Grants fought continually after his bypass surgery. In spite of an optimistic prognosis from his surgeon, Frank was bitterly pessimistic about making a full recovery and therefore full of fear and anger. He

vented these emotions at the most convenient target—Tillie, his wife—lashing out at her at the slightest provocation or no provocation at all. Tillie, who had her own worries, started lashing back. The sickroom turned into a battlefield, slowing Frank's recovery and endangering Tillie's already high blood pressure.

During and after an illness every couple is burdened, but each partner in a different way. Take Patsy and Jake, for example. Patsy is seventy-eight and has just come through an operation for colon cancer. She has to endure pain and discomfort; she must also follow doctors' orders to fight the disease in her body and at the same time deal with a dizzying group of emotions in her mind: anger that her body has betrayed her, fear that she might die, worry about Jake and how he'd manage without her, or resentment that he might manage very well. On his side Jake has to be Patsy's strength and at the same time deal with his own feelings: fear that her cancer may recur, terror of her death and their separation, anger that she might die and leave him, concern for his own welfare if she did, and guilt that he could think of himself at a time like this.

Earlier chapters have discussed the many varieties of loss accumulating in late life. Many losses that cause stress are directly related to poor health and disability. Understandably, significant losses and intense stress can spark strong emotional reactions, the most frequent being depression.

Being *in* a depression is quite different from the moods we all experience and describe by saying "I feel so depressed today." The symptoms of a real depression go beyond feeling blue and are not always obvious or easily diagnosed. They may masquerade and express themselves through prolonged periods of insomnia, loss of appetite, weight loss, forgetfulness, or psychosomatic symptoms. Depression following a profound loss is very often a predictable part of the mourning process, a necessary step in giving up something valued and moving on with life. But when depression is unremitting and unending, professional help may be necessary.

Anxiety often goes hand in hand with loss and with stress, too. Jittery, tense, fearful feelings may also masquerade as insomnia, lack of appetite, or somatic symptoms. Anxiety is to be expected before any threatening situation such as the serious illness of a partner, but it may continue after recovery.

> "Those Petersens! They're like two peas in a pod. You can't pry them loose from each other," people used to say when seventy-seven-year-old Erik and Mara walked down the street together. Mara didn't take such a rosy view of their relationship. This ultra-togetherness really had begun after Erik recovered from prostate surgery. From then on he never let Mara out of his sight. He was driving her crazy. "He sticks to me like glue—I can't get away from him!" He went with her to market; he read a magazine in the beauty parlor while she had her hair done. At home he followed her around the house like a puppy—even into the bathroom and the shower. Whenever she exploded, he had a stock answer: "You don't love me anymore." At Mara's insistence they talked to their doctor and Erik finally admitted that he was anxious and terrified right down to the pit of his stomach all the time. The only antidote was being close to Mara. The doctor prescribed a medication to reduce anxiety, and Mara finally was allowed a little breathing room.

Anger is another common emotional reaction to loss and stress. It is also understandable—there's much to rage about in late life. But this becomes problematic when it is directed at everyone and everything with no letup. The British cartoon character Colonel Blimp was so well known for exploding into apoplectic rage at every provocation that his name has become synonymous with geriatric fury. "You're acting like Colonel Blimp!" a wife may say, hoping to calm down her husband who has just sounded off in fury at a social gathering. If the formerly mild-tempered man never behaved this way until recently, his wife may have reason to be concerned that something is happening to his mind. But perhaps he has never been retired until recently, or never had arthritis until recently, or diabetes or angina or glaucoma. For older people who cannot adjust to the losses in their bodies, to the changes in their lives and in the world around them, rage may be the emotion of choice. Of course, there's a price to pay. Constant anger results in further losses—the steady withdrawal of relatives and friends as well as diminished sympathy from their partners.

ALZHEIMER'S AND RELATED DISEASES

Mental and emotional disturbances are not necessarily chronic in nature. A number can be treated, arrested, or perhaps cured. There is nothing yet, however, to arrest the tragic destructive course of dementing conditions such as Alzheimer's disease.

Dementia is not one single condition, but refers to a series of symptoms produced by a number of diseases all of which run devastating courses. Alzheimer's disease is probably the most familiar to the general public because it has been the subject of so much discussion in print, radio, and television. The best estimates suggest that as many as 15 percent of the over-sixty-five population are afflicted with this dementia, a devastating condition producing marked deterioration of intellectual performance. As with other age-related disorders, dementia occurs with far greater frequency among the very old; 20 percent of the over-eighty population are afflicted. In all, over 4 million Americans suffer from some kind of dementia. Health economists estimated in 1985 that there was an $88 billion loss due to Alzheimer's and related dementias.

People with dementia suffer gradual memory loss, along with loss of problem-solving ability and other aspects of abstract thinking. There may be disorientation in time and space; personality changes; difficulty in communicating, word-finding, and learning; decreased attention span; and impaired judgment.

It's usually hard to pick up dementia when it begins. A woman may suddenly forget her way home for a minute or two. A man may forget why he went into a store. Someone may do something slightly outrageous—become abusive for no apparent reason, wear something inappropriate— for example, a heavy raincoat on a hot summer day. These episodes may be fleeting—coming and going, confusing everyone. Partners often find their own explanations for the bizarre behavior: "He's been working too hard," or "She's been under a lot of strain." Doctors may not pick up quickly since the early symptoms rarely follow a set pattern—a wife may feel generally that her husband is not himself but find it hard to put her finger on the exact problem. She may start wondering if there's something wrong with their relationship.

A husband may decide for himself that his wife's occasional episodes of disorientation are due to the medication she has been taking for depression and insist her doctor try a different prescription. Everyone flounders for a while until symptoms become more alarming and impossible to ignore. Changes become more marked as the disease progresses since it gradually strips away every functioning skill learned from childhood on—dressing, feeding, toileting, reading, following directions, remembering where one lives, using language skills, and finally, perhaps most tragic—no longer recognizing one's partner or other family members.

In addition to the severe impact of advanced dementia on intellectual functioning, the disease also can have profound effects on personality and Alzheimer's patients often display symptoms of depression, paranoia, and agitation that compound problems. These personality changes can make life even more difficult for partners and other caregivers.

Alzheimer's sufferers need increasing care and supervision as time goes on until eventually twenty-four-hour care is required, either at home or in an institution if the situation gets out of control and beyond the physical and emotional stamina of the family.

Although research has increased dramatically and much more is now known about the pathological changes that occur in the brain, there is no known cure or treatment for the symptoms of Alzheimer's disease or any of the other devastating related dementias. This is bad news for the large majority of the elderly now suffering these afflictions.

Making a diagnosis is not a clear-cut process. The symptoms people report to their doctors may seem to indicate dementia but may stem from other conditions that are treatable and hardly the dire life sentence that accompanies a diagnosis of Alzheimer's. Memory loss, confusion, and disorientation can be caused by depression, malnutrition, drug toxicity, or anemia. These conditions can also follow a severe illness or surgery or an accident. It is essential that medical specialists, preferably with geriatric training, be consulted to rule out other possible causes before a diagnosis of an irreversible dementia can be safely made. Moreover, patients need to be observed over a period of time.

One real benefit for victims of AD (Alzheimer's disease) and their relatives is the dramatic growth in the past decade of public awareness of the condition, its devastating effects on the family, and the extraordinary demands it places on the long-term-care system. Contributing to this public awareness has been the advocacy of the Alzheimer's Disease and Related Disorders Association, a national organization composed mainly of the families of AD victims. This association, organized in the mid-1970s, now has over 177 chapters in 46 states which provide essential information and counseling as well as support groups. All these are seen as lifesaving blessings by families who until recently struggled along by themselves. The motto of the association is "Someone to Stand By You."

There is little question that one of the greatest losses experienced by older people is the ability to function intellectually and to keep in touch with the world around them. For couples the destructive powers of AD are probably the most devastating, most tragic, and most feared of all diseases because as they advance they often totally destroy not only the mind but the relationship, too. Couples can no longer interact or communicate with each other. "Sue and I look at our family albums together and this interests her for a while, but she doesn't seem to recognize anyone," a husband remarked sadly at his support group meeting. "She's just as interested in pictures in *Life* magazine. She's forgotten everyone and everything! This damn disease has wiped out our whole life together."

SUBSTANCE ABUSE

We hear all the time about young drug and alcohol users in every community across the country, affluent suburbs as well as inner-city slums. And we know about grown-up users of both substances whose addictions affect their lives at home and at work. But we are less likely to think of Grandma and Grandpa's generation as addicts, except perhaps for a few aging "winos" and derelicts still hanging out on Skid Row.

It might surprise us to learn that 10 to 15 percent of all Americans over the age of sixty are alcoholics, just about the same percentage as in the general population. Alcoholism for some of the elderly is simply a continuation of a lifelong habit, but a significant number of others become alcoholics for the first time in old age. This new late-life dependence may be brought on by one tragic loss—the death of a partner—or by the painful effect of a whole panoply of conditions experienced as losses: retirement, distance from children, financial pressure, declining health. A drink may seem at first to soothe the pain, but then another is needed and another. Soon the latecomer is just as dependent as the lifetime addict. The diagnosis of alcoholism is relative. It depends less on how much is drunk or how often than on its effect on the individual's physical and emotional health.

One partner may notice changes in the other's behavior, which may become hostile, abusive, and uncontrolled at times, but never be willing to admit that alcohol is the cause until someone suggests it, and even then may fight. "What do you mean Daddy's drinking too much? How can a few drinks hurt him? Something else must be wrong!" a mother may reply angrily if her son raises the A-word. She may, indeed, be ignorant, or she may refuse to admit her husband's problem out of shame or anger, or she may even encourage the habit out of a misguided belief that the "few drinks" anesthetize their own troubled relationship.

> Pat and Pete Stein, now that they were both retired, could enjoy a relaxed drink or two before dinner. The "happy hour" became a treasured ritual for them, and friends often joined them. After a while their one or two drinks turned into heavier and heavier drinking. Sometimes they both completely forgot about dinner. As time went on, their health deteriorated, but they blamed "getting old," and continued to reassure each other that their "one or two drinks" every night didn't hurt.

A few drinks *can* hurt because alcohol often does not have the same effect in late life as it did in earlier years. Tolerance decreases with age because older bodies detoxify alcohol more slowly. The moderate drinking of a younger man can turn into an older man's dangerous dependency. Alcoholism may be blamed for an alarming variety of afflictions in addition to inappropriate behavior, including lapses in memory, confusion, insomnia, falls, poor grooming, uncontrolled diabetes, and hypertension.

Drug addiction—with results similar to those of alcoholism—may also be a late-life development. Older people are less likely than younger ones to resort to illegal drugs. They are sometimes called "accidental addicts" because their late-life addiction may come about

through perfectly innocent channels when the drugs obtained completely legally are overused. Prescription or over-the-counter drugs for
insomnia or for pain may become seriously addictive although users,
and sometimes their partners, too, may be unaware of what is happening or refuse to admit a problem.

Substance abuse must not be ruled out as a possible cause of unex-
plained physical complaints or deviant behavior or mental functioning.
But this cause is likely to be carefully hidden and loudly denied
by individual partners or by couples as a team until a crisis forces a
confession.

THE RELUCTANT PARTNER

When physical illness strikes, most people are likely to seek health care.
When mental problems occur, most people do not, or they wait it out
until a serious situation develops. This disparity is particularly strong for
older people, many of whom belong to the generation brought up to
feel there is a stigma attached to needing psychiatric help. They are
often ashamed of their problems, reluctant to admit them, or deny they
exist at all. The same denial plays an important part in seeking help for
sensory impairment. It's not unreasonable to be terrified about facing
the fact that we are losing our minds, our sight, or our hearing. It's
easier to hide from reality as long as we can.

But the piper must be paid! Denial is a Band-Aid at best and the
problems left untreated do not go away. They intensify. Early interventions that might prevent further deterioration have no chance to work.

Well partners can make a critical difference. If they refuse to play the
denial game, they may be able to encourage their ailing partners to ask
for help.

> Harry Gregg kept insisting that his recent lapses of memory were
> due to fatigue. So what if he forgot his own address one day? It
> was just a short lapse—nothing to make a fuss about. His wife,
> calmly but persistently, refused to allow his excuses and eventu-
> ally got him to go to his own doctor, who referred him to a
> neurologist. The diagnosis—an operable brain tumor—ex-

plained his recent lapses, and a successful operation was performed.

Some partners join in the same denial game. They form a denial team with the ailing one. Their teamwork is particularly dangerous when it comes to substance abuse. Because the addiction is far from easy to give up, alcoholics often pretend it doesn't exist. If their partners reject the pretense, there is a better chance for treatment. But partners frequently go right along with the pretense. One may say, "Jack loves to have a few drinks before dinner," dismissing the few drinks as a harmless pleasure and never specifying how many drinks make "a few." Even more serious is the situation where both partners are addicted and both blithely deny any problem exists until a crisis forces the truth.

INFORMATION IS THE BEST DEFENSE

In the good old days before the miracles of late-twentieth-century medicine, health care was in the hands of a relatively small group—physicians, surgeons, nurses, and technicians. It usually involved a personal relationship between doctor and patient. Patients generally did not expect to know much about what was wrong with them. They put themselves in the hands of higher authorities—their doctors—whose words were taken as law. No wonder the image of doctor-as-god came into being.

Today health care is a giant industry with anonymous millions of workers turning out a product to be used by consumers formerly known as patients. The system is a sprawling maze that is bewildering for lay people to comprehend once they get sick. The best defense for the elderly and their partners is to develop some basic understanding of the system, the various professionals who run it, and how to deal with it. They may be surprised to discover that health-care professionals, far from resenting them, expect "consumers" to be armed with information and prepared to make decisions on their own behalf. If patients are unconscious or demented, informed proxies should be on hand to make decisions for them. Research studies and the clinical observations of health-care professionals seem to agree that knowledgeable patients who take an active role in their own recovery usually fare much better.

INFORMED PATIENTS AND THEIR PARTNERS

"Partners in Care" has become the popular slogan of health care in the 1990s; gone are the days of passive obsequiousness to the "expert." Doctors' orders are essential, but they can now be questioned rather than followed blindly. There are several reasons for this transformation. Being sick puts patients in a subservient, dependent position. They get an emotional shot in the arm when they feel they are active participants in their own recovery and may become more optimistic and upbeat. Active participants are more likely to follow directions—taking medicine regularly, keeping to dietary plans, following through on rehabilitation programs.

Finally, let's face it—the squeaky wheel gets attention. Active patients are likely to demand their rights and get better care; this may even involve questioning diagnoses or getting second or third opinions. Doctors, nurses, and other professionals are busy and sometimes overburdened—they have their own problems to negotiate in the system and endless bureaucratic regulations to deal with. They work in a world of complicated high-tech medicine and sometimes their judgments require review. Getting a second opinion need not imply that a physician is inept. It only means there may be more than one way to solve a problem, and feedback from more than one source can be a lifesaver.

Ideally, partners in health care should be a trio, not a duo—the doctor, the patient, and the husband, wife, or companion who is well. An uninformed partner can be a drag on recovery even when the ailing partner is actively in charge. It is essential for both partners to know exactly what's going on, since the healthy one may be called on to make decisions when the patient is comatose, unconscious, or demented.

EXAMINING THE DOCTORS

If we intend to be active consumers, we have to check out the medical care we receive. We may have a beloved family doctor who has taken care of all of us for years, but is he up on the latest in geriatric care? Test him out, and if he does not measure up, remember there's more than one doctor in the world. Ideally, this testing should be done before anyone is ill, but it's never too late to test or to change.

Old bodies are not the same as young bodies; the difference is so significant that a whole new specialty of geriatric medicine has developed. While this specialty has still only a relatively few practitioners, there is plenty that general internists and family doctors can learn about treating older patients. There's nothing wrong with checking out your doctor to see if he or she has had experience treating people your age. The confident physician—probably the competent one—will talk willingly with you and perhaps refer you to a colleague better equipped to help you. The defensive physician will resent "insubordination" and anyone who questions his or her credentials.

At the same time, you might check out how doctors feel about rehabilitation and how interested they are in helping patients function despite their impairments. Do not assume all doctors are sophisticated in these matters; many of them are disease-and-cure oriented and think little about functioning. You may also want to find out what your doctor feels about "life supports," "pulling the plug," "heroic measures," and "death with dignity," issues that have particular significance to many older couples.

If this were a perfect world, our doctors would all be Albert Schweitzers, Mother Teresas, or at least Marcus Welbys—but the world is far from perfect. Too often, doctors are overworked abiding by bureaucratic regulations and overwhelmed keeping up with the latest medical advances. They have to be ready to answer any patient who comes in waving the latest issue of the *New England Journal of Medicine* or a column by the *New York Times* medical writer Jane Brody.

They may tune in with intensity to the progress of a serious disease and give their all to terminal patients, but tune out when it comes to listening to old people's undramatic complaints about everyday aches and pains. They may not even like treating the elderly. Ageism still exists in this country and physicians are not immune from it. They may be terrified of their own old age. One doctor in a thriving practice complained regularly about all the seniors on his list, many of whom had grown old along with him. Since the elderly generally have more

ailments, he was overworked and overburdened. Furthermore, Medicare put a cap on legitimate charges. He talked with wistfulness of his
younger partners and their younger patients. Time for a change?

EXAMINING THE HOSPITALS

Hospitals are not all alike. They vary in quality of facilities, medical,
nursing, and technical staffs, atmosphere, and morale. The one with the
most impressive decor may not have the most impressive track record.
Picking the right hospital may be as important as picking the right
doctor. But even if the hospital has been carefully chosen, it can be an
alien world, especially terrifying to first-time patients. When they enter
the domain of "the experts," they must assume the passive role of "the
patient" twenty-four hours a day. Speaking at all is hard for patients
who are seriously ill and speaking *up* is even harder. It is comforting for
them to know that they have someone to speak up for them and this
is why partners and other relatives play a crucial role.

Whether you are a patient or a partner, there's no need to hang
around passively waiting to see what happens next. Together or separately, you can make some moves on your own, although this may not
be encouraged by the hospital staff. None of these moves may bring the
results you want, but they are worth trying and may be successful.

1. When you are first admitted as a patient, you or your partner
should try to learn as much as you can about the place, introduce
yourselves, and find out the names of staff personnel whenever
possible. Lines of communication are often opened up immediately
just by the exchange of names.

2. One of you should speak with the head nurse or whoever is in
charge of the floor or ward. Find out what the rules are, how you
can ask questions or register complaints without inconveniencing
routines. Ask if there is anything you can do to be helpful. Showing
your consideration for the staff's time and authority helps to
establish a good working relationship.

3. Speak with the medical staff—residents or chief residents—and make sure that communication is open between them and your own private physician. Find out the best way of getting information.

Once you have taken these steps, you and your partner are better prepared to handle problems when they come up. You have let it be known that neither of you will be a tiger, but that neither will be a pussy cat, either. The staff will know that your partner is not likely to lurk in the background sitting helplessly beside your bed or complaining to the wrong people but rather is there on your behalf ready to go to bat for you. Both of you may be full of questions and concerns and the staff will be much more responsive once a relationship has been established. Even if you cannot win over everyone, it's likely that you will identify at least one staff member who will be on your side.

> Moira Tilson was frantic about her husband's continuing high fever three days after his operation. Their physician was out of town and the chief resident was busy in surgery—no one seemed to be on top of his condition. Moira remembered she had established a good relationship with one of the floor nurses when her husband had been first admitted and was able to find her. The nurse made special arrangements for another resident to examine Tim immediately and leave orders for his treatment.

UNMARRIED COUPLES

Unmarried persons—hetero- or homosexual—may not be considered their sick partner's next of kin by hospital staff, and unless special arrangements have been made in advance, they may find themselves in a helpless situation when health-care decisions must be made. As noted in Chapter 9, it is recommended that both partners make arrangements with an attorney for a general and medical power of attorney, each one naming the other to handle medical and financial affairs in case of an incapacitating illness. If serious illness comes and no such legal preparations have been made, a lawyer should be consulted immediately.

EXAMINING HOME CARE

Largely because of escalating hospital costs there is now a greater reliance on home care. Some patients are not being admitted to hospitals at all; others are treated on an ambulatory basis. They are also being discharged much earlier when they have been treated as in-patients. Since the great majority of hospital patients are elderly, and since the recuperative powers of this age group are weak, they are likely to still need care once they leave the hospital, creating serious problems for those at home who must provide that care.

Home health agencies offering nursing and other types of care to patients in their homes have proliferated, but even when this kind of supplementary support is available, the greater burden falls on relatives and usually the patients' partners.

Long-term caregiving is discussed in Chapter 8. The emphasis here is on situations where short-term recovery is expected. Even though short-term, the demands may be heavy on healthy partners who may not be in the best of shape themselves. They may have to prepare special diets, supervise rehabilitation exercises, and perform a variety of nursing duties, including administering medications, monitoring IVs, and even giving injections.

Some insurance policies cover round-the-clock nursing care for a limited period and couples should avail themselves of this help if at all possible. But without this ongoing support, caregiving partners will have to rely on periodic visits of nurses or physiotherapists. Most agencies will take the needs of the family member into consideration and will offer special training.

Even though the burdens on caregivers may be heavy, there are real advantages to home care. Patients and caregivers are in charge in the home setting. They do not have to deal with the hospital bureaucracy or the impersonality of an institutional setting. The food is better! Perhaps most important is the fact that patients tend to do better physically and emotionally in familiar surroundings. They also are not exposed to infections that often are passed around in hospitals.

Unfortunately, there are situations in which the home is the wrong place for an older person who should be in a hospital, possibly having been discharged from a hospital prematurely. This is the time when the well partner, acting on behalf of the patient, may have to contact someone—a social worker or patient advocate in the hospital or the personal physician—who may be able to arrange for readmission to the hospital until a fuller recovery is in sight.

FEELING THE IMPACT

We all know about the possibility of a serious illness or disability in late life. These come with the territory, but even though they are to be anticipated, they are still capable of causing a crisis. Anticipating problems intellectually with our heads is not the same as experiencing them with our bodies. When the crisis comes, it draws all sorts of elements into its orbit—the patients and their partners, their closest relatives, and everyone's emotions. The mix may be explosive.

Negative, painful emotions are no different in older people than in younger ones but may be more prevalent because there's more in late life to trigger them. There is no surefire way to predict how any one individual will react. What is loss to one may not be to another. A wife may applaud a husband's uncomplaining acceptance of his hearing loss but be totally impatient with the ungodly fuss he makes about needing a partial denture. She knows that if she were in his shoes she'd be devastated by the hearing loss but a few teeth wouldn't bother her nearly so much. He may be disdainful of her unhappiness about losing her looks, something he feels is trivial. Or one loss may be taken well, so may the second and the third, but then one day there may be one loss too many:

> Jeff couldn't believe the way his eighty-one-year-old wife Anita carried on when their dog, Boswell, died. He missed the dog, too, but she was inconsolable. He kept urging her to "snap out of it" and commented that she hadn't been this bad when her father died or when she had her mastectomy two years earlier. What Jeff didn't realize was that Anita was mourning her father *and* her mother who had died years before, *and* her hearing that was fading, *and* the five teeth she'd lost to gum disease last winter, *and* the Thunderbird that sat in the garage because

neither she nor Jeff could see to drive anymore, *and* her breast! Now on top of all these she had to mourn Boswell.

Worrying about possible losses ahead, saying "What will happen to us if . . . ?" or "How will I manage if . . . ?," waiting for test results and diagnoses, uncertainty about the future—all these intangibles can trigger negative emotions. These are normal reactions and only become serious problems if they are prolonged and threaten someone's physical well-being. In some cases, however, these reactions may be an extension of lifelong emotional problems, such as manic-depressive or paranoid psychotic disorders. When emotional reactions are prolonged or extreme, regardless of their cause, professional help is advisable. Psychotherapy and/or drug therapy can usually relieve, if not eliminate, problems; no one should be forced to live out his or her life beset by painful emotions, yet this professional help is the kind many older people flatly reject out of ignorance or shame.

CHANGING BEHAVIOR

Sudden illness or declining health can change personality and behavior. It's not unusual to hear such reports as "My uncle's a different person since his stroke," or "I just don't know my grandmother anymore. She's like—dead!" The extrovert may become introverted. The giver may turn into the taker. The optimist may become the pessimist. The withdrawn may demand attention for the first time. It is not always the sick partner who changes—it's just as likely to be the well one. Behaviors never before exhibited in a relationship may come into play; illness may give them license to surface. If these changes are only transitory and eventually everything falls back into place, they can usually be tolerated. But if they are prolonged and unremitting, help may be necessary. Underlying them may be old conflicts that, once understood, would help to ease tensions all around.

Fran couldn't believe that Ed, her husband of forty years, had developed a serious alcohol problem. He'd been feeling blue since his retirement, but she never dreamed he'd resort to drinking as a solution. He never had when times were rough in the past. She was beside herself with anger and was barely able to talk to him. Only when she consulted a therapist and was helped to understand her unresolved lingering anger at her alcoholic father could she be more supportive of Ed.

Even after years of living in deepest intimacy, a new crisis may stir up strong emotions and provoke disturbing behavior patterns.

GOING IT ALONE

No matter how close to each other the two partners are in any relationship, illness is an individual matter. It cannot be shared. One endures the disease—the other stands by. Neither one can know exactly what the other is feeling. Illness happens to *me* or to *you*—it does not happen to *us*. We may have a joint bank account, but we cannot have a joint heart attack. Even if we love each other deeply, *I* cannot put myself in *your* shoes nor can you put yourself in mine. At times, even if genuine empathy and caring are being given and received, each partner is likely to have a sense of "going it alone." Trying to empathize too much with someone who is ill may be just the wrong thing to do. "Stop saying it hurts you as much as it does me! No way it does! I'm the one in pain! Just me! Never forget it! Me! Me! Me!" an invalid has been known to shout at his long-suffering partner.

A close relationship takes on a very different character when illness strikes. A whole set of feelings (hidden or exposed) have to be dealt with and behavior realigned. Consider these thoughts of well partners:

"Jane's sick and frail and I'll do everything I can to help her, but I'm still in great shape. I've got to think about myself, too."

. . .

"I can't believe I resent Pete for having that heart attack! But I do. He should have taken better care of himself. If he didn't want to consider himself, he should have thought of me."

"I try to be sympathetic, but I can't listen to Sally's complaints any more. I'm sick of illness and symptoms. There has to be something else in life."

And now for the other side and the ailing partners:

"He's always saying 'How about a movie? It'll do you good,' or a drive, or a visit. He pretends it's for me, but I know different. When I got sick, he caught cabin fever. He's the one who wants to get out. He's always done what he wanted to."

. . .

"I'm always in pain and Jeanne knows it, but I try not to complain. She tries to be understanding, but I know she tunes me out."

. . .

"I wonder what's in his mind. Is he thinking about what he'll do when I die? Where he'll go? *Who* he'll go with?"

The feelings of the sick and the well partner are usually distorted to a greater or lesser extent by guilt and anxiety. Both are frightened by signs of their own inevitable aging, both may feel guilty, but, like the illness that cannot be shared, their feelings may be difficult to share, too. A special tension enters their relationship, one that may never have been there before. If the two can get to the point of understanding what's going on and what each one can do to cope, they'll have a greater chance of developing a mutually supportive relationship.

SHIFTING ROLES OF THE WELL PARTNER

The healthy partner may suddenly be cast in a variety of new roles, some never even rehearsed before. Furthermore, depending on the sickness of the ailing partner, the healthy one often has to play some of the roles simultaneously.

Occasionally, this is not necessary, since some people, though seriously ill, never give up an inch of control of their health care, business affairs, household tasks, personal care, and even control of their partners, too. At the other extreme are invalids who fall completely to pieces and expect their partners to take over everything. The well partners may be expected to play their roles for the duration of the illness and the recovery, or even longer. The variety of roles include:

BYSTANDER

The poet John Milton's line "They also serve who only stand and wait" applies here to partners relegated to the sidelines. They may feel superfluous but they are not because, as they should be aware, they may eventually have to step in.

SOUNDING BOARD

This is related to the bystander role. Nothing much is asked of the well partner except to be there when needed and above all to listen patiently, if possible, to complaints and symptoms.

NURSE

Healthy partners who may not be in the best of shape themselves may have to give hands-on care to seriously ill ones. When the illness leads to chronic disability, this role assumes added importance. (See Chapter 8.) Even in the short run healthy partners may fulfill critical needs, although in the process their own lives are totally disrupted.

ADVOCATE

When extensive medical care or hospitalization is required, the partner-as-advocate plays an essential role—monitoring care, asking questions, interpreting answers, negotiating improvements in care, or just plain fighting for these.

MANAGER

Depending on the length of the illness, well partners may have to step in and take over tasks normally handled by the invalids. Some household responsibilities, financial arrangements, and business affairs cannot wait until sick partners get better. The manager may also handle medications, arrange for nursing help, and set up doctors' visits and therapy schedules.

ADVISER

Decisions proliferate when illness strikes: whether or not to have surgery, which doctors can be trusted, how much friends and relatives should be told. Some but not all of the decisions affect both partners. Unilateral decisions made by healthy partners may boomerang. They are likely to have greater success when acting as advisers, respecting the autonomy of the invalids, rather than as dictators.

DECISION-MAKER

A point may come—during surgery, coma, or advanced dementia, etc.—when a switch in roles is demanded and the healthy partners move from adviser to decision-maker. They may be asked to give permission for surgery or medications. However, they may not be allowed to make some decisions unless legal proxies have been given in advance. These proxies are particularly important when life-support systems are being considered. (See Chapter 9.)

INTERPRETER

The role of interpreter is of special importance and involves being a go-between for the doctor and the patient. The well partner can describe symptoms in the home situation that the doctor never sees when a patient is in his or her office or reveal problems the patient is too embarrassed to admit. The interpreter can explain doctors' orders and diagnoses that the patient might have been too upset to understand fully.

COMFORTER

A crucial role many partners play with varying success is that of comforter. It may be the hardest, since some people just have no bedside manner and don't know how to put on masks of good cheer. Others automatically know how to "be there" for their ailing partners, to perk them up, distract them from their physical and mental pain. But they cannot be superpeople. It's helpful if others can be brought in—a backup team of friends or relatives—to comfort the comforters.

DISCARDING THE SICK ROLE

Since the healthy partners have to assume such a variety of roles, it would seem as if there's little left for the ailing ones to do except play "patient" or act out the sick role, passively waiting for the care and direction of others. People with some chronic ailments can live quite independently, assuming they want to. Illness and disability, however, cover a wide variety and intensity of conditions. Many illnesses in late life are of short duration and recovery can be expected, although some residual handicap may remain.

The sick ones cannot expect other people, especially their partners, to live their lives for them. No one can enjoy life secondhand. Invalids have a job to do: to get better and to bring their lives back under their own control as quickly as possible. Clinging to the sick role may be a good attention-getter, but it discourages active participation in life and turns patients into dependent, second-class citizens. Some healthy partners have their own reasons for encouraging and perpetuating this dependency. Perversely, they seem to prefer to carry 100 percent of the burdens rather than relinquish any of the total control they have managed to gain at long last.

CAN YOU LIVE WITH IT?

For a host of chronic or degenerative health problems occurring in late life, there is as yet no cure, although new medical advances may change this sad reality one day. But no cure does not mean no help. Much can be done for many of these conditions to alleviate symptoms, control progress, or compensate for diminished functioning, although

Alzheimer's disease still remains beyond relief. Someone with orthopedic impairment can be trained to use special canes, a walker, and even a battery-operated wheelchair. The visually impaired can learn, with the guidance available at any of a growing number of vision-rehabilitation centers, how to utilize special devices that can help them make the best use of the vision that remains, and how to maintain their independence. A wide variety of hearing aids, as well as training in how to use them, are now available in hearing centers across the country.

While none of these appliances or devices promise cures, they can promise to improve the quality of daily life. But despite all the benefits they have to offer, they all have the same drawback: too few older people take advantage of them. Their attitude seems to be "There's no cure, so what's the good of halfway measures," even if the "halfway" measures could give them less pain or improved functioning. Their stubborn refusal has many causes.

REASON 1: I'M JUST GROWING OLD

Some impairments develop slowly, almost imperceptibly, over time. Older people with sensory impairments, or arthritic ones, are lucky. Time is on their side. No sudden crisis descends on them—no stroke, no heart attack, no surgery—that demands immediate attention. There is time to alter the habits of daily life, make accommodations in the home, and investigate devices and appliances to make living easier.

On the negative side, couples may confuse gradual impairment with normal aging. Brainwashed by familiar myths to expect a few things to go wrong as they grow older, both partners make little adjustments to them almost unconsciously. They may even be quite proud of how well they accept life's little infirmities. "What can we expect at our age?" one or the other may state with resignation or good grace. Meanwhile, their hearing or vision impairment or the crippling effects of their arthritis may worsen until the condition is beyond remedy.

REASON 2: COMPENSATING FOR EACH OTHER

Couples not only adjust and adapt to their own impairments, they sometimes find the perfect solution: one partner's strength makes up for the other's weakness.

> Fergie and Al were lucky. They managed well right into their eighties, although no one could say they were in great health. Diabetes had destroyed most of Al's vision, but Fergie's sight was still good so she was the driver. She had progressive arthritis, so he did all the heavy work around the house. His deafness was progressing, so Fergie tried to alert him to sounds he didn't hear. They used to laugh when they said, "We put two half-people together and got one whole person."
>
> When Fergie died, however, Alfred had to go into a nursing home. Because of their interdependent relationship he was only half a person again and could not function without her.

As they grow older, it is essential for both partners to take stock of individual disabilities and then try to improve their own individual functioning so that each one will be able to stand alone whenever this is necessary. Compensating for an impairment when it is not absolutely necessary can be a drawback rather than a benefit and may be one of the reasons widowers tend to function much more poorly.

REASON 3: VANITY! VANITY!

Special glasses, hearing aids, canes, and walkers are often rejected hands down by older men and women out of vanity. They are willing to be left out of conversations, to move with difficulty down the street, to see everything through a blur, rather than accept any device they feel stigmatizes them as old or detracts from their appearance. Designers of these devices have gone to great pains to improve the appearance of glasses and hearing devices just because of the negative attitudes of people who need them.

Partners can help each other see reason, but all too often they share the same prejudices. If so, they are likely to reinforce each other's negativism, thereby allowing deterioration to continue. One partner's positive attitude can play a decisive role in encouraging the other's attempts to be more independent.

REASON 4: GOING OVERBOARD

"You're as old as you feel!" may be a cliché but, like all clichés, it has a basis in truth. A disability may be a true handicap, but in one case it may hardly threaten independence while in another it will lead to total dependence. So much depends on each individual's outlook. One elderly widower, suffering from severely impaired vision in his early eighties, put on a green croupier's eyeshade and, with the help of a specially prescribed magnifier and a high-intensity light, read the *New York Times* every day from cover to cover. His twin sister, similarly impaired, referred to herself as "blind" and retired into total dependence on her even older husband.

With proper training and encouragement the partially disabled can learn to do much for themselves and be less dependent on others for managing daily routines. But it's not easy to change old habits, particularly for someone who enjoys the special treatment a disability inspires.

> After his stroke Frank was treated royally. His wife, Beth, doted on him: feeding, washing, and shaving him, taking him for long walks in his wheelchair every day. She willingly "gave up her life" for him. Beth's nephew, familiar with current poststroke rehabilitation techniques, questioned the need for his uncle's dependency. Soon it became clear to him that Frank really enjoyed being the center of everyone's concern and Beth enjoyed keeping him there. Although the nephew knew that with an electric wheelchair and the use of his good arm Frank could regain much independence and relieve some of the strain on Beth, he saw that he'd never budge them so he bit his tongue and kept quiet.

The climate in this country today is far more receptive to disabled people, young and old. The passage of the Americans with Disabilities

Act in 1990 marked a turning point in the expansion of opportunities and the removal of barriers for the disabled. The act provides for accessible environments not only in the workplace but in all public accommodations—transportation, restaurants, sidewalks, rest rooms. Instigated by vocal groups of younger disabled people, these advances can be shared by older ones as well. They can take advantage of the same rehabilitation techniques as the young—to strengthen impaired functions and to learn to use special devices that can enhance these functions.

A wife may feel she is loving if she can help her husband accept some limitations; her husband may feel he is loving if he can help her compensate for hers. It might never occur to either of them that they would be even more loving if they confronted each other's disabilities and took steps to help the other regain greater independence.

SELF-HELP—MUTUAL SUPPORT GROUPS

"I have no one to talk to—no one who really understands," a wife with advancing Parkinsonism sighs.

"What do you mean? You have me! You know how much I care about you," her wounded husband snaps back.

"Of course you care about me! But you don't have Parkinson's disease. You can't begin to understand what it's like for me!" she insists.

We can learn about a disease, watch its development, sympathize with its pain and discomfort, learn its symptoms, but that still does not make us really understand it. Only those who suffer it themselves know the whole truth. Someone with a disease can offer a fellow sufferer support and encouragement as well as valuable information. This is why increasing numbers of self-help support groups are springing up all over the country, many of them focusing on problems of late life. (See Appendix A.)

Seventy-eight-year-old Libby stopped going out and having company when her deafness became profound. This not only put an end to *her* social life but to her husband Gilbert's, too. She became seriously depressed and passed her despondent feelings over to him. The couple remained withdrawn and depressed until a nurse in their doctor's office began to talk to them about a nearby group of hearing-impaired older people. With some persuasion from Gilbert, Libby joined the group and found she was not alone. She saw how the others were able to deal with their hearing loss, and this encouraged her to go to a hearing-loss clinic to learn ways to deal with her own deafness.

No matter how loving partners are, they can never provide the understanding that comes from a shared experience. The emotional support offered to ailing partners by groups can ease the enormous burdens carried by healthy partners. As a result, they all may be able to enjoy a relationship that was impossible when illness created a barrier. Individual counseling, in addition to group support, may be advisable when couples find that an illness creates strains they cannot handle alone.

PAYING FOR HEALTH CARE

The country is in a health-care crisis, with millions uninsured and costs skyrocketing. While older people generally fare better than their younger counterparts because of the federally sponsored Medicare program, there are still untold conditions and procedures for which they are uninsured, and threatened cutbacks in the program make the future uncertain. Planning in advance to supplement Medicare as well as stockpiling enough savings to cover unpredictable uninsured costs was urged in Chapter 6. It's easier to recommend these suggestions than it is to act on them. For many couples approaching old age today, just keeping up with yearly expenses drains their resources and turns insuring or saving into impossible fantasies.

Couples with only limited income and few assets can apply for Medicaid, a state-federal program of medical support. The local Office on Aging or the United Way can be helpful in negotiating the necessary steps for applying. Voluntary agencies for specific diseases or conditions—vision- and hearing-rehabilitation agencies and the Arthritis

Foundation, for example—may also be helpful. Appliances such as hearing aids and glasses—except after cataract operations—are not covered by Medicare and many insurance policies, although there are states that do provide some coverage.

As of 1992, the time of this writing, justifiably violent criticism is being leveled at the nation's health care. How to revamp the entire system is a major issue in the year's presidential election, with each candidate offering his own version. As yet there is no clear-cut blueprint, but some important issues do come through loud and clear: the country is awake to the need for change in the delivery of health care; public resentment is growing over the ever-soaring costs of care and cure; public awareness is also growing at the disastrous lack of long-term-care provisions for any age. Older couples in particular have to scramble around looking for insurance policies to cover institutional or home care for themselves. When they finally find such policies, they may discover they cannot afford them or they are too late to apply. They may also discover they have only each other to turn to for long-term care.

The Beatles' song "When I'm Sixty-four," mentioned in the first chapter, is relevant now once again in its revised version. It's not unreasonable for wives, husbands, and companions to wonder if their partners will still need them and feed them when they're eighty-four, an age when long-term caregiving may well become a reality, not a hypothetical question.

Did he rage against the cruel fates
who had crippled his limbs and
sapped his strength? And she?
Obeying her wedding vows, did she
dutifully tend his needs? Yet did she
often drift silently to the window to
watch the world live on without
her?

Or, no longer enmeshed in palace
affairs, did they both treasure the
days and hours they had just for
each other, knowing full well that
these would not go on much
longer?

CARING AND COPING

SCENE: A bedroom, obviously a sickroom. Two figures lie in a double bed center stage. Both bodies are motionless, but neither is sleeping—their thoughts keep them awake.

She thinks: Another day finished. Just like yesterday. Just like tomorrow. It's a treadmill—from the sickroom to the bathroom to the kitchen and back again. It'll start all over again in just a few hours. It never stops until I get into bed at night and then I'm too tired to sleep. How long can I go on caring for him like this? It's draining the life out of me. What if I get sick? What'll happen to us then? Some-

He thinks: She's not sleeping either. I can tell. She's just lying there thinking like she does every night. What's she thinking? She won't tell me. We don't talk anymore. Just "Time for your medicine"; "Is the pain bad?"; "The nurse will be here in an hour." Great conversation! God! How we used to talk! But what's to talk about now? Nothing ever happens. I wonder if she hates me. I

times I'm so angry I want to hit out at someone. I know it's not his fault, but sometimes I hate him. On a real bad day I even hope he'll die—just so I'd be free—so I could sleep. No! No! I don't mean that. How could I live without him? I hate what that stroke's done to us. I don't hate him. I love him. If I put my arms around him and hug him, maybe I can sleep.

wouldn't blame her. How many years since that damned stroke? Four? No, five? It must be hell for her. But what about me? What have I got? Nothing. She can dress herself, fix what she wants to eat for herself, get to the bathroom herself. She goes out, she still sees people, takes walks, goes swimming. She still has some life left. Not me. I hate her. No, I don't. I hate what that stroke's done to us. If she puts her arms around me like she does some nights, maybe I'll be able to sleep.

Nowhere is the burden of caregiving heavier than when one partner is permanently disabled or suffers a chronic degenerative condition and the other partner becomes the primary caregiver—a future in store for many couples growing old together. This caregiving is far different from the kind described in the previous chapter, which dealt with serious but short-term illness and partial disability. The care then may be burdensome but has an end in sight. Long-term caregiving goes on and on until the death or institutionalization of one or the other partner—an average of three years.

Most people can deal with crises. Their adrenaline rises and they often surprise themselves at how well they cope with tragedy, adversity, or disaster. But a crisis usually has a time limit. Eventually, things will ease up, perhaps not ideally but at least bearably. Life will resume a normal pattern.

When Sam Parker had his heart attack at sixty-eight, he and Ronnie, his wife, were reassured by the optimistic prognosis they were given by their doctor. Sam would have to take it easy, but if all went well, he'd be back to normal living after a few months. Without a second thought, Ronnie took an unpaid leave from her job and devoted herself to helping Sam through his convalescence. Both of them managed to stay generally cheerful and in good spirits because they knew that everything would get back to normal pretty soon. When Sam's older brother, Syd, developed multiple sclerosis and became increasingly incapacitated, Ronnie and Sam were endlessly concerned and full of helpful advice for Syd and for Janice, his wife. "We understand!" they kept repeating with genuine empathy as they offered still another suggestion. They couldn't fathom why nothing they said or did seemed to improve Janice's or Syd's morale. "We've been there! We know what it's like! Why won't they listen to us?" they kept asking each other in frustration.

The older couple didn't listen because it was obvious that the younger one had not "been there." There was no comparison between their two situations. As the months passed, Sam knew he would get steadily better, and as the months passed, Syd knew he would only get steadily worse. Quite a difference! For one couple there was light at the end of the tunnel; for the other there was nothing at the end of the tunnel—only death. For such couples the old clichés won't work: "You'll feel better soon." "It can't go on forever."

Caregiving comes in many different intensities, depending on the stage of the illness and, to some extent, the needs of the patient. Although the first diagnosis of a chronic disabling illness—mental or physical—usually comes as a devastating shock, intensive care does not start immediately. In the initial stages daily life may seem little changed. The patient may need a watchful eye, ongoing supervision of medication, a special diet, help with tasks that require fine coordination— knotting a tie, lacing shoes, putting on stockings, applying makeup. This can be seen as a warm-up period for caregivers, giving them time to prepare themselves for challenges ahead. It can also be a period of denial. Jane Bendetson described this denial of her husband's illness in a 1991 *New York Times* column, "The Caretakers":

Clinging to hopes, chasing impossible dreams became a triumphant way of life. Those were years of denial on both our parts, pretending to ourselves and to each other that everything was all right. We could still claim walking was difficult because of wind, rain, cold, heat. But there were more and more bottles of pills, more attacks. . . . Gradually the walls of his invalidism enclosed him.

Since the invalid's needs increase in intensity as the disease progresses, the demands on the caregiver therefore intensify, too. By contrast, there is hardly any warm-up period for caregivers of stroke victims, who may go from independence to dependence overnight and need intensive care from the first day they come home from the hospital.

Most of us can picture the duties of a nurse in a hospital, but few of us give a thought to those who perform many of the same duties, plus a host of other ones, in the home. We'd have a hard time imagining what we'd be "in for" if we ever became caregivers. Here's a rough rundown of what can be involved when a patient needs intensive care: Always remember this care knows no letup. It must be given round-the-clock, 7 days a week, 365 days a year. Nurses work in shifts—the caregivers don't know about such luxuries. Sheets may have to be changed several times a day if patients are incontinent, baths and sponge baths have to be given, bedpans emptied, medication administered at regular hours. Special care must be taken of the skin to avoid bedsores. There will be piles of laundry and special cooking. Nutritious meals must be made appetizing enough to tempt listless appetites. Don't forget the between-meal snacks. Doctors' orders must be followed and reports on patient progress prepared.

Patients must be encouraged to maintain as much independence as possible. Their morale must be considered, too. It needs constant boosting. Patients can be difficult, discouraged, irritable, demanding, suspicious, or resentful, but care is still expected to be performed with cheerfulness, compassion, understanding, humor, and, whenever possible, with love.

WHO CARES?

We allow ourselves to be reassured by reports showing that only a small percentage of the nation's elderly, overall, are in nursing homes or need intensive care at home. But other reports are less reassuring. These show that more and more people are living into the later years—eighties, nineties, and above—the decades when serious disabilities can be expected and intensive caregiving is more likely to be needed. More and more couples are thinking these days about such eventualities. The pros, cons, and pitfalls of long-term-care insurance—whether for care at home or in a nursing home—is a favorite topic of discussion at any senior get-together. The need for a caregiver in the future may be a deciding factor for couples, middle-aged and older, to find a "significant other," to marry, remarry, or even to stay married. A seventy-eight-year-old bridegroom thought himself very funny when he introduced his newly acquired bride as "my long-term-care insurance." The joke might lose its humor for him if he ever stopped to realize that one day *he* might also be *hers*.

Traditionally, the caregiver role has been assumed by, or assigned to, women—wives, daughters, and other female relatives. It was understandable why this one-sided caregiving took place in the past when women were at home, but it is somewhat surprising that the pattern continues now that women have joined men in the workplace. Although many wives are indeed cared for by their husbands, many men turn to other relatives to help them out. Some experts suggest that men seem to cope better as caregivers and with less stress, perhaps because they are used to running things, giving orders, taking charge, delegating responsibility. Women may be more stressed because they have always expected to take care of everyone by themselves. Even when they are older and the burden heavier, many would rather martyr themselves than ask anyone for help.

In *Our Kind of People* the critic Jonathan Yardley gives an account of his parents' long and gratifying life together. It was a close and mutually supportive relationship, but when his father's health was beginning to fail, Helen, his mother, surprised everyone. "My greatest fear," she used to say, "is that when Daddy needs someone to care for him all the time and we don't have the money to pay for it, I'm going to have to nurse him myself. I just don't know how I can face it." When she did have to face it, she felt oppressed, but according to her son, she was a coconspirator in that oppression. "Helen was a prisoner, to be sure," he wrote. "But not merely of her husband: she was also a prisoner of her generation and her upbringing, both of which taught that a woman's first duty is to her husband."

Yardley's mother was of the old school, but women today are still seen as the prime caregivers for aging relatives. Wives are seen as the main caregivers for husbands. "I don't need a nursing home!" shouted old widowed Sol Weiner to his exhausted daughter after a stroke left him paralyzed. "Just get me a wife. Any old widow will do. She doesn't even have to be Jewish."

Old patterns are changing. Younger men are expected to share housekeeping and parenting responsibilities when their wives work. Even older men and women who have done little of this sharing in the past are showing signs of change, too. Studies show that some older women, freed from parenting and domesticity, are leaving home for work just at the point when their retiring husbands are leaving work for home, some men even becoming more nurturing in late life while their wives become more action-oriented. Although the current generation of senior wives expect to care for their husbands, there are some older women—independent thinkers or those influenced by the example of their daughters and granddaughters—who resent giving up their freedom in late life and being forced back into the caregiving role.

Despite the changes in attitudes, doctors today are still likely to take it for granted that the woman will automatically accept the main caregiving responsibility for her husband. When the wife is incapacitated, the same doctors are more likely to help her husband locate outside help for her care.

The equilibrium formerly operating between two people is bound to be upset when either of them develops an irreversible chronic condition. One partner then becomes the caregiver and the other the care-receiver. These new roles are likely to dominate their relationship, overshadowing other roles that previously had meaning for them separately or together: breadwinner, parent, grandparent, companion, playmate, sexual partner, etc.

THE CAREGIVER GAINS THE SPOTLIGHT

Unless someone close to us is afflicted, few of us probably give much thought to those suffering from a chronic disabling condition or to the people caring for them. Most of them just drift out of sight. If any concern is shown, it usually goes to the invalids. Their caregivers—partners and close family members—remain shadowy figures lurking in the background even though their efforts make it possible for aging relatives—in the millions—to stay out of institutions. They struggle along alone. A national study updated in the late 1980s showed that 75 percent of all personal care needed by the elderly was provided by an informal unpaid network of family and friends and not by hospitals, nursing homes, clinics, and social agencies.

Although their burdens continue to be heavy, family caregivers are no longer so invisible. They are finally receiving well-deserved and long-overdue credit and concern. Special recognition is going to husbands, wives, and the "significant others" who still provide most of the long-term care at home for their ailing partners. Without this care, more disabled people would face institutionalization much earlier.

This overdue recognition is reflected in the marked increase in services specifically designed for caregiver needs. Among the most beneficial of these are provisions for respite time, a vital safeguard against caregiver burnout since it makes it possible for overworked men and women to have some time just for themselves. Equally beneficial has been the growth of support groups found in a variety of places—nursing homes, day centers, disease foundations—where overburdened partners have a chance to blow off steam. Here they can share their burdens, exchange know-how, and find emotional support. In these groups many caregivers find their first antidote to the loneliness that is so often a consequence of their situation. The Alzheimer's Association began its support groups in 1981 to help caregivers combat burnout. These have now grown into a nationwide network of over two thousand groups. A recent addition to caregiver support is the Well Spouse Foundation, whose slogan is "When One Is Sick, Two Need Help." The foundation has established local chapters in nearly twenty states. (See Appendix A.)

DESIGN YOUR OWN PATTERN

At the early onset of some chronic condition, most of us, like Jane Bendetson earlier in this chapter, keep playing the denial game. We don't want to know what we're in for. When we are actually put to the test and called on to become caregivers, most of us are unprepared and have no idea how we will measure up or if we will measure up at all. Few of us are as forthright as Helen Yardley. Although sharing her fears, we'd probably feel ashamed to admit them. There seems to be something unacceptable about not wanting to care for people we love.

Not everyone is cut out for caregiving, any more than everyone is cut out for parenting. Some people—not just women—seem born to be caring and nurturing. Others become caregivers voluntarily out of a sense of duty or obligation. And still others have the role thrust on them and accept it reluctantly, as Helen Yardley did:

> *She felt obliged to quit her job at St. Michael's so as to devote herself to him full-time, but devotion is not what she felt; she was deeply resentful, because the nursemaid's role she had so feared now loomed before her and because she could see her life slipping away before she had lived it to the full.*

There are plenty of helpful guides for caregiving but no clear universal pattern—one that balances the needs of the receiver with the limitations of the giver. Such a pattern is impossible because couples must find a style suited to their own lives and personal habits. Care must obviously be provided when it is needed, but there is no right or wrong way to give it.

Patterns are woven from many different threads: the marital relationship, the economic circumstances, family values and ethnic heritage. Add to these the egos, strengths and weaknesses, physical and mental stamina of individual caregivers, and never forget the motivation of each one or their hidden agendas.

Take, for example, a hypothetical but familiar situation: A couple—call them Jay and Lori—have been married forty-seven years. They are retired, but with a small pension, their Social Security check, and a few investments, they are reasonably comfortable financially. Jim, at seventy-seven, suffers a stroke and is left partially paralyzed. Lori brings him home from the hospital and cares for him until he dies four years later. These are the bare facts devoid of any real human element—the pain, the tears, the losses. Jay and Lori are stick figures, not flesh-and-blood characters. What were these four years like for them? Let's try out a few possible scenarios.

SCENARIO 1

As a couple, Lori and Jay have always been together-forever types. Even though they had two children—now grown and gone—they have been more wrapped up in each other than in anyone else. Lori, panicked at the thought of losing Jay, was willing to devote her entire life and energy to his care. She gave up her volunteer work at the hospital, stopped playing the organ in her church, and rarely left the house except for shopping or taking Jay to the doctor or physiotherapist. Her children and other relatives, worried about the physical strain on Lori, in time gave up offering help or suggestions because they were always turned down. When Jay died, Lori, although isolated from the world, had no regrets. She and Jay had been inseparables; they were like the pair in "The Old Gray Couple," a poem by Archibald MacLeish:

> *Ours is the late, last wisdom of the afternoon.*
> *We know that love, like light, grows dearer towards*
> *the dark.*

SCENARIO 2

Lori knew that Jay would need constant care, but there was no way she was going to go it alone. The two had always followed parallel tracks. Although they shared many activities, each one had different interests and even different friends. She was unwilling to sacrifice her life for him and was sure he would not do this for her either. "I have to think of myself, too," she often explained almost defensively. But she was determined he would have all the care he needed. She made use of supportive services in their town, enlisted help from friends and relatives, and set up a weekly schedule—a morning here, an afternoon or evening there—for visitors to keep Jay company so she could go out. It wasn't easy, and things got even harder during the last year when Jay became virtually helpless. Lori was aware of criticism, coming mainly from *his* relatives, but she never gave up and as a result had some life left for herself after Jay died. Did she ever have twinges of guilt for having left him alone so much? Yes, but only occasionally.

SCENARIO 3

Jay had always played around and Lori had always known about his affairs. She'd suffered his infidelity in silence through the years, turning a deaf ear to rumors and a blind eye to obvious clues, because she was terrified that one day he would leave her for one or another of his girlfriends. After his stroke she willingly devoted herself to his care night and day, rarely accepting help or even seeming to need much time for herself. Her rewards for her efforts came from the fact that finally, after forty-seven years, she knew where Jay was every night and that she was the only person he needed. He literally could not live without her! That made everything she had to do worthwhile.

SCENARIO 4

Jay had been a tyrant all through their marriage and Lori had been his willing slave, although she knew enough to escape when he was drinking heavily. Despite Jay's semihelpless condition, he still tried to crack the whip. But she was forced to make some decisions on her own and to follow her own instincts. Finally, one day for the first time in forty-seven years, she flatly disobeyed an order from Jay. Eventually, she was running everything—even presiding over the liquor closet, deciding how much Jay could drink and when. She gave him excellent care, even putting her own health at risk, but nothing bothered her because she was in control of her life—and Jay's, too.

THE PLEASURES OF CAREGIVING

It seems hard to believe that there can be much pleasure in a couple's life once one side becomes invalided. But according to firsthand reports, there can be not only pleasure but gratification and satisfaction, too. Although admitting that much changes radically for the worse once a chronic condition takes over, couples are often surprised that there can be changes for the better, too.

> Sylvia Cavell retired after Linc, her husband—a former archi-tect—became wheelchair-bound with arthritis. She was ambiv-alent about this move, because she loved Linc but thrived on the stimulation she received from teaching, too. To their surprise they realized they'd both been so busy first with their children and then with their careers that they'd had little time just for each other, to really talk, to discuss ideas or books or paintings. "Those years after Linc got sick were in some ways the most intellectually stimulating of our marriage," Sylvia used to say. "They weren't easy years for either of us, but I wouldn't have missed them."

Whether intellectually stimulating or not, just having *time together* may be satisfying enough. Life for most couples is full of distractions. The middle years are crowded with work, earning a living, family obligations. Even when retired, differing interests or hobbies pull part-ners in opposite directions. Togetherness is limited. Caregivers often complain about an overabundance of togetherness, but some are grate-ful for the closeness, intimacy, and serenity, particularly when there's so little time left.

"How do you do it? How do you give so much?" a niece asked her weary aunt who was just emerging from her husband's sickroom, carrying his dinner tray. "We still have him with us, and that's the only thing that matters. I'll get plenty of rest later," was her aunt's answer. She was able to feel satisfaction despite the heavy physical and emo-tional burdens because of her deep devotion to her husband and her own strong nurturing personality.

Ironically, a couple's relationship may improve rather than deterio-rate during the caregiving years. The not-so-quiet despairers, for in-stance, whose lives have been spent in an endless tug-of-war and power struggle, may find an end to their war games when one becomes an invalid. Illness may place one permanently on the sidelines while the other gains the crown—but by default. When there is no need to compete anymore, both sides are likely to mellow. Peace at last!

Studies seem to show that caregivers who find rewards in their situation experience a greater degree of well-being than those who find nothing but frustration, depression, and resentment. It isn't necessarily the number of bedpans to be emptied, the number of wet sheets to be changed, the number of back rubs to be given that makes caregiving bearable or unbearable—it's whether the caregivers find pleasure to balance the pain of their burdens.

THE FRUSTRATIONS AND STRESSES

Gerontologists suggest that when healthy partners care for sick ones they suffer less than when children are the caregivers for their aging parents. This does not mean that partners have it easy. Frustration, stress, and negative feelings can be expected by even the most dedicated caregiver—days when patience is stretched to the limit, energies drained, tempers in danger of exploding, tears ready to flow.

Even when the care is not yet intense and a couple's life is not yet seriously disrupted for either the giver or the receiver, caregiving may seem an unwelcome stressful burden that can only become heavier as the need intensifies. So much depends on the relationship of the two people involved. If they have always been adversaries, bitter toward each other or disappointed with each other, it's not surprising that caregiving—at any level—would represent the final blow in a miserable relationship.

The relationship may not have been so unpleasant but simply lacking in closeness and intimacy. When a couple has worked out an amicable yet remote relationship—each one living a somewhat separate life—this satisfying equilibrium gets thrown off balance when one gets ill and needs care from the other. Instead of separate lives, they are now forced to share one life, and what's worse must live it together in unaccustomed closeness and uncomfortable intimacy. The caregiver may accept the responsibility out of a sense of duty, but is bound to feel stressed and resentful at the same time.

Overstressed caregivers often complain of insomnia, depression, fatigue, and emotional instability, but these problems cannot always be blamed on problematic marital relationships or individual personalities. External factors beyond the control of the caregiver can be equally stress-producing:

• *The illness of the invalid.* The heavier the duties, the greater the stress for the caregiver.

• *The financial situation.* If there is no money to pay for extra help, the main burden and therefore the greatest stress falls on the caregiver.

• *Support from other family members and friends.* If this support, emotional as well as practical, is lacking, the caregiver feels more alone and the burdens seem heavier.

• *Criticism from relatives or even from neighbors and friends.* Morale is lowered and stress increased when criticism, direct or implied, undermines the caregiver's efforts.

Perhaps the most important of all the external factors is the health of the caregiver, for if this person breaks down, the whole system breaks down, too. Since caregivers of elderly invalids are usually getting old themselves, they are likely to have some chronic physical ailment of their own. This in itself may not be serious but, coupled with the strain of their responsibilities, can be dangerous. Furthermore, caregivers are often so involved with their partners' health that they tend to forget about their own. Disintegrating knee joints, spinal discs, heart disease, high blood pressure, strokes, and cancer are not infrequent afflictions of caregivers. Gerontologists refer to these men and women as "the hidden patients," who are less likely to watch their weight, follow diets, take regular exercise, and worse yet, more likely to ignore symptoms until these turn into serious or even life-threatening illnesses that force them from the scene temporarily or perhaps permanently.

> Clare Simmons devoted her life to Ben, her husband of fifty-five years, never complaining about her round-the-clock duties as emphysema slowly disabled him. Because she was always focusing on his problems, she paid no attention to her weight loss or her constant thirst, both symptoms of diabetes. Her children put

the weight loss down to catering nonstop to their father's needs and tried unsuccessfully to get her to slow down. Although she saw Ben's doctors regularly, she never mentioned her own symptoms, and one day she was found in a diabetic coma by her daughter. Their children then had to worry about the welfare of two deteriorating parents rather than one.

While everyone, caregiver included, tends to focus concern on the one who is sick, the invalid is not always the first to die. It is not unusual for a caregiver, seemingly strong and in good health, to suffer a sudden and fatal heart attack or stroke. One caregiving wife, who was forced because of her own deteriorating health to institutionalize her husband after eleven years of caring for him, was surprised to see so many men in the nursing home. She was told they were there because their wives had died and that they were still angry at these caregivers for deserting them.

THE INVALID AS STRESS-GIVER

Never underestimate the invalid as a source of stress. The care-receiver's behavior and moods can add to the caregiver's burdens or lighten them. "I don't know her anymore," a bewildered husband may sigh. "She's had a personality change since her stroke. Nothing I do is right! I don't know how to deal with her! What is it she wants?" What she wants, undoubtedly, is for him to give her back her health. That's just what no one can do. She knows it but cannot accept it.

Anger, anxiety, fear, and depression frequently accompany a terminal or disabling illness: rage at the fates, anxiety and fear over the loss of independence, depression at loss of control, loss even of self and identity. There's nothing surprising about these emotions, and it can be a good thing for invalids to ventilate them. It is not a good thing when the sick ones unleash their fury on the well ones who care for them, thereby creating a hostile and depressing atmosphere for everyone. This increases the stress on caregivers, who are not supposed to fight back. If they do relieve their stress by retaliating in kind, they then usually experience great guilt, which in turn increases stress and brings them back to square one. While fighting may have been natural for a couple in the past, caregivers often feel they have been given a gag order and are no longer allowed this luxury.

There may not be any personality changes at all. The invalids may simply keep on behaving the way they've always behaved. The complainers are likely to keep on complaining, the sadistic to keep on giving injury, the bitter to keep on spreading their bile. Their partners, having stuck it out through the years, obviously have learned to handle these destructive traits. But when disability comes and life closes in on them both, the traits are harder to accept and make the caregiving routines harder than ever. Despite advanced Parkinson's disease, the self-centered, egotistic, tyrannical husband may still keep control of his long-suffering obedient wife. He may be disabled and helpless, but her lifelong pattern of subservience makes her incapable of disobedience, and she may eventually break down as she struggles in vain to satisfy him.

LAST STRAWS FOR CAREGIVERS

It's human to have pet hates, things that grate on our nerves or set our teeth on edge—most of us have them. Caregivers, being human, have theirs, too—one particular facet of their situation that is particularly distasteful. If you were to ask a few caregivers what in their situation they find most painful, the hardest to cope with, particularly distasteful, you would get a variety of answers:

> "*The loneliness*. I used to be a people person—so was Jeff—but now we hardly see anyone. He can't get out and hardly anyone comes to visit anymore. Someone told me that Mother Teresa said she'd seen all the pain and suffering in the world and the greatest suffering of all is loneliness. Look at me! I'm proof that Mother Teresa is right!"

> "*The sleeplessness*. That's what's breaking me. I haven't had a full night's sleep since Marie got sick. It's not her fault. It's the pain that keeps waking us both. I dream about sleep. I can taste it! If only I could sleep for a week. That's all I need."

"The wet sheets. I don't mind all the bedpans, but changing those sheets! It's killing me. The worst is getting up in the night when he wets the bed. That's when I think about a nursing home. Maybe one day I'll have to do it."

"That blank look. I think that's the worst. Taking care of her isn't so bad. But that look—it kills me. Sometimes I think she really does know me—her eyes sort of light up. But most of the time she just looks at me like I'm a stranger. We've been married sixty-one years! I'm her husband. I love her. She loves me. Has she forgotten?"

"Me! I'm not the same me anymore. I hate what I am. Some days I'm the great dictator shouting and screaming—some days I'm the martyr bitching and wailing. I wasn't always like this, was I? Cliff and I had a great life once, didn't we? We had fun with the kids, and with each other, too, didn't we? I hate to look at the me in the mirror. I don't know her—I don't like her either!"

GETTING YOUR LIFE BACK

When one partner takes care of the other, there can be a two-way power struggle between the sick one and the healthy one. This struggle may also be three-way, with the illness itself fighting for control. Caregivers are often the losers. A wife reports, "John's emphysema runs our lives!" Another partner admits, "She's down to a hundred pounds and weak as a cat, but when she commands, I obey! I don't dare cross her." Once they have lost out in the struggle, caregivers often feel hopeless, helpless, powerless.

Sarah Miller felt overwhelmed by troubles beyond her control: a sick and cranky husband, Bud, who demanded her constant attention; grown children living nearby who were generous with advice but stingy with help; well-meaning friends who kept hounding her to think more of herself. Worst of all were all those conflicted feelings pulling her apart: guilt that she wasn't doing enough for Bud, anger that she had to give up so much of her life to care for him, resentment toward her children, envy of her friends whose lives continued unchanged. She felt she was floundering, drowning, suffocating. All she could do was pray for things to change.

In her despair Sarah never wondered how things could change. Who or what would come along to perform magic for her? She never said to herself, "Nothing's happening, so it's up to me to make things happen." If anyone had said this to her, she undoubtedly would have been outraged. Not surprisingly, people who are beset by problems resent being told, "Snap out of it!" or "Pull yourself together!" or "Get a grip on things!"

Some things are permanently beyond our control. Sarah would never be able to reverse the illness that was slowly killing Bud; she might never be able to change Bud's demanding behavior, especially if he had always behaved that way. But she could change the way she felt about, and dealt with, his illness, and she could change the way she reacted to his behavior.

Just changing an attitude doesn't change things much, does it? No, not a great deal, but it's a first step. When we feel out of control of our lives, any small changes we are able to make have value. They give us confidence to try for more important ones, proving it's possible to regain at least some of the lost control. First steps are important and can lead the way to more.

STEP 1: LOOSEN THAT EXCLUSIVE BOND

One of the main blocks preventing caregivers from getting back into the driver's seat is that special bond that ties partners together in an exclusive relationship, known among professionals as the "dyadic bond." In spite of the struggles built into the caregiving situations and the obvious need for external support, many couples turn in on themselves as never before, becoming a tight twosome. Paradoxically, having purposefully excluded everyone else from their lives, they often labor under the misguided perception that the rest of the world has forsaken them.

This exclusive bond may stem in part from a misinterpretation of the marriage vows. "In sickness and in health" did not mean that no one but Mom can bathe Pop. "Forsaking all others" concerns adultery, not whether someone else can sit with Grandma while Grandpa gets a haircut. Grown children often complain that they are shut out of their parents' lives. "I have to listen to her complaining all the time, but does she let me give her a break? Never!" a daughter bursts out. "It's not fair—he's my father, too. I love him and I can't get near him. I give up. I don't know her anymore. She's turned into some kind of a martyr. All I hear is: 'My back is killing me, but Daddy says I'm the only one who makes his bed right.' Or 'No, I can't go to Aunt Sally's luncheon even if you do sit with Daddy. You know he won't eat unless I'm there with him.' Or "How I'd love to go for a drive! (Sigh!) But you know I can't leave Daddy.' "

These martyrs paint themselves into impossible corners from which there is no escape. If they constantly reject help, less help will be offered, and then they are more alone and even more martyred than ever.

> When a new doctor came to examine Paula Gleason's bedridden husband, Clint, Paula broke down. "I can't go on!" she sobbed, "I'm on my feet all day and up half the night—and it never stops. It's day after day."
>
> The doctor looked at her with concern. "You don't have anyone to help out—children or relatives?"
>
> "Oh, yes, I have three children," Paula answered.
>
> "They live too far away to help?" asked the doctor.
>
> "No, they're here in Sayville," she admitted.
>
> "And they don't help you?" the doctor said with surprise.
>
> "What could they do? They wouldn't know how to take care of Clint the way I do," Paula insisted.
>
> "Have you let them try?" the doctor asked.
>
> "They're busy with their own lives," was Paula's answer.
>
> "Have you let them try?" repeated the doctor.
>
> "Clint doesn't want anyone but me!" Paula insisted.
>
> "Have you let them try?" The doctor now was raising his voice.
>
> "No, doctor, I guess I haven't."

Closeness and tenderness are gratifying ingredients in caregiving—no one questions their value—but they do not need to operate twenty-four hours a day. The exclusive bond can eventually be hazardous to the physical and emotional health of the caregiver—and of the invalid, too, who might benefit from a transfusion of new faces.

If you find yourself tied up in this exclusive bond, try loosening it a little; then you may find it easier to regain some control. Earlier in this chapter it was said that women caregivers are less likely than men to ask for or even accept help. This may be true because the role of caregiver has traditionally been assigned to them, but never underestimate the importance of this exclusive bond. It may explain why so many women cannot share their burdens with anyone else—they cannot undo the knots they've tied for themselves.

STEP 2: THOSE MIXED-UP FEELINGS—FACE UP TO THEM!

Stanley withdrew, leaving me alone, lonely, obsessed, ceaselessly serving him and his illness. He never thanked me but even if he had, it would not have assuaged my rage as I watched my life ebb away just trying to do what had to be done each day.

I never let him know how I felt, for his was the greater rage, the greater fear. . . . I yearned for freedom—to go, to do, to see. . . . after a while it was hard to remember what I had loved. . . .

Jane Bendetson described these mixed feelings in her column. The feelings are shared—although not always admitted—by many caregivers. The truth is that no matter how much love and devotion exists, the caregiving process is bound to spark ambivalent feelings: "I must be a rotten person," one beleaguered wife reproached herself. "How can I be angry at poor Hank because he's helpless? And he needs me so much. How can I keep on dreaming of packing a bag and taking off forever?"

One emotionally torn husband, feeling pushed to the limit, put on his hat and actually did walk out of the house, leaving his bedridden wife alone and horrifying his family when they found out. He had never been able to admit his rage at her for deserting him and robbing them both of the life they once knew. No one had told either of them it was okay to unburden themselves once in a while, to blow off steam, or that their feelings were normal in the long-term-caregiving experience.

You probably find it easy enough to voice love and caring and sympathy and understanding. But it's much harder, isn't it, to express the opposite emotions? So many of us, especially women, are programmed to feel it's shameful. But when feelings are constantly suppressed, partners may withdraw emotionally or physically and be less effective as caregivers, neglecting their patients or even abusing them.

If, despite being deeply devoted to your partner, you feel such ambivalence, imagine the feelings of couples who have had a generally unsatisfying or antagonistic relationship. What if there has been little love or tenderness or compassion through the years and they have only stayed together for financial reasons or out of habit or fear of being alone? Sparked by the disabled partner's needs, a host of formerly hidden negative feelings may surface in the caregiver's consciousness, or these may have to be buried still deeper because they seem so shameful. The more they are buried and denied, the harder life will become and the more unsuccessful the care.

Negative feelings, whether buried or overt, are neither shameful nor inappropriate, but quite normal. Most caregivers experience them. Once you face up to these feelings and admit them to yourself, the next step is to talk about them. Unburden yourself to someone else—an understanding son or daughter, a relative, a confidant. Even a minister or a doctor or a therapist. Out in the open and no longer shameful, guilty secrets, these feelings may not seem so terrible and you may even be freer to take another step toward control.

STEP 3: TAKE A SELF-INVENTORY

What are you missing now in your life that used to give you pleasure? How much have you given up? Can you get some of it back—even just a little? How many of the things you do could someone else do just as well? What about your friends? Have they drifted away, or have you pushed them off? Without guilt or shame, sketch out—alone or with a confidant, honestly and without guilt or shame—your most bearable scenario. You might even play around with some outrageous fantasies—taking off on a world cruise, getting a full-time nurse, institutionalization or even the death of your partner—but eliminate them quickly because these are unrealistic. Soon you may admit that you have reasonable needs, too, and that maybe you have a right to satisfy at least some of them.

STEP 4: HYPOTHETICALLY REARRANGE YOUR LIFE

Now you are coming closer to a concrete plan. What changes can you make in your current routines so some of these reasonable needs can be met?

> Jan Mantell had given up her part-time job to take care of her husband Jim after his liver transplant. She also withdrew from other activities she used to enjoy because she was unwilling to leave Jim alone. Although she did all this willingly, after a while she found herself getting steadily more depressed and less effective in caring for Jim. He, in turn, became full of self-pity and bitterness. As she thought about her life, she realized she had become a hermit for no reason. Just because Jim couldn't get out, she didn't have to withdraw from the world. She needed a job or a social life or volunteer work—something to boost her own morale not only for her own sake but for Jim's, too.

STEP 5: COMMUNICATE YOUR PLAN AND YOUR FEELINGS

You may find this step harder than the others because it means you'll have to face someone who is disabled with the news that there are going to be changes in the caregiving situation, and also to face children or other relatives with the news that you may need them to pitch in and help out.

> First Jan discussed her feelings with their children and then, after a sleepless night, explained lovingly but firmly to Jim that they both needed a reprieve—some time off away from each other.

The situation they were in was not good for either of them. She explained her plan to go back to work five half-days a week and, out of her salary, pay for a part-time homemaker-attendant. When Jim started to object, Jan interrupted with "I'm not finished! I've also got to have one night off a week."

STEP 6: NEGOTIATE AND COMPROMISE

Don't expect real life to be a clone of your dream plan. Since your patient and your children are part of the solution, they have a right to their input. Depending on their feedback, your plan may go through several revisions before it goes into operation.

Although he wouldn't admit it, Jim was glad to have a rest from Jan—she hovered over him too much. It was suffocating. But a stranger taking care of him all week? No way! Five days were too many. The night off for Jan was no problem for her children, provided she would be flexible and they didn't have to be pinned down to any one night. Jan accepted her children's offer and gave in to Jim's feelings by taking a part-time job for only three mornings a week. It was a compromise for everyone involved, but it worked miracles for all of them.

Jan's first mistake was sitting and waiting for Jim to let her off the hook. Although there are occasionally saintly invalids who do think of their partner's welfare before their own, the majority who have experienced so much pain and loss tend to be self-involved and self-centered. Jan had to start the ball rolling.

These six steps will not necessarily produce perfect solutions, nor will they lead all caregivers in the same direction. But just taking some of the steps can help them break out of the paralysis that comes from a seemingly insoluble situation. The scenarios that develop will have endless varieties. No two couples come out of the same mold. Compromises are to be expected. Negotiating favorable terms is not always possible. You may only be able to make small changes in your routines, but these can have symbolic value, proving that your situation has flexibility; it is not cast in cement.

CARE FOR THE BODY, BUT DON'T
FORGET THE SOUL

A caregiver usually notices the invalid's physical pain. But unless disabled people are asked about their mental pain, or reveal it spontaneously, it may go unnoticed. Other mental tortures may be similarly unnoticed—fear, terror, confusion, doubt. Some people will admit to these, but many will not. They are left to struggle alone and without comfort. The pains and fears of the physically afflicted are agony enough, but think of those whose minds are deteriorating. What's it like to be out of touch with everything and everyone in the world? What's it like when the dividing line between fantasy and reality gets terrifyingly blurred? A few lines from "Extremis," a poem written by a noted rabbi, Byron T. Rubenstein, suffering in his seventies from Parkinsonism, spell out the pain.

> *Do I only dream the years of joy*
> *That other world, that far planet*
> *Where I commanded strength?*
>
> *I could bear the agony*
> *Of being handled gently,*
> *This loving indignity.*
> *. . .*
>
> *If I knew my remembering of joy*
> *And a loud voice*
> *And caresses, and leaps and*
> *Running in the field and triumphs*
>
> *Were something more than the wanderings*
> *Of a mind aged and fever filled.*
>
> *It is not the fear of what lies ahead*
> *That shudders me as the cold water rushes in,*
> *As the sails rend and the lines snap and break,*
> *But the doubting all my youth.*

Basic physical needs have the highest priority. The body must be bathed, fed, medicated, toileted, exercised. But the soul has its basic needs, too, and if these are ignored, the body's overall well-being suffers. Caregivers who have lost control of their lives, who feel martyred and resentful, or who are drained of energy from nurturing physical needs too often completely ignore nonphysical ones. Yet these can be vital elements affecting the morale of caregiver and care-receiver alike, raising it higher or lowering it still further.

> Lila Hopkins had always been a perfectionist in everything—running her house, raising her children, giving her music lessons. When Chet, severely crippled by osteoarthritis, became wheelchair-bound, the care she gave him was, naturally, perfect. He was always perfectly bathed and groomed, his room always immaculate. His medication was given on the button, his meals perfectly prepared and served. Anyone who visited would have been amazed at her devotion. But there were no visitors—there was no time for them. Lila had no time, either, to laugh with Chet, to gossip with him, or to sit with him and hold his hand.

Lila would have been outraged to hear that her caregiving did not rate a perfect 10. Chet's body was kept well fed, but his soul was starved. It lacked basic nourishment.

EMOTIONAL SUPPORT

Successful caregivers know the value of emotional support—some say this is their most important challenge. It may also be the most demanding of their strength. This support involves keeping an upbeat atmosphere, cheering up their invalids, talking to them about things outside the small, shrinking world of illness and disability, empathizing with all those confusions, fears, insecurities, self-doubts. This is obviously easier said than done for even the most dedicated caregivers. Those who are overburdened might voice such resentful reactions as "Who's going to cheer me up so I can cheer him?" or "How can I talk about things outside? I'm in prison with him!" or "What about my fears?"

Stressing the need for emotional support would seem to contradict the importance, mentioned earlier, of loosening the exclusive bond between partners. Actually, the paradox makes sense. Those who have regained control of their lives, faced up to their feelings, and distanced themselves from the stranglehold of their burdens are likely to discover there is time, even if it's brief, for emotional nurturing.

Jan and Jim, described earlier, are a perfect example: Jan arranged things so she and Jim could have time away from each other. Jim enjoyed newfound sociability with the homemaker and his children. Jan, in turn, with more interests and stimulation in her life, was better able to be supportive of Jim and interested in his feelings. He no longer complained that she only gave empty lip service to his misery. The understanding sympathy she now offered him was genuine, not perfunctory as it had been before.

Couples who have never been close emotionally, who have been remote from each other or openly antagonistic, may find it impossible to provide emotional support. It's not easy to reverse the patterns of a lifetime. On the contrary, the strain of protracted caregiving may only add to their alienation. Occasionally, however, a disabling illness can smooth over the "rough edges" of conflicting personalities, allowing the healthy partner to become openly caring and compassionate while the disabled one is able to show gratitude for the unaccustomed concern.

If the caregiver is unable or unwilling to go it alone, the necessary emotional support, like the physical needs, can be delegated to or shared by others: a special relative, an old friend, a favorite child. "He sits like Great Stone Face when I'm with him," a confused wife reports. "You'd think he's forgotten how to talk—but when our daughter's with him, he rattles on forever. I bet she knows more about her father than I do after fifty-three years." In such a relationship the daughter offers the emotional support that the wife cannot and never could provide.

Friends and relatives play an important role in the life of the shut-in whether they tap into the deepest emotional levels or not. Caregivers often complain that their friends have deserted them, and their complaints may be justified. Some people are too self-centered to bother sustaining relationships when others can no longer be the companions they once were. But not all friends are so callous. Many have their own reasons to desert: they may drift away because of their own fears about illness; they may feel unwelcome or rejected when they visit; they may be afraid to face someone who is disabled, depressed, and scariest of all, disoriented. "What should I say? How should I act? What can I do?" they may ask themselves. If maintaining friendships is worth the effort to them, caregivers have to help visitors with sickroom diplomacy and make them feel they make an important contribution.

> Although he regained most of the use of his right hand and leg after a mild stroke, Sherman Gerson lost much of his ability to speak. He had been a highly articulate, highly sociable journalist, but now that he could hardly get the words out, he became depressed and withdrawn from everyone. Friends rallied around, but it was a struggle to keep any conversation going. Sally, his wife, finally figured out a plan that cut conversation to a minimum but gave his friends a chance to be with him. Since he could no longer drive and had to go to a speech therapist every day, Sally suggested to his friends that instead of just visiting and trying to talk, they take turns driving Sherman to the clinic. Sally's plan kept his social contacts alive, lifted his depression, and strengthened his motivation to regain his speech.

When caregivers complain, as they often do, "that the phone never rings" or "no one ever visits," it might be justifiable to reply, "There are two ends to the telephone. Why don't you make some calls?" Some caregivers might actually make the opening gambit: "It's been so long! Dave and I would love to see you. How about coffee Friday morning?" The first call is likely to be hard to make, but if it works, the next ones come easier. Having the companionship of others is a tonic for care-receiver and caregiver alike.

> Lizzie Franck made sure that she and Max had company for dinner at least once over the weekend, and friends in for a drink several times a week. Everyone was amazed that even though Max, who was half-paralyzed, needed so much care, Lizzie was able to cook gourmet dinners and all sorts of fancy appetizers. "You've got enough to do. Why knock yourself out?" friends kept repeating, but Lizzie had a stock answer. "When Max and I are alone all the time, we get like zombies. We don't talk—just

sit and stare at the TV. But when we have company, we both come to life. It's worth knocking myself out if the payoff is feeling alive a few times a week."

You don't have to be a gourmet cook to keep social life going. An Oreo cookie and a cup of tea may be just as satisfying. The value of friends and social interaction is considered of such importance that in some communities, when couples have no friends or relatives to depend on, volunteer groups may be found that are organized specifically to give this kind of social support to the chronically disabled.

QUALITY TIME TOGETHER

In most caregiving situations partners usually spend a lot of time in each other's company. "Too much togetherness!" is a frequent complaint. But even though your body is obviously right next to your partner's when you are busy bathing or dressing or feeding or pushing a wheelchair, your mind may be miles away. The two of you may rarely be on the same wavelength.

It takes special efforts to pull away from a day-to-day preoccupation with disability, to find out if there is anything left that can be shared or enjoyed together.

> Marni Schultz and her husband Alec, who was partly paralyzed, refer to their life as BS (Before Stroke) and PS (Post-Stroke). Determined to keep on doing things together, they tried to figure out which of their BS interests could be enjoyed PS. Plenty had to be eliminated, but not everything. Since they always loved exploring their city, they didn't wander aimlessly when she took him out in his wheelchair. Each walk became an excursion—window-shopping in high-fashion boutiques, rediscovering their favorite bookshops and art galleries or finding new ones, watching for signs of spring in the park, visiting a school playground and remembering the days when they were young parents. In the evenings and in bad weather they picked out TV programs to watch together or Alec chose the book and Marni read to him. Although no longer sexual partners, they still shared the same bed and both found comfort in closeness and

intimacy. The enjoyment the two found in each other kept Alec's morale high and this, in turn, lifted Marni's spirits.

Although Alec was physically disabled, his mind was unaffected, so it was possible for him and Marni to maintain a high level of sharing and interaction until the end. For patients with advanced dementia these possibilities are sadly limited, although through trial and error some can still be maintained—through music, old family albums, and even through food. One caring husband, whose wife had advanced Alzheimer's, discovered that she seemed livelier and more responsive when he served ice cream, so a visit to a nearby ice cream parlor became part of their daily schedule. She obviously enjoyed her treat and his enjoyment came from seeing her response.

CHALLENGING THE PATIENT

Close relatives and oversolicitous caregivers may be hazardous to the health and welfare of care-receivers, who often complain that people hover over them, never giving them a chance to do or even to think for themselves.

The source of oversolicitous caring may simply be love: "I can't bear to see you like this. I will do everything for you because I love you." Or fear: "I'm afraid you'll fall if I leave you alone for a minute," or "You won't eat if I'm not there." Or ignorance: "No one ever told me someone in a wheelchair could do any housework." Or impatience: "You're having such a hard time getting your socks on—let me do it for you."

But there may be more complicated emotions:

• *Guilt,* as in: "I'm really angry that our life is ruined because of your illness, but I feel badly because you're in pain. If I take extraspecially good care of you, then maybe I won't feel so badly."

• *The need to control,* as in: "I'm terrified that this illness is going to kill you and then I'll be alone, but if I knock myself out and do everything for you, maybe I can fight it."

• *Obligation,* as in: "You've always taken such good care of me and now it's my turn. I owe you. I don't know if I'll be able to pay off the whole debt, but I'm going to do everything I can for you."

Loss of independence is one of the hardest losses for the chronically disabled. Some say this is worse than any pain they suffer. Hovering over them, catering to their every need, may seem like the most loving behavior, but it may be the most destructive. What the disabled need and what most of them want instead is constant encouragement to maintain whatever independence they have left. The tonic that boosts their morale and preserves their physical strength is proof that they can still play a part in their own care.

> When Kitty Barnard, after fighting it for weeks, finally gave in and agreed she needed a wheelchair, her grown children insisted she hire a homemaker. "How can Daddy run the house and take care of you, too?" they kept saying. Kitty flatly refused the homemaker. "I'm not out of commission yet!" she announced, and proceeded with Lance's help to make a list of the "possibles" and the "impossibles" in their day-to-day routines: how much she could realistically handle herself between her wheelchair and her walker, and how much she would have to leave to Lance. Granted, it took her well over an hour to give herself a sponge bath every morning and dress herself, but she did not need him for this. She couldn't handle vacuuming and washing floors or windows, but she polished silver, washed dishes, and could even put a meal on the table herself. Bookkeeping, bill-paying, Christmas cards, and letter-writing were also her department. They both knew they were in a holding pattern. Kitty's functioning would inevitably diminish as her condition deteriorated, but for the time being she took pride in her declaration of independence.

BE PREPARED FOR INTERFERENCE

FROM OUTSIDERS:

If you and your partner are scoring well on the independence scale, you still should be prepared to receive flak undermining your efforts not only from your children but from friends, relatives, neighbors, and assorted know-it-alls who are often quick with criticism and slow with help. Such comments as

"Do you really expect him to wash the dishes? That's inhuman!"

"I can't believe you make her feed herself. She can hardly manage her fork! Here darling, Sister's here and she'll feed you!"

"You're going to the movies and leaving him alone? For two whole hours?"

are likely to infuriate you or, worse yet, shake any confidence in your own decisions. You may never be successful in convincing everyone that your method of caregiving gets the best results. But if it works for you—stick with it.

FROM PARTNERS, TOO:

Independence is not necessarily valued by everyone. The afflicted partner, like a recalcitrant child, may literally curse the well one who every day makes a list of tasks that have to be done. One husband, recently diagnosed with Parkinson's disease, immediately gave in to his fate of becoming helpless. Every morning he stood naked waiting for his wife to dress him after she had helped him take a shower. Every morning she left the room saying pleasantly over her shoulder: "Come on, dear, get your clothes on. I'm going down to make breakfast." Disabled people may throw in the towel too quickly, willing to be dependent long before they have to. Some, while complaining about being coddled by their caregivers, invite the solicitude, sending out a contradictory message: "Leave me alone! But don't go far." Or that well-known guilt-producer: "Don't worry about me! I'll just sit here in the dark alone!" or simply begging for pity and attention with a subtle "Poor me!" attitude.

WHAT THE CARE-RECEIVER CAN DO

Caregivers are normally expected to play "active" roles and care-receivers "sick" ones, passively accepting care, humoring, catering, and concern. They may be grateful for the care, resentful because they need it, or even demanding of more. Some act as if there were a law decreeing that the disabled shall be forever on the receiving end. There is no such law.

The relationship between the two partners need not, and should not, be a one-way street. It might sound unreasonably callous to want to say to a wheelchair-bound man or woman, "Don't just sit there! Do something!" The remark is neither callous nor unreasonable because, short of abject pain and advanced dementia, even chronically disabled partners can share their care to some degree and be active participants rather than bystanders in the life around them. The previous chapter stressed how technological advances have helped to make this possible. Even victims of Alzheimer's in the earlier stages can be encouraged to take care of some tasks and follow through on some routines themselves.

And when it comes to their morale, care-receivers cannot assume this is wholly someone else's job. They have a responsibility to make at least some effort to keep up their own spirits. The very process of taking an active role in their own welfare may be the best all-around morale booster, not only for themselves but for everyone else. An invalid who is somewhat cheerful, somewhat uncomplaining, and somewhat self-reliant is easier for everyone to be with and is likely to have more social interaction than the obligatory "duty visits" from relatives and friends.

When their own morale is reasonably high, disabled partners may be able to give more than a passing thought to the morale of the partners who care for them. When both understand each other's feelings and what each is going through, the whole emotional climate of the house clears up. Few care-receivers are as insightful or empathetic as one woman steadily deteriorating from multiple sclerosis. She was able to say gently to her stressed-out partner, "I don't blame you for being so angry. Life's a drag for both of us. But I'm too dependent on you for you to be so angry at me all the time. Please! Get some help!"

COPING WITH DEMENTIA

It's hard for us to imagine a more painful and difficult challenge than caring for anyone, especially someone we love, suffering from dementia. This mental condition, usually but not always associated with Alzheimer's disease, puts the heaviest burden on caregivers and accounts for a great portion of nursing-home placements.

Dementia may start with occasional instances of inappropriate behavior and memory lapses which, though disturbing, can be excused. But gradual and profound personality changes usually follow and cannot be ignored. Dementia's advanced stages are accompanied by physical deterioration. Ongoing medical and psychiatric care are essential and, at home, round-the-clock supervision and care are required. Furthermore, the care changes as the condition worsens. Even the most devoted caregivers are bound to be frustrated, drained of energy, depressed. They are in great need of emotional and physical support because they are truly alone—often the ones they care for no longer recognize them.

GRIEVING IN ADVANCE

We are expected to grieve when someone we love dies, but we usually do not associate mourning with long-term illness when death is not imminent. Yet when dementia takes hold, something does die—the most meaningful parts of a relationship. What's left when our partners do not know us, cannot understand us, talk to us, remember our shared history? There's good reason to mourn.

> When Harvey began to lose his memory, Louise felt she had lost part of him. As his disease progressed, she told her friends the husband she knew had really died. There was no more sharing, no reminiscing. They had no future together, she knew that, but they really had no past left, either. Louise often broke down into bitter tears.

She was lucky she could cry. A mourning process had started for her and it was a healthy one. It allowed her to see Harvey in a different way, and not to keep on being bitterly disappointed that he was no longer the person he used to be. She could accept him for what he was now. This allowed her to think of herself and to reach out for other interests in her life.

NONVERBAL COMMUNICATION

Once they stop longing for what can never be and accept their partners' limited abilities, caregivers may be more receptive to developing new ways of communicating. People with dementia are not necessarily totally out of touch with the world around them just because they cannot process information logically the way the rest of us do or communicate rationally. They may respond in different ways to nonverbal stimuli. Comforting words may not help the mentally impaired if they are agitated, but they may be soothed if someone holds their hands or gently strokes their foreheads or gives a tender hug.

An alert caregiver will watch for nonverbal stimuli that are effective: tasty foods, smells pungent or sweet, music or other comforting sounds. Those suffering from dementia may respond well to a quiet, peaceful atmosphere, to the voices if not the words of people they love. They may even be able to dip back through their disoriented memories and respond to a lullaby or a tattered teddy bear.

Partners and other close relatives are vital resources in caring for an Alzheimer's patient because they are the keepers of family history. They are the ones with an intimate knowledge of their relatives' history and what used to gratify them the most.

HELP BEYOND THE FAMILY

It's hard to ask for help, particularly help with something we've always been able to do by ourselves before. Couples who have taken care of each other through the years often expect to continue when they get older. They may be able to do just that, even when this care becomes more burdensome, if they are willing to accept extra support and not keep on insisting "I can do it myself!" Today, in contrast to yesterday, there is help out there that can support caregivers' efforts without usurping their role.

> Carol Denzer had managed to care for her husband Harry since the early days of his Alzheimer's in the home they had shared for over fifty years. They had always cared for each other in the past during short illnesses, and she had no intention of stopping, even though his condition was chronic and steadily deteriorating. But as Harry's dementia worsened and he became physically out of control, she became desperate. Finally, and with a sense of having failed, she knew she could not keep on going alone. She needed help but had no idea how to find it.

Carol was an aging human being struggling with a superhuman job. Carol kept on going without help because four roadblocks were standing in her way: being of the "old school," she had been programmed to believe that the role of the good wife is to do everything for her husband to the bitter end. Next, she was convinced that no one would understand Harry the way she did and give him the loving care he needed. Thirdly, she worried about eating into their limited savings— what would happen to them when these were gone? And finally, she didn't have a clue about what kind of services were available in her community or how to go about looking for them.

By admitting they need help, caregivers like Carol have taken the first step, bypassing the first roadblock. The remaining roadblocks translate into three questions: What services are there to turn to? How good are they? How much do they cost?

AVAILABILITY OF SERVICES

Almost everyone now knows about the long-term-care needs of the elderly. Public awareness has been steadily growing over the last two decades. Community, nursing-home, and care-management services have mushroomed until recently, although now a lid has been put on this growth. Little further expansion is expected through the 1990s because of the nation's serious economic problems—there may even be cutbacks. The first step to take when looking for help is to find out what the community has to offer.

This first step is likely to lead to a care-management service that operates privately or through local agencies. Such a service includes a counselor, usually a trained social worker or nurse, who is knowledgeable about community resources and evaluates the mental or physical problems a couple deals with and what kind of help the two of them need. Skilled care managers usually try to zero in on both partners—the one giving and the one needing care—and to help the caregiver sort out his or her own complex feelings. Once they have a clearer picture of the situation, care managers are then able to work out a plan that the couple's financial resources can realistically handle. The plan may make use of a variety of community services. (Sources for locating care-management services, private and agency, are listed in Appendix A.)

SUPPORT GROUPS AND COUNSELING SERVICES

A support group can be a lifesaving outlet for caregivers, perhaps the only place where they can let down their hair and blow off steam in a nonjudgmental atmosphere with people who understand and share the same experiences. Tips on coping are also exchanged. As a member of one group commented, "There is no misery index here. No one claims 'My misery is greater than your misery.' It's a luxury to be able to talk about our own feelings openly and without guilt." Support groups are valuable for healthy men and women whose partners face illness or disability for the first time (as mentioned in the previous chapter), but these groups are especially important for anyone locked into years of caregiving. For those who find themselves especially overwhelmed, individual or group counseling with professional therapists may be advisable.

HOME CARE

Home-care services, which include a wide range of supportive help, can be brought right into the home: skilled nursing care, home health aids, home attendants. Caregivers can get help with their partners' physical needs a few hours a day or around the clock. Even a few hours can make a world of difference, lifting the crushing weight of solo care without intruding on a couple's treasured privacy.

Home-care services are not limited to patient care alone but may include meals on wheels, transportation, housekeeping, shopping, visiting, all of which relieve caregivers, allowing them a reprieve from an endless round of duties, some of which they are no longer physically able to carry out.

DAY PROGRAMS

In communities where they are available, day programs can be lifesavers for families who want to keep disabled relatives—usually, but not always, those with dementia—at home. Many couples are able to keep going thanks to a local day program to which their disabled partners can go several times a week or even daily. These programs not only provide a structured therapeutic program for their patients but also give the caregivers much-needed respite time. Thanks to day programs, some caregivers even go back to work; others take classes, go to church, play the piano, visit friends, play bridge, or sit peacefully by themselves doing nothing.

NURSING HOMES

Nursing-home care is always an option but, according to studies, one that couples choose only as a last resort when coping becomes impossible. It spells physical separation for couples who may have been to-

gether fifty years or more. For some it seems like divorce, abandonment, even death. Some give in and never forgive themselves.

> "You couldn't keep going, Ma," a devoted son said to his
> mother when they left the nursing home after settling his father
> in. "It would have killed you."
> "I should have died trying!" was her only answer.

Yet there comes a time when the caregivers have to admit "I can't
go on" voluntarily, or have the admission forced out of them by
concerned children. The caregiver's inability to cope, rather than the
condition of the disabled partner, may tip the scales.

The decision to resort to nursing-home placement is an agonizing
one. It carries a heavy load of guilt and other painful emotions. But
these must be put aside while those most closely involved try to examine the advantages and disadvantages from every angle. The caregiver
has to raise and try to answer such questions as:

• Can I keep on going without jeopardizing myself—physically or
mentally?

• Will my partner receive as good care in a nursing home? Better
care?

• Is there a decent one nearby that I can visit easily? If so, can I
afford it?

• Have I exhausted all my options? Could I get more home care,
day care, or help from my family?

Once these questions are answered and the decision is made, the
process is not over, nor the anxiety. The first challenge is locating a
good nursing home within affordable range. It must be a licensed
facility meeting state codes. But even once the home is selected,
concerns continue—and guilt. The specter of the much-publicized
nursing-home scandals still haunts anyone considering placement. "Will
they really take care of her there?" "Are they just out for his money?"
"How will I know if they're treating him right when my back is
turned?"

These are valid questions pertinent to the welfare of every nursing-home resident. The regular presence, concern, and attentiveness of people from the outside world—partners and relatives—is critical to ensuring ongoing high-quality care. Good homes now depend on corrective feedback from relatives and are more willing to involve family members in decisions on care.

The same kind of close supervision is essential at home when caregivers depend on outside help. The questions asked about nursing-home care should be asked and answered about home care and day programs as well.

WHO PAYS THE BILLS?

The question of who covers the costs of long-term care haunts almost everyone except the very affluent. Middle-class assets cannot be depended on to cover the tab of long-term care—it can rise to astronomical proportions and could wipe out a lifetime of savings. As of 1992, the picture is hardly encouraging. Medicare provides very limited coverage for the cost of home-care services vital to the well-being of the disabled elderly. The greater part of federal funding for institutional care is channeled through Medicare and Medicaid, but Medicare coverage has a time limit while Medicaid has none. Long-term health insurance for nursing-home stays and home care is being widely publicized today, but unfortunately it is beyond the reach of most people who are already past sixty.

The whole subject of health care and its costs is making dire headlines today and the picture for all ages gets worse every year as costs rise and too many people lose out on care. The natives are getting restless and something must be done for them. Changes, hopefully beneficial ones, are in the wind but will not occur overnight or, sad to say, in time for couples who need help right now.

Caring for those who are slowly losing their independence is always a challenge, testing the physical and emotional endurance of anyone who accepts the job. But there are as many ways to give care as there are to receive it. Caregiving patterns are as varied as the marital patterns each couple have designed for themselves. Togetherness takes on a new meaning—it is suffocating for some couples, gratifying for others. Life is not doomed to be chronically miserable for either side.

Regardless of the variety, patterns of caregiving for irreversible conditions have one element in common—all lead to one inevitable end.

> *Everything they know they know together—*
> *everything, that is, but one:*
> *their lives they've learned like secrets*
> *from each other,*
> *their deaths they think of in the nights alone.*
> —Archibald MacLeish, "The Old Gray Couple"

9

Did he lie beneath embroidered coverlets retelling over and over the stories of battles he had won in days gone by and enemies he had vanquished long, long ago? Did he fear his name would have no place in history, that he would pass away forgotten?

And she? Did she assure him of the value of his life, of the love of his people, his children, and his grandchildren? Or was she beset by her own terrors? Of the lonely days and nights ahead? How could she live without him? What meaning would life hold for her after he had gone?

T H E   F I N A L
C H A P T E R

Marcia: Let's face it—we're not getting any younger and we're going to die one of these days. Why can't he talk about it? He knows I've signed a living will— no one's going to keep me alive when I'm really dead. And no fancy funeral—just a simple cremation. He doesn't have to do things my way. I've told him that. I'll do whatever he wants. All he has to do is tell me. But he won't. His regular will? Sure, he's got one—the same one he made thirty

Justin: Paperwork! Haven't we got enough of that? Insurance forms, tax forms, Medicare forms. Now she's at me all the time with more: A living will! Medical power of attorney! Fine! If she wants that stuff, let her go ahead! Maybe I don't. Can't she think of anything but dying? I'm only seventy-four, for God's sake, and she's even younger. We've still got plenty of time! Maybe if we hang in there long enough, they'll invent something to keep us going forever.

years ago when the kids were little. What's the matter with him?

And that freezing idea. Maybe I'll get myself frozen and wake up and start living again a hundred years from now. She laughs at that, but who knows? They went to the moon, didn't they? And about my will—I guess she's right. I've got to revise it. I'll get to it one of these days.

*D*eath is a touchy subject. We each have our own ways of looking at it. Two poets offer totally opposed views:

Under the wide and starry sky
Dig the grave and let me lie.
Glad did I live and gladly die,
And I laid me down with a will.
—Robert Louis Stevenson

Do not go gentle into that good night.
Old age should burn and rave at close of day;
Rage, rage against the dying of the light.
—Dylan Thomas

Most people find themselves somewhere in the middle ground between these two poles as they contemplate the end of their lives. Their emotions may be mixed: fear of the great unknown ahead, sadness at what must be left behind, dread of pain in the final moments, anxiety about unfinished business, unresolved relationships. Some fight the inevitable and manage to postpone it by their sheer will to live. Others passively drift along, accepting whatever comes. We all know death gets closer every year. There's no escape. But we can't be blamed for hoping it won't catch up with us for a long while.

Some couples deal with death in yet a different way: like Justin, they ignore it or even deny it. This is not hard to understand, since so many are not only living longer but more healthily. At sixty or even seventy they do not feel or act the way their parents did if they were lucky enough to live past sixty. They often feel in body and mind more like their thirty- or forty-year-old children. They seek—and then follow— any new commands assuring longer, better lives: Floss those teeth! Expand those lungs! Run those marathons! Cut that cholesterol! Eat those beans! Watch those pounds! Don't forget those seat belts or those sunscreens. No wonder they expect these efforts to pay off in long life or even immortality. Why waste time dwelling on death or even thinking about it at all?

But whether we react with fury or gladness, reaching toward it or backing away, death, paradoxically, is the only guaranteed universal fact of life. We know, furthermore, that even though the scientists are performing miracles and will perform more before the end of this century, the secret of true immortality will not come in time for us.

IMMORTALITY HAS A PRICE

Close to three hundred years ago the satirist Jonathan Swift in *Gulliver's Travels* introduced his hero to a mythical tribe of immortals, the Struldbruggs. Gulliver was at first envious:

> *But happiest beyond all Comparison are those excellent Struldbruggs, who . . . have their Minds free and disengaged, without the Weight and Depression of Spirits caused by the continual Apprehension of Death.*

Gulliver soon discovered the error of his assumption. Firsthand acquaintance with the Struldbruggs proved that there is indeed a fate worse than death. Although immortal, they were declared legally dead at eighty and lived thereafter on the fringes of society. They were "opinionative, peevish, covetous, morose, vain, talkative," incapable of friendship, and full of envy—of the young who could enjoy life and of the old who could die.

At Ninety they lose their Teeth and Hair; they have at that Age no Distinction of Taste but eat and drink whatever they can get without Relish or Appetite. The Diseases they were subject to still continue without increasing or diminishing. In talking they forget the Common Appellation of Things and the Names of Persons. . . . The Language of this country always being upon the Flux, the Struldbruggs of one Age do not understand those of another . . . and thus they lye under the Disadvantage of living like Foreigners in their own Country.

We've come a long way since 1726 when *Gulliver's Travels* first appeared and Swift painted that sorry picture of life over eighty and of immortality. According to the Bible, life after *seventy* did not promise much pleasure either:

The days of our years are threescore years and ten; and if by reason of strength they be fourscore years, yet is their strength labour and sorrow; for it is soon cut off, and we fly away.
—Psalms 90:10

Today we know that life needn't stop at seventy. It can go on thirty or forty more years—but not forever. These later decades, however, are high-risk. Once a disease is diagnosed, it may no longer be a death sentence—good medical treatment can slow down its course. But the reward for life may be chronic disability. A great-grandmother in her late eighties, physically incapacitated and ready for death, plaintively asked her daughter, "Do you think they've forgotten me?" Modern medicine performs miracles today by keeping alive people who in the past would have certainly died years earlier. But concerned professionals are questioning the heavy price that is being paid for these extended years, and not only in dollars. There are few miracles transforming the diminished quality of the years remaining for the survivors. Too many are condemned to a kind of half-life as they wait for death.

THE OLD TABOOS

Death used to be a family affair, part of life for everyone, grown-ups and children alike. Without the benefit of modern medicine, people died at every age and died at home with those closest to them keeping the death watch at the bedside. But in post-industrialized society and especially in the second half of this century, with the advent of high-tech health care, the death watch moved away from the family and into the hospital. Deeply religious people continued to say "He's in God's hands" about some beloved relative, but more often the feeling is "He's in the doctor's hands" or "He's on a respirator." Death and dying became remote events—less familiar, more unknown, and therefore more terrifying. They became taboo subjects to be avoided like sex once was before its recent revolution. Freud wrote about this taboo in his essay "Obscure Thoughts on War and Death":

> *We were of course prepared to maintain that death was the necessary outcome of life . . . that death was natural, undeniable and unavoidable. In reality, however, we were accustomed to behave as if it were otherwise. We showed an unmistakable tendency to put death on one side, to eliminate it from life.*

The word "death" itself became taboo and euphemisms replaced it—"passed on," "departed," "at rest," and "lost"—often to the confusion of young children. One little boy, after brooding for days, finally burst out, "Isn't anyone ever going out to look for Grandpa? What if *I* get lost? Who'll find me?" He had heard his mother repeat to friends, "I lost my father!" A wall of silence built up, preventing everyone, even the mourners, from mentioning the name of their dead relative. A recent widow burst into tears because a friend made a passing reference to Stan, her husband, who had been dead for several weeks. "No one ever mentions his name to me! It makes me feel that he never lived. I want to talk about him, but when I do, everyone is in a hurry to change the subject." Because adults found death such a mysterious, frightening event, they were determined to "protect" their children, often keeping them in quarantine, away from funerals and from the sobs and grief of mourning grown-ups. No wonder the children then grew up and passed on their own terror of the unmentionable D-word.

NO LONGER TABOO, DEATH IS "IN"

Like the Berlin Wall, the Wall of Silence shrouding death from view has fallen, but only very recently and not for everyone. Since mid-century more and more concern has been shown for the emotions of the dying and of those closest to them, not only by physicians but by psychiatrists, social workers, philosophers, and theologians. The no-no's of generations past—sex, homosexuality, and death—have slowly emerged as familiar and perfectly acceptable topics of general conversation in many circles, although plenty of people are still quite uncomfortable with them.

A little over twenty years ago *On Death and Dying* by Dr. Elisabeth Kübler-Ross offered nonprofessional readers one of the first open discussions of the subject. The book flouted taboos and brought those two words—"death" and "dying"—back into general usage. Kübler-Ross realized from her work with terminal patients that they usually go through five emotional stages before they can accept the fact of their own death—denial, isolation, anger, bargaining, and depression—and that those closest to them experience similar emotions. Many have trouble working through these stages alone and need the support of some understanding person—a partner or other close friend—who is willing to *be* there for them, to listen when they want to talk.

The dying may want more than just plain talk. They may want to reminisce, to review past glories, to be forgiven for past mistakes. They may want reassurance that they will not die without leaving a ripple behind them, a sign to show that they have "made a difference," if not to the world, or the nation, or even the community, at least to someone somewhere, thereby gaining a shred of immortality.

This yearning for shreds of immortality often plagues the elderly even when dying is not imminent. Writers wonder if their books will be read in future centuries; composers, if their music will live on; artists, if anyone will look at their paintings. Two eminent retired scholars, well known for their rivalry, competed endlessly about whose work would receive more footnotes one hundred years after their deaths.

"Look, Granny! She has your eyes!" says the young mother as her frail grandparents hover over the bassinet of their newest great-grandchild, "and she's got Gramp's dimple!" The two frail old people smile at each other, knowing something of themselves will live on through the eyes and dimple of a tiny girl.

IF SOMEONE TALKS, WILL ANYONE LISTEN?

While talking of death in general terms may now be easier—even with all the thorny issues it involves today—it may be a different story when it comes to talking about *my* death or *your* death. Partners may find themselves in disagreement about practical, objective issues—like Marcia and Justin—or they both may feel incapable of dealing with them. Subjective emotional matters may encounter roadblocks, too. Even though talking can be good therapy for those who are approaching death, the person who brings up the subject is often stopped cold: "When I'm gone . . ." a husband may start, but before he can say another word, his wife may interrupt with, "Oh, stop talking like that—you know I hate it."

The gag order may be given even when death is still a distant event. *She* may want to talk about her future if she should survive her husband. *He* may be unable to contemplate a future in which he will have no part. She may then try the opposite tack: what about his future if she should die first? He cannot contemplate a future without her, so that subject is closed, too. She never gets a chance to talk.

Grown children have their own taboos, too, inhibiting frank discussion. If Mother says, "Daddy and I won't be around much longer," hoping to have a serious talk about her own worries, she's likely to be silenced by her daughter's outburst: "What are you talking about! You're both in terrific shape! I bet you outlive me!"

PLANNING FOR DYING—DECISIONS, DECISIONS!

In the past decade we have become increasingly aware of such issues as living wills, the right to die, euthanasia, assisted suicide, DNR (do not resuscitate), medical power of attorney, hospice care, and the still-unanswered question, "What defines death?" Those who prefer to avoid knowing about these subjects would have to eliminate from their lives radio, television, newspapers, and magazines, for all the formerly tabooed issues are now regularly discussed in the media.

If talking about emotional issues and feelings is painful, dealing with practical issues can be equally thorny. People are being called on to make choices, perhaps the most truly vital of their lives. In the past the dying may have indicated some preferences about their funerals—where they wanted to be buried and by whom—but except for these wishes they had very little involvement in their own deaths. They did the dying and everything else was taken care of by others—doctors, nurses, relatives, lawyers, funeral parlors, ministers, priests, and rabbis.

Today the dying are not necessarily cast in such a passive role. They can play an active part—if they want to—in directing the final act of their lives. They have options to consider and momentous choices to make about where to die, when to die, and how to die. An increasing number of hospitals and physicians expect patients to make their choices not when death is imminent but well ahead of time, perhaps years before they are likely to die. The choices may be practical and concrete, but they are nevertheless fraught with emotion.

We may find it easy to speak of death in a vague, undefined way as in "After I'm dead," but it's much harder to weigh the pros and cons of using mechanical supports to keep our very own heart and lungs and kidneys alive. In the process we are forced to come face-to-face with ourselves as dying bodies. "I hate this," a wife whimpers as she and her husband sign living wills. "I feel like I'm fast-forwarding our life to the last frame and seeing my dying body on a TV screen. I'm not ready." Both of them may have said in the past that they never wanted to be hooked up to machines, and without such a document their wishes might not be respected. But their signatures on the dotted lines make death a reality.

Since death is a solitary venture for all human beings, decisions should be made according to each individual's own religious beliefs, cultural heritage, ethical values, and personal preferences—not according to the preferences of husbands, wives, significant others, and children.

Growing old together, if it is to be satisfying, demands planning ahead for a variety of future possibilities, including retirement, illness, and caregiving. This planning has been discussed in previous chapters and concerns life. The ultimate plan concerns death and the choices available before the final irrevocable separation. Making out a will is such a scary reminder of mortality that only one-third of the population leaves one behind at death. So it's not surprising that this ultimate plan has been, until recently, too painful and frightening for most couples to consider. The tide seems to be turning—more couples are weighing their options now, although the partners may not agree on the final choices.

HOW LONG SHOULD LIFE BE PROLONGED?

Through the wizardry of modern technology, life can begin in a laboratory test tube and through similar wizardry, also known as "heroic measures," death can be delayed. People of all ages who would have died of some trauma or disease in the past are being saved and returned to some form of normal living.

Physicians have been trained to put the highest value on life. They and millions of nonprofessionals agree with the old saying "While there's life there's hope." But how long should life be prolonged when there is no hope? This question is being hotly debated by doctors, lawyers, theologians, and philosophers. When advances in biology and medicine turned science fiction into fact, thereby posing ethical questions never raised before, bioethics, a new field of medicine, was born. What is the value of a lifeless life, dependent on mechanical supports? Should radical surgery be performed on an eighty-year-old cancer patient when all it can promise is a few more weeks or possibly months of pain and suffering? What should we call a man who listens to the life supports clicking away the minutes and the hours as he sits at the bedside of his wife, deep in a coma from which she will never wake? Is he a husband or a widower? How long must he postpone his mourning for her? Days? Weeks?

Sue Halpern, in her book *Migrations to Solitude,* describes a man dying in an ICU whose

> *life is going to end, not with a bang and not with a whimper, and not with fire or ice, but with a hose down his throat and the hiss and rattle of a breathing machine in his ears and an unlimited, unobstructed view*

of the ceiling. He will wither under the twenty-four-hour grow-lights. It might take a while. This while is what will be referred to as his life.

There are those who treasure life at all costs—even in comas and vegetative states. They frankly admit they will accept anything and everything that will keep their bodies going, and their partners', too. A husband may be able to accept his wife's death only if he knows every attempt has been made to save her. Why would a recent widow keep asking anyone who would listen, "We *did* do everything we could for him, didn't we? Was there anything else we could have done?" after a stroke killed her husband when he was recovering from lung-cancer surgery. Theirs had been a stressful marriage from which love and compassion had vanished over sixty years before. Did she agonize out of guilt because she had so often prayed for his death? Was she asking for forgiveness?

A man may speak with bravado when dying is still a remote possibility, repeatedly telling his wife and friends, "None of those heroics for me! Let me go quickly—don't drag out the misery." But he may change his tune when he comes face-to-face with death. The bravado may vanish and abject fear take its place. Or he may suddenly love whatever extra minutes of life he can be given, and beg for time to smell one more flower, see one more dawn, hug one more grandchild. He may be willing to subject himself to procedures and indignities he had recoiled from before.

Other people remain consistent to the end, adamantly wedded to their conviction that death is preferable to living on—in name only— by grace of machines and tubes and other heroic measures. Since most hospitals and their staffs have been trained to treasure life, those who prefer death are unlikely to have their wishes obeyed when a crisis comes unless these wishes have been clearly spelled out in writing that leaves no room for misunderstandings.

THE LIVING WILL

A living will, one or two pieces of paper signed, witnessed, and sometimes notarized, states clearly the signer's wishes. Such a document applies only to the care of the terminally ill. It cannot affect the treatment of seriously ill patients who have a good chance of recovery even though they may suffer some permanent incapacity. As one lawyer put it, "It is not a statute to let people die if they are going to live. It is a statute to let people die if they're going to die."

When these documents were first distributed over twenty years ago, they had no legal power—doctors and hospitals held the power; they dictated treatment. Sometimes this coincided with the patient's stated wishes and more often it did not. Over time the living will has gained in recognition and it now has legal status in most states. There may be further changes ahead, broadening the scope of a state statute. A new statute enacted in 1991 in Connecticut, for instance, allows the terminally ill to refuse nutrition and hydration. This provision was not included in the previous statute.

Individuals can compose their own living wills, find a printed form of their state statute in a stationary store, or ask their lawyers to prepare one. A number of organizations, including Concern for Dying and the Euthanasia Educational Council, distribute millions of their own forms, which vary in wording but carry the same message. One such document is addressed to "My family, my physician, my lawyer, my clergyman. To any medical facility in whose care I happen to be. To any individual who may become responsible for my health, welfare or affairs." It states:

> If the situation should arise in which there is no reasonable expectation of my recovery from physical or mental disability, I request that I be allowed to die and not be kept alive by artificial means or "heroic measures." I do not fear death itself as much as the indignities of deterioration, dependence and hopeless pain. I, therefore, ask that medication be mercifully administered to me to alleviate suffering even though this may hasten the moment of death.

Although people of all ages sign living wills, these documents carry more urgency for the elderly—death has stark reality for them. A Connecticut lawyer specializing in estate planning reports that the living will is a small part of any overall plan, but seems to carry the heaviest weight with her clients over sixty. She also comments that although most of her clients want such a will, she sometimes has to referee serious disagreements between husbands and wives.

MEDICAL POWER OF ATTORNEY

Uneasy that their living wills may not be strong enough to persuade the medical community to abide by their wishes, many people are now backing up their wills by appointing some trusted person to speak on their behalf—a partner, a relative, a doctor, a lawyer, a friend. These appointees, who have legal recognition in fifty states, but not the District of Columbia, go under different names in different states—*medical power of attorney* in New York State and *health-care proxy* in Connecticut. They are empowered to speak on behalf of patients who are comatose, demented, or paralyzed and unable to speak for themselves. Without such a spokesperson, the hospital staff may not be aware that an unconscious patient has a living will at all, or forget that there is one, or mislay it. These wills are, after all, just pieces of paper that can easily get lost or buried within the stack of papers clipped to the patient's chart. The health-care proxy has clout, knows about the will, can produce it, and can insist that its wishes be observed.

A husband often appoints his wife as his proxy and she appoints him as hers—assuming they have trust in each other. One wife recently paused, pen in hand, ready to sign the document naming her husband as her proxy. She looked at him long and hard, then refused to sign. She never explained her reasons. Perhaps she felt it was too cruel a job to give him. Perhaps she didn't trust him to follow her wishes. Or did she have a lurking worry that he'd pull the plug on her too soon? Any one of the three reasons is possible. There have been cases where one partner has been emotionally unable, when the crisis came, to follow the expressed wishes of the other, or has even tried to countermand them. Doctors and other relatives then have to step in, and fireworks can be expected.

Since so many questions of law are now involved with dying—once such a simple process—do-it-yourself documents may not stand up legally. Couples who hope to avoid loopholes usually feel safer when they consult lawyers to help them draw up watertight documents which are most likely to ensure that their intentions will be followed. Additional documents can be prepared, setting forth an individual's wishes about autopsy, organ donations, funerals, and cremation.

WHEN TO PULL THE PLUG

Life, liberty, and the pursuit of happiness are rights intended for all citizens. Should they also have the right to die? This question is being furiously debated everywhere, along with the previous question, "Should life be prolonged?" Emotions flare over both questions, one side hotly insisting that life at all costs is sacred and the other—equally passionate—arguing that a vegetative existence is not life and that death is a sacred alternative. The controversy has made ongoing headlines over the past years as the families and lawyers, first of Karen Quinlan and later of Nancy Cruzan, kept fighting—the Cruzans up to the Supreme Court—for permission to remove life supports from their comatose daughters. They finally won, but only after an endless series of legal battles.

Although this may seem like a modern dilemma born from the marriage of medicine and technology, there's nothing new about the subject of euthanasia—literally "beautiful death"—which goes back centuries. The words of the sixteenth-century English humanist Sir Thomas More, sometimes called the Father of Euthanasia, may have an archaic ring, but they are still timely today:

> If the disease be not only incurable, but also full of continual pain and anguish, then the priests and magistrate exhort the man that . . . he will determine with himself no longer to cherish that pestilent and painful disease. . . . And in doing so they tell him he shall do wisely, seeing by his death he shall lose no happiness, but end his torture. . . . They that be thus convinced finish their lives willingly, either by fasting, or else they are released by an opiate in their sleep without any feeling of death. But cause none such to die against his will.

While there are plenty of forces debating for or against the question, there is no unanimity even among the supporters of the right to die. Some favor only *passive* euthanasia for a terminal patient: withholding vital medication, sometimes including food and water, and removing life supports while continuing to use painkillers and other measures to make the patient comfortable. These steps are taken with the consent of patients or their proxies.

More radical supporters are fighting to legalize *active* euthanasia: taking deliberate steps—in other words, pills or injections—to end the lives of the hopelessly ill, an act that was legal in ancient Greece. As of 1992, active euthanasia is a criminal act in almost every country, and people engaging in it—physicians or family members—are sometimes, but not always, accused of murder. Holland is the rare exception to the rule and permits active "mercy killing," but only according to certain special guidelines. These were reprinted in *Scientific American* in March 1991:

• The patient must repeatedly and explicitly express the desire to die.

• The patient's decision must be well informed, free, and enduring.

• The patient must be suffering from severe physical or mental pain with no prospect of relief.

• All other options for care must have been exhausted or refused by the patient.

• Euthanasia must be carried out by a qualified physician.

• The physician must consult at least one other physician.

• The physician must inform the local coroner that euthanasia has occurred.

Passive euthanasia, though legal in most places, is no simple or clear-cut matter. Even if a wife who holds his proxy can bring herself to agree that her elderly husband is terminal and has a right to die with dignity—a phrase in common use today—things do not necessarily move ahead smoothly. Unanswered questions can be barriers. Who decides when a condition is hopeless? How much longer should life be kept going? Who should make these decisions? The appointed proxy can insist that the patient's intention be followed, but this intention does not specify details. Dr. Robert Butler believes that each case is different and should receive individual attention from a panel that might include not only physicians but psychiatrists, social workers, legal advisers, and family members.

To date there is no uniformity of opinion or law about questions of life and death. Confusion is rampant across the country. Regulations differ from state to state, hospital to hospital, and doctor to doctor. In 1991 the columnist Ellen Goodman wrote in the *Boston Globe:*

> *But when you talk about ending treatment and ending life, you have entered a Middle-Eastern bazaar of medical ethics. It is as if every state carried a different message on its license plate. . . . Not only do states have different laws and guidelines, so do counties, hospitals, even doctors. In some places, a family can walk down a hospital hallway and find a second and third contradictory opinion.*

The dying can find themselves trapped in a maze of bureaucratic red tape and conflicting medical ethics. A further roadblock is an ongoing argument about the exact definition of death. Is a man alive as long as his heart and lungs are functioning? Is a man dead if his brain function is flat? Violent disagreement among family members frequently compounds the confusion.

The controversy surrounding the right to die, euthanasia, and death with dignity will probably continue into the twenty-first century, with batteries of professionals on both sides trying to establish their cause as the true gospel.

WHOSE LIFE IS IT ANYHOW?

Legal documents offer one way for the elderly to maintain control over their lives, and therefore over their deaths. They have another option: to end their lives by suicide, deciding for themselves when and how to die. This option is not frequently chosen, although suicide rates are higher among the elderly—especially older men—than in any other age group. The over-sixty-five segment, although only 12 percent of the total population, accounts for 25 percent of reported suicides. (The total may actually be higher, because suicide figures are traditionally under-reported.)

Society in general is shocked by any instance of suicide because it goes counter to most religious and ethical principles. Some psychiatrists see it as an act of hopeless despair or of aggression, not only against the self but against survivors—partners, children, parents.

Others dispute traditional opinions and describe suicide as a rational act under certain desperate circumstances. This view was dramatically underscored in 1975 when Dr. Henry P. Van Dusen, a noted theologian, and his wife committed suicide together. They had been ill for some time and, fearing they might both soon become dependent on others, could see little meaning or dignity in the life remaining to them. The Van Dusens left a letter behind to explain:

> *Nowadays it is difficult to die. We find this way we are taking will become more usual and acceptable as the years pass. Of course, the thought of our children and our grandchildren makes us sad, but we still feel this is the best way and the right way to go.*

Norman Cousins, editor of the *Saturday Review,* commented on the Van Dusen suicide: "What moral or religious purpose is celebrated by the annihilation of the human spirit in the triumphant act of keeping the body alive? Why are so many people more readily appalled by an unnatural form of dying than by an unnatural form of living?"

Many suicides pass unnoticed with little more than a short item on the obituary page. While the Van Dusens' act was given wide coverage, no one was prepared for the bombshell that came in 1991 when *Final Exit* by Derek Humphry, founder of the Hemlock Society, an organization disseminating advice on suicide, was published and made front-page news in the *New York Times* by rising straight to the top of that paper's best-seller list. Books from small publishers with little advance publicity rarely appear on any list, so *Final Exit*'s success must have come because it is literally the last word in how-to books, offering for the first time a variety of specific ways the terminally ill can commit suicide.

Demand for the book was so great that most stores had a list of customers waiting for the next shipment. While no one would claim that all the book-buyers were potential suicides, many stores did report most customers were over sixty. Several salespeople, however, commented with surprise that the elderly buyers seemed perfectly cheerful and not as if they were about to commit a fatal act.

Experts in medical, legal, philosophical, and other allied professional circles have been struggling to explain the unexpected response from the reading public. Why was the book gobbled up so greedily? Dr.

Arthur Caplan, a bioethicist at the University of Minnesota, quoted in the *New York Times,* suggests that the popularity of this book underscores the depth of public concern about euthanasia today. "It is frightening and disturbing and that kind of sales figure is a shot across the bow. It is the loudest statement of protest of how medicine is dealing with terminal illness and dying."

Many are justly concerned that the book will reach the wrong readers and be used not only by the terminally ill, whose future is hopeless, but by those who merely feel hopeless or are deeply depressed and have a chance for recovery. This argument is used by the opponents of both passive and active euthanasia.

Assisting someone to commit suicide still stands as a crime, but there are no figures available on how often a physician has been willing to go one humanitarian step further than the act of omission—withholding medication or life supports—to an act of commission—hastening death. No figures show how many couples exact promises from each other: "Promise you won't let me suffer the way my mother suffered!" "Promise you won't let me be a vegetable!" "Promise I'll never go to a nursing home!" Similar promises are often exacted from children by their aging parents. No figures show how many of these promises are ever put to the test and, if they are, how much anguish is suffered by the survivors who keep them.

WHERE DO WE GO TO DIE?

Death can come anywhere, at any time: an elderly man suffers a fatal heart attack and dies instantly on a street corner before help can come; a frail grandmother is killed by a runaway taxi; an aging couple is killed in a plane crash and their wish to die together is granted.

In general, death comes in a hospital, in a nursing home, at home, or in a hospice program functioning in any of these three places. Occasionally, the terminally ill have the rare advantage of choosing where to die. Those with uncommon forethought may even have indicated their preference long in advance in documents attached to their living wills.

IN THE HOSPITAL

Patients in good hospitals, and even in not-so-good ones, can expect to find the most sophisticated life-support equipment, state-of-the-art intensive care units, and highly trained medical staffs—physicians, nurses, technicians. They can also expect to find strangers. Those closest to the patients—partners, close relatives and friends—feel progressively more and more remote—cut off, banished—as the lifesaving equipment becomes more and more high-tech. "You can go in and see her now, but don't let her talk. And five minutes—no longer," whispers the ICU nurse to the elderly husband of a dying woman. "She's not my wife anymore," mutters the desolate man as he comes out exactly five minutes later, "she's *their* patient."

The dying process, like the birth process, has come full circle. In the past, babies were born at home surrounded by their closest family. Today most births, although not all, take place in hospital settings, but fathers, formerly the forgotten men, now are encouraged to participate in their wives' labor, and other family members crowd in soon after to share the excitement of the arrival. Family support for the dying has regained its importance and is now encouraged whenever possible. Professionals have come to realize that mechanical support cannot replace human support. Being surrounded by the love, compassion, comfort, and understanding of people who care about them may be of greater value to the dying than the high-tech know-how of skilled strangers manning machines. Unfortunately, too many people have grown up behind the wall of silence about death and have no idea how to act, what to say, or how to behave when someone they love is dying—even someone deeply loved whose death is agony to contemplate.

Because of the impersonality of the hospital setting, many people let it be known that they do not want to die there even if it means their death may come sooner. Although life supports can only be used in a hospital, some families with relatives who are already settled into a nursing-home life try to avoid a move to a sterile, impersonal hospital setting when a crisis comes. "Mac could have lived a little bit longer, I guess, if I'd let them hospitalize him and put him on a respirator," a widow admitted sadly, "but he was finally settled in the nursing home, and I couldn't bear to see him terrified again at being in a new place with all those machines on him." Any home—their own or a nursing home—seems to some people a better place to die.

AT HOME

The terminally ill may be brought home or kept out of hospitals altogether for another reason—expressly to avoid any chance of life supports and "heroic measures." "Choosing Death at Home," another front-page feature in a 1992 *New York Times,* reported this recent trend and described the strains as well as the benefits involved. Partners and other family members interviewed admitted the emotional and physical exhaustion of watching someone they love die, but were quick to add that the chance for intimate exchanges and cherished moments together usually outweighed the trauma and fatigue. Tending the dying, however, is not something everyone can take on.

> If eighty-three-year-old Sy Lansing knows his cancer is going to kill him soon, and his doctors know there is nothing more they can do for him in the hospital except keep him going a while longer, why shouldn't he go home to die if that's what he's begging to do and that's what Rose, his eighty-one-year-old wife, has promised him?

This seems like the ideal scenario, but there are several barriers standing in the way of its success: What if Rose had never given serious thought to that promise when she made it? What if she just can't face it when the time comes? What if they'd never been close? What if she'd always been afraid of him and gave her promise because she was afraid to refuse? What if she loves him, but not quite enough to make such a sacrifice for him? What if their grown children and other relatives have their own problems to deal with and let her know she cannot count on them except occasionally? What if there isn't enough money to pay for extra help? What if her own health is precarious and she barely has enough strength to take care of herself? How can she take care of him, too? Rose might feel better able to bring Sy home if there is a hospice program where she lives and she finds out whether or not it can give her enough help with Sy's care.

THE HOSPICE

The hospice movement began in London in 1967 when St. Christopher's Hospice first ushered in a whole new approach for treating the terminally ill. The movement crossed the Atlantic seven years later. In 1974 the first hospice was established in the United States. Now there are over seventeen hundred programs spread over fifty states. Some are independent, some sponsored by hospitals, and others affiliated with home-health agencies.

A hospice program has its choice of locations, too, because it is not a place but a system of care providing physical, emotional, and practical support. It can function in a private home, in a hospital, or in a nursing home. Some programs are fully staffed with a battery of physicians, nurses, psychiatrists, and social workers as well as homemakers and specially trained volunteers. To qualify for a program patients usually must have no more than six months to live. Medicare and private insurance cover some of the cost of hospice services. While a full staff may not be found everywhere, all hospice workers are trained to comfort and support not only the dying but those closest to them as well.

> "You're crazy! It'll kill you!" everyone said to Betty Angelo when she took Bud out of the hospital and brought him home to die. "I owe him," she explained. "Look what he's done for me!" Ironically, Betty had gone through her own cancer four years earlier and Bud had been with her all the way, even helping her learn to accept a colostomy bag. Two years later she developed macular degeneration, and although she had some vision, she was declared legally blind. "How can a half-blind semi-invalid take care of a dying man?" her friends kept asking, but they soon found out that Betty could get all the help she needed from hospice workers. Nurses came in every day to bathe Bud, give him injections for pain, and make him comfort-

able. Homemakers helped with the housework and marketing. Betty was alone at night and able to manage, although quite often when she couldn't help him get out of his wheelchair and onto the bed, she had to dial the hospice number—help came at any hour she called. Bud was able to die peacefully, four months later, in the home they had built when they married forty-eight years before. Medicare and private insurance helped with some of the costs.

The total of those who die at home is not large—80 percent of all deaths in the United States are in hospitals—but the number is growing, as proven by the growth in hospices, some of which have doubled their workload in recent months. The increase is partly due to changes in Medicare and insurance rulings that since 1983 have allowed reimbursement for hospice care.

Hospice workers help to ease the strain on caregivers, who often go through weeks, sometimes months, of demanding day and night routines—bathing, feeding, toileting, medicating, lifting, cooking. Without hospice support, the stress can drain even the sturdiest caregivers, but for frail and aging partners, struggling against all odds to keep going, it can be overwhelming.

WHEN THE TIME COMES

The time will come—if not today, it will come tomorrow. Of the many aging couples who hope to die together, only a fortunate few have their wish granted. The majority are fated to endure permanent separation because one partner—usually the woman, according to actuarial figures—will outlive the other. The survivor is left behind to mourn, to grieve, and to wonder what to do with the leftover years. There is no sure way to predict which partner will go first. It may be the frail partner, invalided and dependent for years; it may be the healthy one; or both partners may seem strong, active, vital, but . . .

"Let's set the alarm for 6 A.M.," eighty-one-year-old Sam said the night before their fishing trip. The alarm didn't wake him. Neither did his wife. He never woke up again.

"Look at that butterfly," seventy-seven-year-old Kurt shouted to his companion, who was right behind him on the trail in the Swiss Alps. As he turned around, she dropped at his feet. A massive heart attack killed her in minutes.

. . .

"I'm going for your ice cream—I'll be right back!" eighty-eight-year-old Jerry called out reassuringly to his wife as he left the house. He suffered a cardiac arrest in the ice cream store. The emergency medical service responded quickly, but it was too late.

The sudden death of a deeply loved partner is a savage body blow. It sends us reeling, blacking out the world we know. A chronic, disabling, and ultimately terminal disease is also savage, but in a different way. Instead of a sudden blow, we are forced to witness the slow deterioration of a deeply loved partner, slipping slowly downhill to death. No one can say which manner of dying is easier for survivors to accept; both are filled with pain. It might seem that a slow deterioration lets partners get used to mourning, to anticipate grief and start to deal with it. Perhaps this is true. But there is a price to pay for the rehearsal, as one widow came to realize:

There's nothing worse than the way Harry died—in a minute without a warning. That's what I used to think. If only I could have had some warning, something to get me a little prepared. Now I'm watching my brother waste away from cancer. I can hardly remember the way he used to look. He's not the same person. When I visit him, I feel better about the way Harry went. He never changed. I'll always see him just as he always was—healthy and strong and happy. He'll stay that way for me forever.

When death comes slowly, mourning may begin but it cannot be completed, and it may also carry with it a burden of guilt: "Did I do enough?" "Why wasn't I more patient?" "When I prayed to be able to sleep all night, did I really want her to die? I didn't mean it, did I?"

When death is sudden, grief may also be mixed with painful emotions: *Guilt*—"Did I miss something, some hint there was something wrong?" *Anger*—"Did he know he was sick and not tell me? How dare he keep it to himself? I'll kill him!" *Regret*—"If I'd known, I would have spent more time with her. Why did I make such a big deal about my poker games?" *Paralysis*—"I've nothing left—no reason to get up in the morning. I can't go on without her." *Outrage*—"Damn him! He promised me he'd let me go first! He double-crossed me."

IT'S A BUSY TIME

The full impact of death may be postponed because there is likely to be endless activity bustling around the surviving partner. Some homes become like Grand Central Station, with friends and relatives coming and going, bearing a variety of items appropriate to the occasion which, coincidentally enough, all begin with the letter *C*: candy, cake, casseroles, comfort, condolence, and counsel. Some visitors are less welcome than others. "Where were they when I needed them?" a widow asked, remarking with bitterness that people who were conspicuously absent when she and her late husband longed for a little companionship during his years of illness returned in droves for his wake.

When death comes after a long illness, plans for funerals or memorials may have been made in advance. People with unusual forethought may have made these long before they had any intention of dying. A seventy-five-year-old man not only left plans for cremation and for a memorial service, but drafted his own obituary, too. When there are no advance arrangements on file—especially when death has come suddenly—close family members have to rush into buying cemetery plots, writing obituaries, debating burial versus cremation, and then making funeral or memorial plans accordingly. The rush is even more urgent for observant Jews, who must bury their dead before sundown of the following day.

Disagreements may slow things up and draw the bereaved parent or grandparent into a tangle of family discord. Hot arguments often arise over who will deliver the eulogies, what kind of coffin is needed, how many limousines should be hired. While some family members insist on a simple ceremony, others demand a lavish funeral, including an ornate coffin and a fleet of limousines, to display their devotion to the deceased. "How can you be so cheap? I thought you loved Daddy!" a son may shout at his mother who knows her dead husband's feelings about wasteful rituals. Mother and son may become estranged at the very time when they need to console each other.

Special discord may be expected when the ones who have died leave behind children from a previous marriage or relationship. *His* children or *her* children may have their own ideas about the funeral arrangements they want for *their* own dead parent, ideas that may run counter to the wishes of their dead parent's partner. Many stepchildren are as supportive as any children, but some may rush in to claim what is legally due them from their inheritance. While a prenuptial arrangement may have been made to protect the security of each partner, there have been instances where the surviving partner, lacking such protection, has been literally evicted from the house by the children from the dead partner's first marriage.

Even after the endless stream of condolence callers has dwindled to a trickle, life may continue to be busy. The terms of the will have to be put into motion, insurance benefits collected, death benefits from Social Security, pensions continued. The traditional "little woman" with no head for finances may need help, while the grieving widower may find it hard to keep the wheels of housekeeping rolling. Children and other close relatives may pitch in, lending a hand with everything, but beware of hands that are too helping! You may discover when you finally catch your breath that you have turned control of your life over to someone else, even though that "someone" may be truly well-meaning. Not infrequently, a widow may admit regrets such as, "I couldn't think straight after Arthur died. I must have lost my mind. My kids sold my house out from under me and moved me to a condo! And I let them."

Widows, widowers, and other bereft partners, once they get their lives back into their own hands and have a chance to face their loneliness directly, may find they are lonely in hundreds of different ways: they may miss their dead partners because they no longer have companionship, or someone to cook, clean, and sew for them, someone to fix things, or to travel with or play bridge with or go to church with. Ask three surviving partners what they miss most and you'll get three different answers:

"What I miss is someone to share things with—bad things and good things, too," one may answer. "Someone to nudge and say

'Hey, look!' to when there's a new flower coming up in the garden—or to say 'Taste this—how is it?' to when I've tried a new recipe. Someone who's just always there for me."

. . .

"I have a Squeeze Box with an alert system," a second may explain, "and I know I can call 911 if I have chest pains, but what I miss most is a warm body next to me in bed—not just for sex, although that, too—and a voice that whispers, 'Are you all right? Do you need something? Is the pain bad again?' "

. . .

"I miss Frank in so many different ways," the third may sigh, thinking of her companion of many years. "But what I miss most is that he promised he'd never let me linger—he was the one I counted on to give me 'the pill' when the time came."

DON'T CONSULT A TIMETABLE

There is no school for mourners, no place to go to learn how to deal with grief and accept it in advance so that when it comes we can be ready. Writers, philosophers, and poets have all dealt with grief and mourning, but their words, beautiful though they may be, convey secondhand emotions. Only with the firsthand experience can one really know what grief feels like personally.

If you expect to be in hysterics and never to stop weeping, you may be amazed to find yourself dry-eyed, frozen, stunned, without any feeling at all. If you expect insomnia, to lie awake night after night tortured by loneliness, you may be surprised to discover that grief can be exhausting and all you want to do is sleep. If you have always been able to keep yourself under control, you may be shocked that sudden wild, primitive impulses come over you, as one widow revealed. "Now I know why people used to tear their hair out, rip their clothes, cover themselves with sackcloth and ashes, throw themselves wildly on the grave and howl at the moon! That's just what I wanted to do—but of course I didn't."

Survivors sometimes describe their suffering in metaphors. One widow sees grief as a foreign country—alien, cold, and frightening—

and mourners as explorers groping their way blindly through its dark landscape, trying to find familiar landmarks. A widower says when his wife died it seemed that the whole world came to a dead stop—like a "still" in a movie. And then when the world picked up and resumed a normal pace, he was forever out of step, moving only in slow motion.

How long did the widow feel alien? How long was the widower in slow motion? Weeks? Months? It's almost impossible to give grief a timetable, to determine how long is long enough, how long is too long. We are accustomed to knowing the timing of things in other areas of life: education—six years for grade school, four years for high school; cooking—four and a half minutes for a boiled egg, fifteen minutes per pound for roast beef (rare); pregnancy—nine months if you're a human, sixty-four days if you're a dog.

Grief does not follow the clock or the calendar; furthermore, it cannot be counted on to move in a straight line. It usually follows a zigzag course—one month of reasonable well-being may revert to a week of despair. Friends who have not experienced grief themselves, who have forgotten what it felt like, or who have learned pop psychology from magazines or television may do more harm than good with: "I know just what you're feeling, but it will pass." "You'll get over it soon! Just give it time!" "Stop brooding—it's not good for you." "What you need is exercise!" "Meditation!" "Whole grains and beans!" "Come on—snap out of it! He's been dead over a year."

One ninety-four-year-old great-grandfather who had himself endured many personal tragedies understood the erratic progress of mourning. He always wrote one note of condolence immediately to a newly widowed relative. But nine or ten months later he made a practice of sending a second note. His words varied, but his message was always the same as in a note to a favorite niece:

> It's nine months since Rob's death, and from my vast experience with such events, I'm sure that by now the "condolence brigade" has moved on to comfort someone else and you are now left to your own devices to sink or swim. Knowing you as I do, I'm sure you will swim, but rather than feeling better now, I suspect you may be feeling worse. Don't be surprised and do be patient with yourself. These periods of feeling worse may very well come and go over the next years. So if you need a hand to hold or a shoulder to cry on, I offer you both.

Some survivors are unable to deal with their grief at all; their mourning goes out of bounds. Their families may watch them sink into deep depression. Under such circumstances it may be necessary to seek professional help from doctors, social workers, psychiatrists, ministers, or rabbis.

NEW LIVES FOR OLD

Research seems to indicate that surviving partners generally do make a reasonable adjustment and the majority manage to work out a bearable pattern of living. Most studies agree that widowers, unless they remarry or form a new intimate relationship quite quickly, make a poorer adjustment. Many die within the first year or are prone to disease and physical disorders.

It might be expected that the widowed who had the stormiest relationships would make the best and quickest adjustment once they are relieved of the burden of marital conflicts. This, however, does not seem to be the case, since they are the ones who often have most trouble dealing with their conflicted feelings about their dead partners, which can never be resolved. As Robert Anderson wrote in his play *I Never Sang for My Father,*

> *Death ends a life . . . but it does not end a relationship which struggles on in the survivor's mind . . . towards some resolution which it never finds.*

The odds for making a satisfying new life favor the survivors of positive relationships. Some experts suggest that these men and women are even more likely to look for and find a new partner. That's a logical theory. However, this theory is more likely to work out in practice for widowers than for widows. Even if an older widow is interested in finding a new partner, the odds are against her because of the dwindling supply of men in her age group. The odds against her are even higher if she hopes to find one who can measure up to her dead husband.

In the book *Vital Involvement in Old Age,* Erik Erikson and his coauthors give an honest appraisal of aging women widowed after long marriages, but their words could apply to anyone who, after a vital relationship is over, must face going on—and growing old—alone. They write that the surviving partners

> *of long-intimate marriages never really finish with the re-experiencing that is so much a part of mourning. Rather, they seem to reach a point at which these feelings no longer dominate every minute of every day. At this juncture, they find themselves able to begin to build upon the lifelong strength of marital love, in developing new kinds of mutuality with relatives and friends who are still alive. Still, even those individuals who successfully organize their lives . . . often find themselves missing their partners profoundly, after many years of widowhood. . . . These individuals cannot feel like themselves in old age without considering the partners who were part of their lives for so long. In the absence of these partners, a measure of isolation seems to be a necessary dimension of widowhood identity.*

E P I L O G U E

> Had they not both pledged themselves one to the other forever and sworn their union would last "till death do us part?"
>
> But one day, did they come to realize that they no longer found pleasure in each other? Did they then confess to themselves in secret that discontent had replaced the happiness of their earlier days? Did they indeed honor their vow "till death do us part" and live on together, but had the spirit of their union died long years before?

*N*o one needs to be told that the death of a beloved partner is a tragic blow at any age, and never more devastating than in late life. It is less obvious that the death of a rewarding relationship can be almost as devastating. Once the spirit of a couple's relationship dies, it leaves behind two people under one roof destined—

unless they change—to live through late life together without the crucial benefits of mutual devotion and emotional support.

"Unless they change!" That's the stumbling block in late life for too many couples who feel too old to change. The previous chapters have looked at the many challenges facing couples as they move on through the various stages of life, the adjustments they may have to make to each other and the variety of patterns their relationship may follow. What has been a constant throughout the years is the need, and the willingness, on both sides to change, to renegotiate, to readapt to new stages. Why should being old stop the process?

We all know couples who never adjust to each other. Unwilling to divorce, unable to compromise, they go through life as quiet or not-so-quiet despairers. We also know that some partners who have had positive relationships—inseparables, parallel pairs, collaborators—find themselves out of step with each other as they deal with their own aging. Late life is a dangerous stage; it has the power to make a bad situation worse or turn a good relationship sour. Once this happens, too many of us feel there's nothing we can do to improve things, so we resign ourselves to a bitter future. We often compound our unhappiness by blaming our partners for wasted years and brooding about all the pleasure of life we are denied.

Couples who are always in conflict may not even think about changing their patterns. They may unconsciously gain some perverse gratification from their mutual friction. Or they look for outside satisfactions to compensate for the dissatisfactions inside their marriage: turning to children and grandchildren, burying themselves in books or hobbies, busying themselves with church or charitable work.

Those in the most painful turmoil are couples who want to improve their lives but do not have a clue as to how to start. So instead of taking action they waste their energies complaining about each other, their friends and relatives who have let them down, their bodies which no longer function smoothly, the outside world where they have no place.

A first step for such partners might be to stop recriminating and start communicating. A plaintive question might get things started. "What's happened to us?" "Are we over the hill?" "Can anyone call this *living*?" Or one partner might even say bluntly, "We've already outlived our parents and we may have twenty more years to go! What's the good of all this extra time if we're going to drag through it like a couple of zombies? Let's do something before it's too late!'' Once each side knows that the other wants change and is willing to make the effort, the two may be surprised to find themselves collaborators instead of antagonists. Communication and collaboration are likely to result in another word beginning with *C—change!*

As collaborators, we may be able to see our partners more clearly and to accept them as the people they really are, not as the people we always hoped they'd be. We may understand how aging has limited them, yet recognize the strength that remains. In the process we may also come to understand ourselves better and to be honest in our appraisal of our own strengths and limitations. We may even learn to be more realistic in our expectations of our partners and of ourselves.

When both partners work together to renew their ties, they may be surprised to find that even small changes in behavior and attitude can help to put new life into a lackluster relationship.

Some couples who relish challenge make renewing their relationship a do-it-yourself project, proud to take charge of their own destiny; others need professional guidance to get started; and still others ask for help if they stumble along the way. Marriage counselors, therapists, doctors, ministers, rabbis, priests, can be found in most areas. These professionals are trained to deal with such difficulties, but many older couples are reluctant to ask for help because they are ashamed to admit they have problems at their age or because they feel they are too old to change. Admittedly, many marriage counselors and other therapists have shared, even perpetuated, this old myth and until recently have not been eager to work with older people, individually or in couples. As the older population has escalated, however, more men and women have looked for professional help and proved that they can benefit from it as much as younger people, albeit a little more slowly.

If two people can successfully renew their relationship and come to see themselves realistically, accepting each other as the people they are, will romance and illusion be gone from their lives? Not necessarily. The glass slipper has been for centuries a dazzling symbol of love and fantasy. But it's only a symbol, after all. We can make it stand for a deeper love, for commitment, for loyalty, closeness, caring. When a man looks at his wife and murmurs, ''I don't know why, but you excite me as much as ever!" does he really see her or does he see instead the slim, blond bride she once was? Does she see a sturdy athlete with a full head of hair? Does either one believe—in reality—that the glass slipper still fits?

But the reality does not matter. In reality, she is wrinkled, gray, and eighty-one. He is paunchy, bald, and eighty-three. What matters is the way the two still feel about each other. If the spirit of their relationship can stay alive, neither one needs to worry about footgear. After all, glass slippers are likely to pinch before long, while comfortable, worn jogging shoes are probably a safer choice for going the distance.

W H E R E   T O
F I N D   H E L P

1. STATE AND TERRITORIAL
AGENCIES ON AGING

These agencies will provide information about local resources, including Area Agencies on Aging.

ALABAMA

Commission on Aging
136 Catoma Street
Montgomery 36130
(205) 261-5743

ALASKA

Older Alaskans Commission
Department of Administration
Mail Station 0209, Pouch C
Juneau 99811-0209
(907) 465-3250

AMERICAN SAMOA

Territorial Aging Program
Government of American Samoa
Pago Pago 96799
011 (684) 633-1252

ARIZONA

Aging and Adult Administration
Department of Economic Security
1789 West Jefferson, 950A
Phoenix 85007
(800) 352-3792 (Arizona only)

ARKANSAS

Arkansas Office on Aging and
   Adult Services
Donaghey Building, Suite 1417
Seventh and Main Streets
Little Rock 72201
(501) 682-2441

CALIFORNIA

Department of Aging
1600 K Street
Sacramento 95814
(916) 322-3887

COLORADO

Aging and Adult Services
   Division
1575 Sherman
Denver 80218-0899
(303) 866-5905

CONNECTICUT

Department on Aging
175 Main Street
Hartford 06106
(203) 566-3238

DELAWARE

Division on Aging
Department of Health and Social
   Services
1901 North DuPont Highway
New Castle 19720
(800) 223-9074 (Delaware only)

DISTRICT OF COLUMBIA

Office on Aging
1424 K Street Northwest, 2nd
   Floor
Washington 20005
(202) 724-5626

FLORIDA

Department of Health and
   Rehabilitation Services
1317 Winewood Boulevard
Tallahassee 32301
(800) 342-0825 (Florida only)

GEORGIA

Office of Aging
Room 632
878 Peachtree Street Northeast
Atlanta 30309
(404) 894-5333

GUAM

Office of Aging/Social Services
P.O. Box 96910
Agana 96910

HAWAII

Executive Office on Aging
335 Merchant Street, Room 241
Honolulu 96813
(808) 548-2593

IDAHO

Idaho Office on Aging
Statehouse, Room 114
Boise 83720
(208) 378-0111

ILLINOIS

Department on Aging
421 East Capitol Avenue
Springfield 62701
(800) 252-8966 (Illinois only)

INDIANA

Commission on Aging and Aged
251 North Illinois Street
P.O. Box 7083
Indianapolis 46207-7083
(800) 622-4972 (Indiana only)

IOWA

Iowa Department of Elder Affairs
914 Grand Avenue, #236
Des Moines 50309
(800) 532-3213 (Iowa only)

KANSAS

Department on Aging
Docking State Office Building
122 South
915 Southwest Harrison
Topeka 66612
(800) 432-3535 (Kansas only)

KENTUCKY

Division for Aging Services
275 East Main Street
Frankfort 40601
(502) 564-6930

LOUISIANA

Office of Elderly Affairs
4528 Remington Avenue
P.O. Box 80374
Baton Rouge 70898
(504) 925-1700

MAINE

Bureau of Maine's Elderly
State House No. 11
Augusta 04333
(207) 289-2561

MARYLAND

Office on Aging
Room 1004
301 West Preston Street
Baltimore 21201
(800) 338-0153 (Maryland only)

MASSACHUSETTS

Executive Office of Elder Affairs
38 Chauncy Street
Boston 02111
(800) 882-2003

MICHIGAN

Office of Services to the Aging
300 East Michigan Avenue
P.O. Box 30026
Lansing 48909
(517) 373-8230

MINNESOTA

Minnesota Board on Aging
444 Lafayette Road, 4th Floor
St. Paul 55155
(800) 652-9747

MISSISSIPPI

Mississippi Council on Aging
301 West Pearl Street
Jackson 39203-3092
(800) 222-7622 (Mississippi only)

MISSOURI

Division on Aging
Department of Social Services
2701 West Main Street
Jefferson City 65102
(800) 235-5503 (Missouri only)

MONTANA

Department of Family Services
48 North Last Chance Gulch
P.O. Box 8005
Helena 59604
(800) 332-2272 (Montana only)

NEBRASKA

Department on Aging
301 Centennial Mall South
P.O. Box 95044
Lincoln 68509
(402) 471-2306

NEVADA

Division for Aging Services
505 East King Street, #101
Carson City 89710
(702) 885-4210

NEW HAMPSHIRE

Division of Elderly and Adult
    Services
6 Hazen Drive
Concord 03301
(800) 852-3345 (New Hampshire
    only)

NEW JERSEY

Division on Aging
Department of Community Affairs
CN 807 South Broad and Front
    Streets
Trenton 08625
(800) 792-8820 (New Jersey only)

NEW MEXICO

State Agency on Aging
224 East Palace Avenue, 4th Floor
Santa Fe 87501
(800) 432-2080 (New Mexico only)

NEW YORK

Office for the Aging
Empire State Plaza, Building No. 2
Albany 12223
(800) 342-9871 (New York only)

NORTH CAROLINA

Division on Aging
Kirby Building
1985 Umpstead Drive
Raleigh 27603
(800) 662-7030 (North Carolina
    only)

NORTH DAKOTA

Aging Services
Department of Human Services
State Capitol Building
Bismarck 58505
(800) 472-2622 (North Dakota
    only)

OHIO

Department on Aging
50 West Broad Street, 9th Floor
Columbus 43266
(614) 466-5500

OKLAHOMA

Special Unit on Aging
P.O. Box 25352
Oklahoma City 73125
(405) 521-2281

OREGON

Senior Services Division
313 Public Service Building
Salem 97310
(503) 378-4728

PENNSYLVANIA

Department of Aging
231 State Street
Harrisburg 17101-1195
(717) 783-1550

PUERTO RICO

Department of Social Services
P.O. Box 11398
Santurce 00910
(809) 721-4010

RHODE ISLAND

Department of Elderly Affairs
79 Washington Street
Providence 02903
(800) 752-8088 (Rhode Island
only)

SOUTH CAROLINA

Commission on Aging
400 Arbor Lake Drive,
#B-500
Columbia 29223
(803) 735-0210

SOUTH DAKOTA

Office of Adult Services and
Aging
Kneip Building
700 Governors Drive
Pierre 57501
(605) 975-2222

TENNESSEE

Commission on Aging
706 Church Street, Suite 201
Nashville 37219-5573
(615) 741-2056

TEXAS

Texas Department on Aging
Capitol Station, P.O. Box 12786
1949 IH 35
South Austin 78741-3702
(800) 252-9240 (Texas only)

TRUST TERRITORY OF THE
PACIFIC

Office of Elderly Programs
Government of the Trust
Territory of the Pacific
Saipan, Mariana Islands 96950
Telephone 9335 or 9336

UTAH

Division of Aging and Adult
Services
120 North 200 West
Box 45500
Salt Lake City 84145-0500
(801) 538-3910

VERMONT

Office on Aging
103 South Main Street
Waterbury 05676
(800) 642-5119

VIRGINIA

Department on Aging
700 East Franklin Street, 10th Floor
Richmond 23219
(800) 55-AGING (Virginia only)

VIRGIN ISLANDS

Commission on Aging
6F Havensight Mall
Charlotte Amalie
St. Thomas 00801
(809) 774-5884

WASHINGTON

Aging and Adult Services
Administration
OB-44A
Olympia 98504
(800) 422-3263 (Washington only)

WEST VIRGINIA

Commission on Aging
Holly Grove-State Capitol
Charleston 25305
(800) 642-3671

WISCONSIN

Bureau on Aging
217 South Hamilton Street, #300
Madison 53703
(608) 266-2536

WYOMING

State Office on Aging
Hathaway Building, Room 139
720 West Eighteenth Street
Cheyenne 82002-0710
(307) 777-7986

2. NATIONAL ORGANIZATIONS

American Association of Homes for the Aging (AAHA)
1129 20th Street NW, Suite 400
Washington, DC 20036
(202) 296-5960

Association of not-for-profit housing, continuing care communities, nursing homes, and community services for the aging. Provides information to consumers and professionals on not-for-profit homes and services.

American Association of Retired Persons (AARP)
1909 K Street NW
Washington, DC 20049
(202) 872-4700

Consumer organization composed of members age fifty and older, with local chapters around the country. Provides information to consumers on all aspects of aging, influences public policy, and offers travel, insurance, pharmaceutical, and other programs to members.

American Society on Aging (ASA)
833 Market Street, Suite 516
San Francisco, CA 94103
(415) 543-2617

Membership organization of professionals in the field of aging, and other interested individuals and organizations. Provides information, education, publications, and other resources on aging.

Asociación Nacional Por Personas Mayores (National Association for Hispanic Elderly)
2713 Ontario Road NW
Washington, DC 20006
(202) 293-9329

Provides information and resources concerning the Hispanic elderly.

Gerontological Society of America (GSA)
1275 K Street NW, Suite 350
Washington, DC 20005
(202) 842-1275

Interdisciplinary scientific membership organization of professionals and scholars in the field of aging. Provides information, education, publications, and other resources on aging.

Gray Panthers
1424 16th Street NW, Suite 602
Washington, DC 20036
(202) 387-3111

Grass-roots advocacy organization of people of all ages, with local chapters around the country. Provides information and advocates for the right of all Americans to decent, affordable health care, housing, and services.

National Association of Area Agencies on Aging (NAAAA)
112 16th Street NW, Suite 100
Washington, DC 20036
(202) 296-8130

Association of local area agencies on aging that provide information and referral, and plan and coordinate services for older people in communities across the country. Provides information and resources on aging services.

National Association of State Units on Aging (NASUA)
2033 K Street NW, Suite 304
Washington, DC 20006
(202) 785-0707

Association of state agencies on aging responsible for planning and coordinating services for the aging in their respective states. Provides information and resources on aging services.

National Caucus and Center on Black Aged (NCCBA)
1424 K Street NW, Suite 500
Washington, DC 20005
(202) 637-8400

Provides information, resources, training, and housing for older black Americans.

National Citizens Coalition for Nursing Home Reform
1424 16th Street NW, Suite L2
Washington, DC 20036
(202) 797-0657

A coalition of over three hundred groups and five hundred individuals across the nation, organized to improve care for nursing-home residents. Publishes a newsletter and provides information on legislative and regulatory developments and issues of concern to nursing-home residents and their families.

National Council of Senior Citizens
925 15th Street NW
Washington, DC 20005
(202) 347-8800

Membership organization of 4,800 senior citizens' clubs around the country. Advocates of decent, affordable health care, housing, services, and programs for older people and for people of all ages.

National Council on the Aging
West Wing 100
600 Maryland Avenue SW
Washington, DC 20024
(202) 479-1200

Membership organization of professionals in the field of aging, and other interested individuals and organizations. Provides information, technical assistance and consultation, education, advocacy, and resources on all aspects of aging.

National Indian Council on Aging
6400 Uptown Boulevard NE, Suite 510W
Albuquerque, NM 87110
(505) 888-3302

Provides information and resources concerning older Native Americans.

National Pacific/Asian Resource Center on Aging
1334 G Street NW
Washington, DC 20005
(202) 393-7838

Provides information, training, and resources concerning the Pacific/Asian elderly.

Older Women's League
730 11th Street NW, Suite 300
Washington, DC 20001
(202) 783-6686

National membership organization with local chapters around the country, focusing on women as they age. Provides information, education, resources, and advocates for policies that will improve the image, status, and quality of life of mid-life and older women.

3. DISEASE- OR CONDITION-SPECIFIC ORGANIZATIONS

Alzheimer's Association (Alzheimer's Disease and Related Disorders Association)
70 Lake Street
Chicago, IL 60601
(800) 621-0379 *or*
(800) 572-6037 (in Illinois)

Provides information and resources for people with Alzheimer's disease and other dementias, and their families. Local chapters around the country sponsor support groups and other programs and services.

American Diabetes Association
Diabetes Information Service Center
1660 Duke Street
Alexandria, VA 22314
(800) ADA-DISC
(703) 549-1500 (in Virginia and Washington, D.C., metro area)

Voluntary health organization concerned with diabetes and its complications, with affiliates and chapters around the country. Funds research and provides education and other resources to people with diabetes, their families, health-care professionals, and the public.

American Heart Association
7272 Greenville Avenue
Dallas, TX 75231
(214) 373-6300

Provides information on the prevention and treatment of heart disease.

American Speech-Language-Hearing Association
10801 Rockville Pike
Rockville, MD 20852
(301) 897-5700

Membership organization of speech, language, and hearing professionals. Publishes a journal and provides information on the treatment of speech, language, and hearing problems.

Lighthouse National Center for Vision and Aging
800 Second Avenue
New York, NY 10017
(800) 334-5497
(212) 980-7832 (TDD for deaf and hearing-impaired individuals)

Provides information and resources on vision and aging to consumers and professionals. Services include training, technical assistance, and consultation, and the dissemination of educational materials.

Society for the Right to Die
250 West 57th Street
New York, NY 10107
(212) 246-6973

Provides information and education on ethical, legal, and policy issues related to the right to die with dignity. Provides sample living wills and other advance directives upon request.

4. ORGANIZATIONS FOR FAMILY CAREGIVERS

Aging Network Services
4400 East-West Highway
Suite 907
Bethesda, MD 20814
(301) 657-4329

Provides consultation and referrals to long-distance caregivers of aging parents or other relatives.

Family Caregivers of the Aging
National Council on the Aging
600 Maryland Avenue SW
Washington, DC 20024
(202) 479-1200

Membership group that provides information and resources to family caregivers.

National Association of Private Geriatric Care Managers
655 North Alvernon, Suite 108
Tucson, AZ 85711
(602) 881-8008

Association of professionals in private practice who provide care management
to families of older people needing assistance.

5. NATIONAL SELF-HELP CLEARINGHOUSES

American Self-Help Clearinghouse
25 Pocono Road
Denville, NJ 07834-2995
(201) 625-7101
TDD (201) 625-9053

National Self-Help Clearinghouse
City University of New York Graduate Center School
25 West 43rd Street, Room 620
New York, NY 10036
(212) 642-2944

Self-Help Center
1600 Dodge Avenue, Suite S-122
Evanston, IL 60201
(708) 328-0471

~~~~~~~~~~~~~~~~~~~~~~~~~~~~~~~~~~~

C H E C K L I S T S
F O R   E V A L U A T I N G
S E R V I C E S

1. NURSING HOMES

I. Where to start
    A. Get a list of nursing homes in your area from
        1. Hospital social service departments
        2. Local Department of Health and Department of Social Services
        3. State Department of Health and Department of Social Services
        4. County medical society
        5. Social Security district office
        6. State and local Office of the Aging
        7. Your physician, clergyman, relatives, friends
    B. Visit several before making a decision.

II. What to notice about the general atmosphere
    A. Are visitors welcome?
        1. Are you encouraged to tour freely?
        2. Do staff members answer questions willingly?
    B. Is the home clean and odor-free?
    C. Is the staff pleasant, friendly, cheerful, affectionate?
    D. Are lounges available for socializing?

III. Is attention paid to the patients' morale?
    A. Are they called patronizingly by their first names or addressed with
        dignity as "Mr.," "Mrs.," "Miss ————"?
    B. Are they dressed in nightclothes or street clothes?

C. Do many of them appear oversedated?

D. Are they allowed to have some of their own possessions?

E. Are they given sufficient privacy?

    1. Are married couples kept together?

    2. Are "sweethearts" given a place to visit with each other in complete privacy?

F. Is good grooming encouraged?

    1. Are a beautician and barber available?

G. Is tipping necessary to obtain services?

IV. What licensing to look for

A. State Nursing Home License

B. Nursing Home Administrator License

C. Joint Committee on Accreditation of Hospital Certificate

D. American Association of Homes for the Aging

E. American Nursing Home Association

V. Location

A. Is it convenient for visiting?

B. Is the neighborhood safe for ambulatory residents?

C. Is there an outdoor garden with benches?

VI. Safety considerations

A. Does the home meet federal and state fire codes?

    1. Ask to see the latest inspection report.

    2. Are regular fire drills scheduled?

B. Is the home accident-proof?

    1. Good lighting?

    2. Handrails and grab bars in halls and bathrooms?

    3. No obstructions in corridors?

    4. No scatter rugs or easily tipped chairs?

    5. Stairway doors kept closed?

VII. Living arrangements

A. Are the bedrooms comfortable and spacious?

B. Is the furniture appropriate?

    1. Is there enough drawer and closet space?

    2. Are doors and drawers easy to open?

    3. Can residents furnish their rooms with personal items?

C. Can closets and drawers be locked?

D. Is there enough space between beds, through doorways, and in corridors for wheelchairs?

E. Are there enough elevators for the number of patients?

    1. Are elevators large enough for wheelchairs?

VIII. Food services

A. Is there a qualified dietitian in charge?

    1. Are special therapeutic diets followed?

    2. Are individual food preferences considered?

B. Are you welcome to inspect the kitchen?

C. Are menus posted?

    1. Do the menus reflect what is actually served?

D. Are dining rooms cheerful?

    1. Are patients encouraged to eat in the dining room rather than at the bedside?

    2. Is there room between the tables for the passage of wheelchairs?

E. Are bedridden patients fed when necessary?

    1. Is food left uneaten on trays?

F. Are snacks available between meals and at bedtime?

    1. Are snacks scheduled too close to meals in order to accommodate staff shifts?

    2. Is there too long a period between supper and breakfast the next morning?

IX. Medical services

A. Is there a medical director qualified in geriatric medicine?

B. Are patients allowed to have private doctors?

C. If there are staff physicians, what are their qualifications?

    1. Is a doctor available twenty-four hours a day?

    2. How often is each patient seen by a doctor?

D. Does each patient get a complete physical examination before or upon admission?

E. Does the home have a hospital affiliation or a transfer agreement with a hospital?

F. Does each patient have an individual treatment plan?

G. Is a psychiatrist available?

H. Is provision made for dental, eye, and foot care as well as other specialized services?

I. Are there adequate medical records?

X. Nursing services

A. Is the nursing director fully qualified?

B. Is there a registered nurse on duty at all times?

C. Are licensed practical nurses graduates of approved schools?

D. Is there adequate nursing staff for the number of patients?

E. Is there an in-service training program for nurses' aides and orderlies?

XI. Rehabilitation services

A. Is there a registered physiotherapist on staff?

    1. Good equipment?

    2. How often are patients scheduled?

B. Is there a registered occupational therapist on staff?

    1. Is functional therapy prescribed in addition to diversionary activities?

C. Is a speech therapist available for poststroke patients?

D. Is the staff trained in reality orientation, remotivation, and bladder training for the mentally impaired?

XII. Group activities

A. Is the activities director professionally trained?
B. Are a variety of programs offered?
    1. Ask to see a calendar of activities.
C. Are there trips to theaters, concerts, museums for those who can go out?
D. Are wheelchair patients transported to group activities?
E. Is there a library for patients?
F. Is there an opportunity to take adult education courses or participate in discussion groups?

XIII. Social services

A. Is a professional social worker involved in admission procedures?
    1. Are both the applicant and family interviewed?
    2. Are alternatives to institutionalization explored?
B. Is a professional social worker available to discuss personal problems and help with adjustment of patient and family?
C. Are social and psychological needs of patients included in treatment plans?
D. Is a professional social worker available to the staff for consultation?
    1. On social and psychological problems of patients?
    2. On roommate choices and tablemates?

XIV. Religious observances

A. Is there a chapel on the grounds?
B. Are religious services held regularly for those who wish to attend?
C. If the home is run under sectarian auspices, are clergy of other faiths permitted to see patients when requested?

XV. Citizen participation

A. Is the Patient Bill of Rights prominently displayed and understood?
B. Is there a resident council?
    1. How often does it meet?
    2. Does it have access to the administrator and department heads?
C. Is there a family organization?
    1. How often does it meet?
    2. Does it have access to the administrator and department heads?
D. Do the patients vote in local, state, and federal elections?
    1. Are they taken to the polls?
    2. Do they apply for absentee ballots?

XVI. Financial questions

A. What are the basic costs?
    1. Are itemized bills available?
    2. Are there any extra charges?

 B. Is the home eligible for Medicare and Medicaid reimbursement?
  1. Is a staff member available to assist in making application for these funds?
  2. Is assistance available for questions about veterans' pensions? Union benefits?
 C. What provision is made for patients' spending money?

2. HOMEMAKER–HOME HEALTH AIDE SERVICES

Adapted from the "Basic National Standards for Homemaker–Home Health Aide Services" established by the National HomeCaring Council, Foundation for Hospice and Homecare, 1990.

1. Does the agency from which you are seeking services have legal authorization to operate? Is it licensed or certified?

2. Is the agency in compliance with legislation that relates to prohibition of discriminatory practices?

3. Does the agency have written personnel policies, job descriptions, and a wage scale established for each job category?

4. Does the agency provide supervision of the homemaker–home health aide service that ensures safe, effective, and appropriate care to each individual or family served?

5. Does the agency provide every homemaker–home health aide training for each task performed for the client?

6. Does the agency have written eligibility criteria for service and written procedures for referral to other resources?

7. Does the agency evaluate all aspects of its service and provide ongoing interpretation to the community?

8. Does the agency provide a written statement of clients' rights and clear evidence that it is fully implemented?

COMMON DISEASES AND SYMPTOMS IN LATE LIFE

1. DISEASES AND CONDITIONS

Some diseases, although they may occur earlier in life, are much more likely to appear in the later years. Listed below are a number of common diseases that afflict older persons and some ways in which they may be treated. *All patients should, of course, consult their physicians for diagnosis and treatment of their own individual conditions.*

ALZHEIMER'S DISEASE

Alzheimer's disease is the best-known and most common of the dementias that afflict older people. It is a neurological disease affecting the cerebral cortex, the outer layer of the brain. At the outset there are only minor symptoms—forgetfulness is one of the most noticeable. As the disease progresses, memory loss increases. Some personality and behavior changes appear: confusion, irritability, restlessness. Judgment, concentration, orientation, and speech may be affected. In severe cases patients eventually become incapable of caring for themselves.

The causes of Alzheimer's disease are not known, nor is there yet a cure, but all patients should be under the care of physicians who can carefully monitor their progress and suggest supportive measures as well as routines that will help make life easier for both the patients and their families. Self-help groups for families of Alzheimer's disease patients, under the auspices of the Alzheimer's Association, can be found in many parts of the country.

ARTERIOSCLEROSIS (ATHEROSCLEROSIS)

Arteriosclerosis is a general term for hardening of the arteries. *Atherosclerosis,* one type of arteriosclerosis, causes the narrowing and closing of a blood vessel due to accumulation of fats, complex carbohydrates, blood and blood products, fibers, tissues, and calcium deposits in its inner wall. Other types of arteriosclerosis are uncommon and will not be discussed here.

Arteriosclerosis is also related to hypertension (high blood pressure) and diabetes. The extent of arterial involvement in arteriosclerosis increases with age and can affect all the arteries of the body, especially those of the brain, heart, and lower extremities. When the blood supply to the brain is reduced by narrowing of the arteries supplying the brain, disturbances in behavior and cognition may result.

Arteriosclerosis in older people is treated by attempting to lower the blood fats by diet when they are significantly elevated. Elevated blood pressure should be treated with a low-salt diet and, when necessary, the milder antihypertensive drugs. Cigarette smoking should be discontinued. A program of supervised physical activity is helpful, as is the control of obesity and diabetes. Surgical procedures to relieve or bypass obstructed blood vessels in the chest, neck, heart, and extremities may be of value after careful workup and evaluation of the benefits and risks involved.

ARTHRITIS

Arthritis is a general term referring to any degeneration or inflammation of the joints. It is classified according to its acuteness or its chronicity and also according to the joints involved and specific laboratory and X-ray findings. Many older persons suffer from arthritis, some to a mild degree and others severely.

The most common form, called *osteoarthritis,* involves primarily the weight-bearing joints and is due to the wear-and-tear process that accompanies aging. Inflammatory involvement of the joints, *rheumatoid arthritis,* is less common in the aged. *Gout,* a metabolic disease of the joints accompanied by severe pain and signs of inflammation, may also be seen in the aged. Treatment of arthritis varies with the cause and includes physiotherapy, use of certain anti-inflammatory medications, and orthopedic devices. There are specific drugs for treating gout.

BRONCHITIS AND EMPHYSEMA

Bronchitis is an inflammation of the cells that line the bronchial air tubes. It may be caused by infection, or by chronic irritation from cigarette smoke or following the inhalation of some harmful substance. Infectious bronchitis may be treated with antibiotics. In the case of chronic bronchitis, cessation of smoking is, of course, imperative. If untreated, chronic bronchitis may progress gradually to pulmonary emphysema.

Pulmonary emphysema, which results when the air sacs in the lungs are distended and damaged, is often found in heavy smokers. The patient suffers from shortness of breath and a cough. Treatment focuses on relief of chronic bronchial obstruction by use of devices that help the emphysema patient to breathe. A variety of drugs and exercises are of value.

CANCER

Cancer (malignant neoplasm or *tumor)* is an uncontrolled growth of a tissue or portion of an organ that can spread (metastasize) to another part of the body. Cancer can occur in the throat, larynx, mouth, gastrointestinal tract, skin, bones, thyroid, bladder, kidney, and so forth. Because cancer symptoms in the aged may be atypical, or may be ignored by the aged patient afflicted with other symptoms and often with a poor memory, comprehensive annual examinations are vital for early detection and treatment.

Cancer may be treated with surgery, radiotherapy (X-ray), chemotherapy (medication), or by any combination of the three modalities. Because life expectancy is limited and the growth of many cancers is slow in very old persons, the value and potential side effects of potent methods of therapy should be carefully considered before they are undertaken.

CONGESTIVE HEART FAILURE

Congestive heart failure occurs when the heart muscle has been so weakened that its pumping performance is impaired and it cannot provide sufficient circulation to body tissues. This condition may result from many years of untreated high blood pressure, heart attacks, or rheumatic heart disease. It may also be produced by diseases such as chronic lung diseases, anemia, infection, and alcoholism.

Treatment for congestive heart failure is directed at improving the heart's pumping efficiency and eliminating excess fluids. Digitalis derivatives are often used to strengthen the heart muscle, and diuretics and salt restriction to remove excess fluid from the body. Treatment of a precipitating disease, such as hypertension, overactivity of the thyroid gland, or anemia, may also be necessary.

CORONARY ARTERY HEART DISEASE

This disease, which is present in almost all individuals over the age of seventy in the United States, involves atherosclerosis of the arteries that supply blood to the heart muscle. In older persons coronary heart disease is superimposed on a heart where there may be a general decrease in muscle-cell size and efficiency.

A heart attack *(myocardial infarction)* happens when a portion of the blood supply to the heart muscle is cut off. In older people it is not unusual for there to be hardly any symptoms accompanying an infarction, in contrast to the crushing pain experienced by younger persons. Substitution symptoms are also common in the elderly. For example, when the older heart fails because of a heart attack, blood may back up behind the left side of the heart into the blood vessels of the lungs, causing shortness of breath instead of chest pain. In other cases, the flow of blood from the weakened heart to the brain is diminished, with resultant dizziness or fainting rather than chest pain.

Modern treatment of the complications of acute myocardial infarction (which include irregular heartbeat and heart failure) with drugs, oxygen, and electrical equipment is saving many lives and enabling the period of bed rest to be shortened. Patients with uncomplicated cases now get up out of bed and into a chair much earlier than before, and cardiac rehabilitation is begun early with good results. Cardiac shock (intractable heart failure), however, remains a difficult problem with a high mortality rate.

Common in individuals with coronary heart disease is *angina pectoris*. This condition results from a temporary inadequacy in the blood supply to the heart muscle. Angina is characterized by severe but brief pain over the mid-chest region; the pain may radiate to either or both arms, the back, neck, or jaw. Angina is treated commonly and safely with nitroglycerin.

DEPRESSION

Depression, as a clinical problem, is the most common manifestation of mental illness in the elderly. Its symptoms can include feelings of hopelessness, anxiety, and self-deprecation, insomnia, anorexia, weight loss, apathy, and withdrawal. At its most severe, it can include suicidal thoughts. At its mildest, it can be confused with normal mourning following a serious loss. Its symptoms also resemble those of the early stages of dementia. For older people there is a close relationship between poor physical health and depression. Depression can also be a reaction to inter- or intrapersonal conflicts. Psychotherapeutic intervention is often helpful. In the case of severe depression, the use of psychotropic drugs is advisable.

DIABETES MELLITUS

Diabetes mellitus occurs commonly in older people, and the usual form is Type II. Although it is called non-insulin-dependent diabetes, insulin may be required in certain instances, such as surgery, infection, or trauma. While inheritance is an important factor in Type II diabetes, environmental factors, such as obesity and decreased physical activity, are also involved.

The older diabetic may present few or no clinical symptoms of the disease. In fact, complications arising from diabetes may be the first signs of this disease in the elderly. These complications include retinopathy (which can be mild to severe), cataracts, glaucoma, strokes, heart diseases, neuropathy (nerve damage, which can occur in different parts of the body), kidney disease, and impotence.

The prevalence of diabetic retinopathy increases with advancing age from 10 percent at age fifty-five to over 30 percent by the age of eighty. Therefore, regular visits to an ophthalmologist are essential. Foot care should be managed by a podiatrist, since nerve damage or poor circulation can lead to trauma, infection, and possibly amputation. Since exercise improves glucose control and can contribute to weight loss, a prudent exercise program should be discussed with the person's internist and ophthalmologist.

DRUG MISUSE

Drug misuse causes widespread problems among the elderly. It results from misdiagnoses by doctors, faulty prescriptions, and improper use by patients. Fifty-one percent of deaths from drug reactions involve those over sixty, who comprise only 17 percent of the population. A particular problem for older people, who often seek treatment for multiple conditions, is the adverse effect of combining drugs. Alcoholism and dependence on hypnotic drugs to induce sleep are the most frequent types of drug misuse.

Helpful steps include consultation with a physician who is knowledgeable about geriatric medicine and appropriate drug dosages for older people, and who can coordinate multiple drug use. Self-medication even with nonprescription drugs should be avoided.

EAR DISEASES

The ear consists of the external, the middle, and the inner ear. Problems in each of these parts may affect hearing. Any condition that prevents sound from reaching the eardrum can cause a hearing loss. Common problems affecting the external ear include impacted ear wax and swelling of the tissues lining the canal caused by inflammation. Problems that frequently affect the middle ear include fluid accumulation and infection within the inner-ear cavity. Hearing losses caused by conditions of the external or middle ear are known as *conductive* losses, since they affect the pathway by which sound is conducted to the inner ear.

Conductive hearing losses are frequently treatable by a physician. Hearing problems involving the middle ear in the aged are similar to those occurring earlier in life. The most common cause is infection. Hearing loss in the middle ear that is not due to infection can often be corrected by surgery. Lesions of the inner ear, if not too extensive, can be helped by the proper use of hearing aids.

Another type of hearing loss results from damage to the inner ear. That is *sensorineural* hearing loss, often called *nerve deafness*. The inner ear houses the nerve structures that receive the sound waves and begin to transmit them to the brain. In most instances, sensorineural losses are irreversible. Recent technological advances have increased the usefulness of hearing aids for people with sensorineural hearing losses.

EYE DISEASES

Cataracts, glaucoma, macular degeneration, and diabetic retinopathy are the four leading causes of vision loss in the elderly. *Cataracts* are cloudy or opaque areas in part or all of the lens of the eye through which light cannot pass. Often cataracts present no problems, but when they do, surgery is usually very successful. The implantation of intraocular lenses is an out-patient procedure at present, well tolerated by most older persons.

Glaucoma is a disease in which too much fluid accumulates inside the eyeball, causing increased pressure and at times internal damage. It is an insidious disease, difficult to detect in its early stages, when it is best treated by medication. Therefore, regular checkups for glaucoma are important.

The retinal disorders, including *macular degeneration* and *diabetic retinopathy,* increase sharply with old age. The retina is the thin lining on the back of the eye made up of nerves that receive visual images and pass them on to the brain. Macular degeneration adversely affects the part of the retina that permits the perception of fine detail. Diabetic retinopathy, one of the possible consequences of diabetes mellitus, occurs when the small blood vessels that nourish the retina leak fluid or release blood, thereby damaging the retina. In the early stages of these retinal diseases laser treatment can be avoided through control of diabetes. There is no known cure for macular degeneration, which accounts for 70 percent of cases of low vision in older persons. Rehabilitative low-vision care, therefore, is an important intervention to maximize residual vision.

HYPERTENSION

Hypertension, otherwise known as high blood pressure, when present over long periods of time can lead to arterial disease and eventually to heart failure, stroke, or kidney failure. In older people, high blood pressure is unlikely to be of recent origin, and much of the damage to the arterial system has already been done.

Hypertension in the aged should be treated by moderate dietary salt restriction and, if necessary, by drugs. Only the milder drugs should be used in very old persons, since the more powerful ones can cause sudden and severe lowering of blood pressure, which may lead to fainting spells or even strokes or heart attacks—the very complications such drugs are used to prevent.

MALNUTRITION

Malnutrition can mean either overnourishment or undernourishment. In cases of obesity, drastic caloric reduction is not recommended for older persons. Those with high blood pressure and diabetes mellitus can benefit from gradual weight reduction while maintaining a balanced diet.

Undernourishment is a not uncommon problem for the elderly and is often due to a decline in activity or to loneliness, depression, or disability. Severe cases of malnutrition can result in illness and acute mental disorders. The maintenance of a balanced diet is important for all older persons, who are particularly susceptible to nutritional deficiencies.

NEURITIS

Neuritis is a disease of the peripheral and cranial nerves characterized by inflammation and degeneration of the nerve fibers. It can lead to loss of conduction of nerve impulses and consequently to varying degrees of paralysis, loss of feeling, and loss of reflexes. Although the term *neuritis* implies inflammation, this is not invariably present. Neuritis may affect a single nerve or involve several nerve trunks.

Diagnostic workup by a neurologist is indicated. Treatment of specific causes, such as diabetes, pernicious anemia, or alcoholism, may be helpful.

OSTEOPOROSIS

Osteoporosis is an age-related condition that predisposes bones to fracture with little or no trauma. Four times more prevalent in women than in men, it is characterized by a marked reduction in bone mass. A total of 24 million Americans suffer from all forms of osteoporosis, including the kinds that lead to crippling hip and wrist fractures.

The causes of osteoporosis are unknown, but the condition is associated with a deficiency of dietary calcium and with metabolic imbalance. Interventions found to reduce bone loss in some cases include maintenance of calcium balance, estrogen therapy, and exercise.

STROKE

Stroke is a cerebrovascular disorder due to thrombosis, hemorrhage, or an embolism. Eighty percent of those who suffer a stroke survive, but most have residual impairment. The most common impairment is paralysis affecting one side of the body. Speech, perception, and vision can also be affected, and aphasia is often present. The patient's ability to think, however, may not be impaired. Early and ongoing rehabilitation is important to prevent secondary complications and to restore functional abilities.

2. SYMPTOMS AND COMPLAINTS

The following are some of the more common symptoms and complaints of older persons. Wrongly regarded by many older patients and their families as being the natural consequences of aging and therefore not worth mentioning to a busy doctor, these symptoms—and indeed, all others—should be reported to a physician.

BREATHLESSNESS

Breathlessness, known as *dyspnea,* is common in the aged and may reflect heart failure, disease of the lungs, or anemia. It is exaggerated by obesity.

CONFUSION AND MEMORY LOSS

Confusion and memory loss as well as disorientation and poor judgment represent changes in intellectual functioning that can stem from a variety of conditions. Abrupt changes in any older person from his or her customary state of functioning should be investigated for a possible physical disorder. These *acute brain syndromes* may result from almost any physical ailment or drug problem. The symptoms are often transient and reversible if the underlying condition is diagnosed and treated. However, these symptoms are also the hallmarks of *dementia,* which can be diagnosed only through ruling out other underlying disorders and observing gradual deterioration of intellectual functioning over time.

CONSTIPATION

Perhaps no part of the body is as misunderstood as the lower digestive tract, which is involved in absorption of nutrients and elimination of solid waste matter. Many people still believe that a daily bowel movement is needed for good health. This belief is false. Not everyone functions on a once-a-day schedule—or needs to. It is common to find people in perfect health who defecate regularly twice a day and others who have a bowel movement only once every two or three days without the slightest ill effects. There are some people who have regular bowel movements at still longer intervals without any health problems. Marked changes in individual habits should be investigated.

DIFFICULTY IN SWALLOWING

Dysphagia, or difficulty in swallowing, is a common complaint of elderly persons that cannot be ignored. Its onset in old age calls for examination to rule out cancer of the esophagus. Dysphagia may indicate the need for a change in diet to soft, minced, or liquid foods. Bedridden or wheelchair-bound aged persons with marked dysphagia should be fed only by properly trained personnel, to avoid possible aspiration of food into the lungs, which may cause a secondary severe pneumonia or even death by suffocation.

FAINTING

Fainting, or *syncope,* may result from a variety of circulatory, neurological, or surgical causes in the aged, as well as from anemia. A careful neurological workup is indicated. Transitory disturbances of the circulation to the brain may be overlooked unless special testing is done. Major injury may result from falls accompanying fainting spells in the aged.

FALLS

Accidents are an increasingly important cause of death and disability in the elderly, with one-half of accident fatalities occurring in the home. The most frequent accidents are falls due to poor vision or visibility, vertigo, sedation, mental confusion, or the adverse use of drugs. In addition to medical and rehabilitative care, helpful interventions include sufficient lighting (particularly on stairs), installation of handrails, and proper carpeting.

FATIGUE

Fatigue is sometimes a symptom of boredom. If it is coupled with marked inactivity and negativism, it may strongly suggest depression. However, fatigue may also be a symptom of organic disease. It is a particularly prominent symptom of heart disease, anemia, and malnutrition. Persistent fatigue should therefore be checked into by a physician.

GIDDINESS OR DIZZINESS

Dizziness, or *vertigo,* may occur even in old people who are well, but there are innumerable possible causes, and this condition should always be looked into. Even when it is not a symptom of illness, vertigo is a common cause of falls, with consequent injuries such as the too-frequent, disabling fracture of the hip.

HEADACHES

Headaches seem to be less common in later life, and it follows that when severe headaches do occur in an older person, they are not to be ignored. They may be due to muscle strain resulting from poor posture, or to infection of the sinuses. Some severe headaches may be caused by lesions within the skull or by inflammation of the walls of blood vessels in the head.

HEARING LOSS

Impaired hearing is not inevitable in old age, although some degree of hearing loss is common, especially for high-pitched sounds. Every effort should be made to determine the cause of hearing loss in the aged. Careful examination by an ear specialist should be followed, if necessary, by audiometry and the painstaking process of being fitted for a hearing aid. Loss of hearing may lead to physical danger—for instance, from an unnoticed approaching car. Hearing loss may also lead to isolation and even to paranoid behavior, as those who are not able to understand others will feel cut off from them and may even mistake what they are saying as being of a hostile nature.

INABILITY TO SLEEP

The inability to sleep, or *insomnia,* may be a consequence of various discomforts, or else it may be evidence of a psychiatric upset. Persons suffering from anxiety often experience some difficulty in falling asleep, and those who are depressed tend to wake early and toss and turn. Both anxiety and depression are common in the elderly. Some older people are convinced that they must, above all things, have a great deal of extra repose. Others, because of loneliness or boredom, tend to go to bed early at night after having slept during the afternoon as well, and cannot understand why they wake early and cannot get back to sleep. They do not appreciate the lessened need for sleep that accompanies aging.

LACK OF APPETITE

Although there are wide variations in older persons' eating habits, just as in those of the young, a sudden change in appetite should be considered a symptom to be reported. Lack of appetite, or *anorexia,* is a symptom of physical or mental difficulty. A thorough medical workup is needed, followed by a psychiatric evaluation.

SEIZURES

Seizures, or convulsions, may involve the entire body, or only a part. Whatever the extent, there are involuntary twitchings of the muscles and usually unconsciousness. Seizures may have their onset in old age. Since they may be a symptom of some underlying disease or abnormal condition, they call for a careful examination by a neurologist. Seizures are often successfully treated with appropriate medication.

SEXUAL PROBLEMS

The capacity for sexual response normally slows down in late life, but definitely survives. Dissatisfaction on the part of either partner should be investigated. Problems can range from inhibitions stemming from negative stereotypes about aging to misunderstandings between partners and physical difficulties. Among the latter are lubrication problems in women and vascular insufficiencies in men. Certain medications and alcohol misuse can affect sexual functioning. Frank communication between partners, with professional help if needed, and consultation with a knowledgeable physician are recommended.

VISION LOSS

Normal age-related vision changes include a decline in visual acuity; a decline in the ability to adapt to the dark and to function in low levels of light; increased difficulty in judging distances and focusing on objects at various distances; and a decline in color discrimination. These changes do not typically result in major functional limitations if appropriate correction is made through regular prescription lenses. However, increasing numbers of older people are experiencing visual impairments that result from age-associated eye diseases. Medical, surgical, and rehabilitative low-vision interventions can be very effective in preventing and correcting these diseases or sustaining and improving visual functioning.

S E L E C T E D
R E A D I N G S   A N D
R E F E R E N C E S

AGING/LATE LIFE

Ade-Ridder, Linda, and Hennon, Charles. *Lifestyles of the Elderly*. New York: Human Sciences Press, 1989.

Averyt, Anne. *Successful Aging*. New York: Ballantine Books, 1987.

Belsky, Janet K. *Here Tomorrow: Making the Most of Life After Fifty*. Baltimore and London: Johns Hopkins University Press, 1988.

Bengston, Vern L., and Schaie, K. Warner, eds. *The Course of Late Life: Research and Reflections*. New York: Springer Publications, 1989.

Binstock, Robert H., and George, Linda K., eds. *Handbook of Aging and the Social Sciences*. 3rd ed. San Diego: Academic Press, 1991.

Birren, James E., and Schaie, K. Warner, eds. *Handbook of the Psychology of Aging*. 3rd ed. San Diego: Academic Press, 1991.

Birren, James E.; Sloane, R. Bruce; and Cohen, Gene D., eds. *Handbook of Mental Health and Aging*. 2nd ed. San Diego: Academic Press, 1991.

Butler, Robert N. *Why Survive? Being Old in America*. New York: Harper & Row, 1975; Harper Torchbooks, 1985.

Hendricks, Jon, and Hendricks, C. David. *Aging in Mass Society: Myths and Realities*. Boston: Little, Brown, 1986.

Henig, Robin Marantz, and Editors of *Esquire*. *How a Woman Ages*. New York: Ballantine Books, 1985.

Karp, David A. "A Decade of Reminders: Changing Age Consciousness Between Fifty and Sixty Years Old." *The Gerontologist* 28, no. 6 (1988).

Maddox, George L., et al., eds. *The Encyclopedia of Aging*. New York: Springer, 1987.

Palmore, Erdman. *Ageism: Negative and Positive*. New York: Springer, 1991.

———, ed. *Handbook on the Aged in the United States*. Westport, Conn.: Greenwood Press, 1984.

Perlmutter, Marion, ed. *Late Life Potential*. Gerontological Society of America, Washington, D.C., 1990.

Pesman, Curtis, and Editors of *Esquire. How a Man Ages*. New York: Ballantine Books, 1984.

Schneider, Edward L., and Rowe, John W., eds. *Handbook of the Biology of Aging*. 3rd ed. San Diego: Academic Press, 1991.

ALZHEIMER'S DISEASE/DEMENTIA

Aronson, Miriam K., ed. *Understanding Alzheimer's Disease*. New York: Charles Scribner's Sons, 1988.

French, Carolyn J.; King, Nancy Long; and Levine, Eve B. *Understanding and Caring for the Person with Alzheimer's Disease: A Practical Guide*. Atlanta: Alzheimer's Disease Association, 1985.

Mace, Nancy L., and Rabins, Peter V. *The 36-Hour Day: A Family Guide to Caring for Persons with Alzheimer's Disease, Related Dementing Illnesses, and Memory Loss in Later Life*. Rev. ed. Baltimore: Johns Hopkins University Press, 1991.

CAREGIVING/HOME HEALTH CARE

Crichton, Jean. *Age Care Sourcebook: A Resource Guide for the Aging and Their Families*. New York: Simon & Schuster, 1987.

Golden, Susan. *Nursing a Loved One at Home: A Caregiver's Guide*. Philadelphia: Running Press, 1988.

Hogstel, Mildred O., ed. *Home Nursing Care for the Elderly*. Bowie, Md.: Brady Communications, 1985.

Kaye, Lenard W., and Applegate, Jeffrey S. *Men as Caregivers to the Elderly: Understanding and Aiding Unrecognized Family Support*. Lexington, Mass.: Lexington Books, 1990.

Lawton, M. Powell; Brody, Elaine M.; and Sapersteen, Avalie. *Respite for Caregivers of Alzheimer's Patients: Research and Practice*. New York: Springer, 1991.

Lustbader, Wendy. *Counting on Kindness*. New York: Free Press, 1991.

Nassif, Janet Zhun. *Home Health Care Solution: A Complete Consumer Guide*. New York: Harper & Row, 1985.

Strong, Maggie. *Mainstay*. New York: Penguin, 1989.

DEATH/DYING/LOSS

Boyle, Joan M., and Morriss, James E. *The Mirror of Time: Images of Aging and Dying*. New York: Greenwood Press, 1987.

Humphry, Derek. *Final Exit*. Eugene, Ore.: Hemlock Society, 1992.

Kalish, Richard A. "Young, Middle, and Late Adulthood." In *Death, Grief, and Caring Relationships*. 2nd ed. Monterey, Calif.: Brooks/Cole, 1985.

Lewis, C. S. *A Grief Observed*. New York: Bantam Books, 1963.

Rosen, Elliot J. *Families Facing Death: Family Dynamics of Terminal Illness: A Guide for Health-Care Professionals and Volunteers*. Lexington, Mass.: Lexington Books, 1990.

Sankar, Andrea. *Dying at Home*. Baltimore: Johns Hopkins University Press, 1991.

Thornton, James E., and Winkler, Earl R., eds. *Ethics and Aging: The Right to Live, the Right to Die*. Vancouver: University of British Columbia Press, 1988.

Viorst, Judith. *Necessary Losses*. New York: Fawcett/Gold Medal, 1986.

Weizman, Savine G., and Kamm, Phyllis. *About Mourning: Support and Guidance for the Bereaved*. New York: Human Sciences Press, 1984.

RELATIONSHIPS WITH FAMILY AND FRIENDS

Banks, Steven, and Kahn, Michael. *The Sibling Bond*. New York: Basic Books, 1982.

Bengston, Vern L., and Robertson, Joan F., eds. *Grandparenthood*. Newbury Beach, Calif.: Sage Publications, 1985.

Brubaker, Timothy H., ed. *Family Relationships in Later Life*. Newbury Beach, Calif.: Sage Publications, 1990.

Bumagin, Victoria E., and Hirn, Kathryn F. *Helping the Aging Family: A Guide for Professionals*. New York: Springer, 1990.

Cherlin, Andrew J., and Furstenberg, Frank F., Jr. *New American Grandparent: A Place in the Family, a Life Apart*. New York: Basic Books, 1986.

Edinberg, Mark A. *Talking with Your Aging Parents*. Boston: Shambhala Publications, 1987.

Kirschner, Charlotte. "The Aging Family in Crisis—A Problem in Family Living." *Social Casework* 60 (April 1979): 209–16.

Kornhaber, Arthur, M.D. *Between Parents and Grandparents*. New York: Berkley Books, 1986.

Matthews, Sarah H. *Friendships Through the Life Course: Oral Biographies in Old Age*. Newbury, Calif.: Sage Publications, 1986.

Silverstone, Barbara, and Hyman, Helen Kandel. *You and Your Aging Parent: A Family Guide to Emotional, Physical, and Financial Problems*. 3rd ed. New York: Pantheon, 1989.

Strom, Robert D., and Strom, Shirley K. *Becoming a Better Grandparent: A Guidebook for Strengthening the Family*. Newbury Beach, Calif.: Sage Publications, 1991.

Troll, Lillian E., ed. *Family Issues in Current Gerontology*. New York: Springer, 1986.

HEALTH/MENTAL HEALTH/DISABILITY

Berg, Robert L., and Cassells, Joseph S., eds. *The Second Fifty Years: Promoting Health and Preventing Disability*. Institute of Medicine. Washington, D.C.: National Academy Press, 1990.

Blazer, Dan. *Emotional Problems in Later Life: Intervention Strategies for Professional Caregivers*. New York: Springer, 1990.

Brody, Stanley J., and Pawlson, L. Gregory, eds. *Aging and Rehabilitation II: The State of the Practice*. New York: Springer, 1990.

Butler, Robert, and Lewis, Myrna. *Aging and Mental Health*. New York: Merrill (Macmillan), 1991.

Dunkle, Ruth E.; Haug, Marie; and Rosenberg, Marvin, eds. *Communication Technology and the Elderly*. New York: Springer, 1984.

Genevay, Bonnie, and Katz, Renee S., eds. *Countertransference and Older Clients*. Newbury Beach, Calif.: Sage Publications, 1990.

Hellman, Susan, and Hellman, Leonard H. *Medicare and Medigaps: A Guide to Retirement Health Insurance*. Newbury Park, Calif.: Sage Publications, 1991.

Hogue, Kathleen, et al. *The Complete Guide to Health Insurance: How to Beat the High Cost of Being Sick*. New York: Walker & Co., 1988.

Hughston, George A.; Christopherson, Victor A.; and Bonjean, Marilyn J., eds. *Aging and Family Therapy: Practitioner Perspective on Golden Pond*. Binghamton, N.Y.: Haworth Press, 1989.

Murphy, Robert F. *The Body Silent*. New York: Henry Holt, 1987.

MARITAL RELATIONSHIPS

Bell, Robert R. *Marriage and Family Interaction*. 2nd ed. Homewood, Ill.: Irwin, 1983.

Bernard, Jessie. *The Future of Marriage*. New York: Bantam, 1973.

Lederer, William J., and Jackson, Don D. *The Mirages of Marriage*. New York: Norton, 1968.

L'Engle, Madeleine. *Two-Part Invention: The Story of a Marriage*. New York: Farrar, Straus & Giroux, 1988.
Melville, Keith. *Marriage and Family Today*. New York: Random House, 1988.
Scarf, Maggie. *Intimate Partners: Patterns in Love and Marriage*. New York: Ballantine Books, 1987.
Sussman, Marvin B., and Steinmetz, Suzanne K., eds. *Handbook of Marriage and the Family*. New York: Plenum Press, 1987.

RETIREMENT/ACTIVITY

Butler, Robert N., and Gleason, Herbert P., eds. *Productive Aging: Enhancing Vitality in Later Life*. New York: Springer, 1985.
Erikson, Erik, et al. *Vital Involvement in Old Age*. New York: Norton, 1986.
Flatten, Kay; Wilhite, Barbara; and Reyes-Watson, Eleanor. *Exercise Activities for the Elderly*. New York: Singer, 1988.
Morris, Robert, and Bass, Scott, eds. *Retirement Reconsidered: Economic and Social Roles for Older People*. New York: Springer, 1988.
Szinovacz, Maxmiliane; Ekerdt, David J.; and Vinick, Barbara H., eds. *Families and Retirement*. Newbury Beach, Calif.: Sage Publications, 1992.

SEXUALITY

Brecher, Edward M., and Editors of Consumer Reports Books. *Love, Sex, and Aging: A Consumers Union Report*. Boston: Little, Brown, 1984.
Butler, Robert M., and Lewis, Myrna I. *Love and Sex After Sixty*. Rev. ed. New York: Harper & Row, 1988.
Travis, Shirley S. "Older Adults' Sexuality and Remarriage." *Journal of Gerontological Nursing* 13, no. 6 (n.d.): 9–14.
Weg, Ruth B., ed. *Sexuality in the Later Years: Roles and Behavior*. New York: Academic Press, 1983.

HELPFUL PAMPHLETS AND ARTICLES

American Association of Homes for the Aging.
Choosing a Nursing Home: A Guide to Quality Care
Community Services for Older People Living at Home
Continuing Care Retirement Community: A Guidebook for Consumers
Available from the American Association of Homes for the Aging, 1050 17th Street NW, Suite 770, Washington, DC 20036.

American Association of Retired Persons.
AARP Educational and Community Service Programs, 1990. Order no. D990.
Checklist of Concerns/Resources for Caregivers. Order no. D12957.
Coping and Caring: Living with Alzheimer's Disease. Order no. D12441.
Growing Old Together: An Intergenerational Sourcebook. Order no. D12342.
Handbook About Care in the Home. Order no. D955.
Miles Away and Still Caring—A Guide for Long Distance Caregivers. Order no.
D12748.
On Being Alone: AARP Guide for Widowed Persons. Order no. D150.
Portrait of Older Minorities. Order no. D12404.
Profile of Older Americans. Order no. D996.
    Available free from AARP Publications, Program Resources, Department/BV, 1909 K Street NW, Washington, DC 20049.

American Health Care Association.
Guide to Nursing Home Living. Order no. 00024.
Thinking About a Nursing Home? A Consumer's Guide to Long Term Care.
    Available from American Health Care Association, P.O. Box 35050,
Washington, DC 20013.

Bern, Mercedes. *Guide to Choosing Medicare Supplemental Insurance.*
    Available from United Seniors Health Cooperative, 1334 G Street NW,
Suite 500, Washington, DC 20005.

Consumer Information Center.
Diet and the Elderly. Order no. 516T.
Guide to Health Insurance for People with Medicare. Order no. 529T.
Health Care and Finances: A Guide for Adult Children and Their Parents. Order
no. 459T.
Safety for Older Consumers. Order no. 425T.
Turning Home Equity into Income for Older Americans. Order no. 137T.
Your Social Security. Order no. 514T.
    Available from Consumer Information Center, P.O. Box 100, Pueblo,
CO 81002.

Consumers Union. "Who Can Afford a Nursing Home." *Consumer Reports*
53, no. 5 (May 1988): 300–311.

Johnson, Michael. *I'd Rather Be Home: A Practical Guide for Individuals, Families, and Professionals.*
    Available from Consulting Opinion, 375 Northeast 163rd Street, Seattle, WA 98155.

National Council on the Aging.
   Caregiver Tips. Set of eight booklets. Order no. 2032.
   Facts and Myths About Aging. Order no. 121.
   Family Home Caring Guides. Set of eight guides. Order no. 2023.
   Ideabook on Caregiver Support Groups. Includes directory of 300 caregiver groups in the U.S. Order no. 2010.
   Memory Retention Course for the Aged. Order no. 4160.
      Available from NCOA Family Caregiver Program, Department 5087, 600 Maryland Avenue SW, Washington, DC 20024.

Public Affairs Committee.
   Home Health Care: When a Patient Leaves the Hospital. Order no. 560.
   Protecting Yourself Against Crime. Order no. 564.
   Right to Die with Dignity. Order no. 587A.
      Available from Public Affairs Committee, Inc., 381 Park Avenue South, New York, NY 10016.

Richards, Marty, et al. *Choosing a Nursing Home: A Guidebook for Families.* Seattle, Wash.: University of Washington Press (P.O. Box C50096, Seattle, WA 98145), 1985.

U.S. Congress, House Select Committee on Aging.
   Where to Turn for Help for Older Persons: A Brochure.
      Available from U.S. Government Printing Office, Superintendent of Documents, Washington, DC 20402, or from Administration on Aging, 330 Independence Avenue SW, Washington, DC 20201.

U.S. Congress, House Select Committee on Aging. Subcommittee on Human Services.
   Exploding the Myths: Caregiving in America. Order no. 99-611.
      Available from U.S. Government Printing Office, Superintendent of Documents, Washington, DC 20402.

U.S. Department of Health and Human Services, Health Care Financing Administration.
   Your Medicare Handbook, 1992. Order no. HCFA 10050.
      Available from U.S. Department of Health and Human Services, 6325 Security Boulevard, Health Care Financing Administration, Baltimore, MD 21207.

U.S. Department of Health and Human Services, National Institute on Aging.
   Age Pages. Collection of fact sheets on disorders and diseases, sexuality, hearing, incontinence, foot care, accidents, nutrition, crime prevention, etc.

Self-Care and Self-Help Groups for the Elderly: A Directory.
    Available from NIA Information Center/PL, 2209 Distribution Circle,
Silver Spring, MD 20910.

U.S. Department of Health and Human Services, National Institute on Drug
Abuse.
    Using Your Medicines Wisely: A Guide for the Elderly.
    Available from Elder-ED, P.O. Box 416, Kensington, MD 20740.

U.S. Department of Health and Human Services, National Institute of Mental
Health.
    Maintenance of Family Ties of Long-Term Care Patients.
    Available from National Clearinghouse for Mental Health Administra-
tion, Public Inquiries Section, Room 11-A-21, 5600 Fishers Lane, Rockville, MD 20857.

U.S. Department of Health and Human Services, Social Security Administration.
    Social Security Handbook. 15th ed. Washington, D.C.: U.S. Government
Printing Office, 1992.

I N D E X

Grateful acknowledgment is made to the following for permission to reprint previously published material:

Henry Holt and Company, Inc.: Excerpt from "The Death of the Hired Man" by Robert Frost from *The Poetry of Robert Frost,* edited by Edward Connery Lathem.

Houghton Mifflin Company: Excerpt from "The Old Gray Couple" from *New and Collected Poems 1917–1976* by Archibald MacLeish. Copyright © 1976 by Archibald MacLeish. Reprinted by permission of Houghton Mifflin Company. All rights reserved.

New Directions Publishing Corporation: Excerpt from "Do Not Go Gentle into That Good Night" from *Poems of Dylan Thomas* by Dylan Thomas. Copyright 1952 by Dylan Thomas. Reprinted by permission of New Directions Publishing Corporation.

Scientific American: Excerpt from Holland's Euthanasia Guidelines from "Death with Dignity" by John Horgan, March 1991.

Washington Post Writer's Group: Excerpt from syndicated columnist Ellen Goodman. Copyright © 1991 by The Boston Globe Newspaper Co./ Washington Post Writers Group. Reprinted by permission.

ABOUT THE AUTHORS

Barbara Silverstone, D.S.W., is President of The Lighthouse Inc., which includes among its diversified vision-rehabilitation programs the Lighthouse National Center for Vision and Aging. She is a member of the National Association of Social Workers, a Fellow and past President of the Gerontological Society of America, a Fellow of the American Orthopsychiatric Association, and formerly a member of the House of Delegates of the American Association of Homes for the Aging. Dr. Silverstone has addressed national audiences on topics such as family relations of the elderly, long-term care for the frail elderly, the psychosocial implications of aging, and age-related vision loss. Her professional experience has encompassed a wide variety of settings from private practice to psychiatric and rehabilitaiton services, and has included individual and group psychotherapy with children, young adults, and the elderly and their families. Her other publications include *You and Your Aging Parent*, co-authored with Helen Kandel Hyman; the textbook *Social Work Practice with the Frail Elderly and Their Families*, co-authored with Ann Burack-Weiss; and a chapter, "The Social Aspects of Rehabilitation," in *Aging and Rehabilitation*, edited by Dr. Frank Williams.

After graduating from Barnard College, Helen Kandel Hyman first was a staff writer for CBS for eight years and then switched to a career as a free-lance writer and editor. Since then she has written extensively on mental health, medical, and family subjects, including over a hundred radio and television scripts, documentaries, and pamphlets for CBS, NBC, UNICEF, the Family Service Society, the American Hospital Association, and the public health department of the Equitable Life Assurance Society. Her work in recent years has been concentrated on the two opposite ends of the life cycle, writing mainly for or about the young and the elderly. Her translation from the Italian of *A Treasury of the World's Greatest Fairy Tales* (Grolier) appeared shortly before she met Barbara Silverstone and they began work on the first edition of *You and Your Aging Parent*. Since then she has written and lectured on various aspects of intergenerational relationships, and she is now working on a book about old age for young readers. She was married for forty years to the late Herbert H. Hyman, professor emeritus of sociology, Wesleyan University in Middletown, Connecticut, and has three children and three grandchildren.